The Outdoorsman's Emergency Manual

The Outdoorsman's Emergency Manual

by Anthony J. Acerrano

Line drawings by Helene E. Walker and Dwight Walles

Stoeger Publishing Company

Illustrations from Advanced First Aid and Emergency Care,
© 1973 by the American Natural Red Cross, reproduced with
permission.

Photographs by Anthony J. Acerrano, unless otherwise noted.

Library of Congress Cataloging in Publication Data
Acerrano, Anthony J.
      The outdoorsman's emergency manual.
      Includes index.
      1. Wilderness survival. I. Title.
GV200.5.A3   613.6'9   77-84334
ISBN 0-88317-036-1

Published by Stoeger Publishing Company
55 Ruta Court
South Hackensack, New Jersey 07606

This Stoeger Sportsman's Library edition is published by
arrangement with Winchester Press.

Third printing, May 1983

Distributed to the book trade and to the sporting goods trade
by Stoeger Industries, 55 Ruta Court, South Hackensack,
New Jersey 07606

In Canada, distributed to the book trade and to the sporting goods
trade by Stoeger Canada, Ltd., 165 Idema Road, Markham,
Ontario L3R 1A9

Printed in the United States of America

Acknowledgments

First, I have a bunch of Walkers to thank: My sister, Helene Walker, was invaluable as an artist, and produced most of the fine drawings that appear in this book. Gene Walker, my brother-in-law, deserves a hearty thank you for photographic and mechanical-art contributions. Thanks also go to Mrs. Alice Walker for typing parts of the manuscript, and to David Walker for being a patient photographic subject. I'm especially grateful to Barbara Walker, who spent many hours reading and editing the rough-draft manuscript, criticizing it ruthlessly, but also thoughtfully and intelligently.

Sincere thanks go to many others: To Judy Hensel, a former editor and present friend, whose abundant kindness, patience and warmth never fail to amaze me, and who helped this book through its planning stages; to Warren J. Brier, who coached the book outline through several revisions, and in general provided seasoned advice on the craft of book writing; and to John Faltus, a good friend and perfect outdoor companion, who served as an incredibly patient and cooperative photography assistant.

I'll be forever indebted to Norman Strung, who has helped in more ways than he realizes, and who provided invaluable encouragement, advice and tutelage whenever they were needed.

Joe Kieffer, my uncle, contributed by assisting with photography, serving as cook, housekeeper, tour guide and philosopher-in-residence for the duration of a writing and picture-taking session at his Tennessee home; and I am grateful beyond words.

Finally, I give a sweeping thank you to the many friends, agencies, state fish and game departments, manufacturers and private organizations who contributed much-needed information, photographs and encouragement to this project.

ANTHONY J. ACERRANO

This book is dedicated to my mother and father, who helped in this effort as they have in all others; with patience, assistance and, most of all, with love.

Contents

PART I

*Understanding
Emergencies*

1

Introduction to Emergencies

As the boughs of the forest part before you, a stage is formed in an opening in the underbrush. The floor is littered with spruce needles, brown and burnt, and scattered about are boulders of granite. Lichens grow atop them in scabrid patches. The ceiling is a dark canopy of spruce tops.

Through a wall of backstage trees emerges the leading player; bearded, wide-eyed, breathing in gulps and pushing through a tangle of blackberry. Not until one of the thorny branches catches a rip in his tattered shirt does the bush register. He stops, eyes the pocked berries, then descends, willing to fight off bear, beast or spirit for his rights to the life-saving morsels.

This scene needs no explanation. You've seen or read variations of it dozens of times. Here is a poor chap lost in the wilderness—scared, hungry, facing life in its rawest form. Only through animal reaction and low cunning will he extricate himself.

Put yourself in this unfortunate fellow's moccasins. What would you do? Would you try to find food first, or water, or shelter? Would you attempt to walk out or would you stay put and wait for help? What about fire? You have no matches, and it's beginning to rain—cold, soaking rain. The berries you ate helped, but they didn't relieve the angry growling and the aching of your stomach.

All right, let's try shifting scenes . . . something less dramatic, perhaps, and something more likely to happen to the average outdoorsman.

The stage has melted into a stream—*your* favorite trout stream—and you're standing hip deep in fast water. You've fished this run before, and although the current is powerful, the occasional two-foot rainbows you pull from it make the effort of wading worthwhile. A slip could be dangerous, but you've been trout fishing for years and never had an accident yet.

Yet.

But this isn't your day. Halfway across the stream you run into trouble. The bottom has become difficult—slippery, irregular boulders that offer only the shakiest foothold. The water is fast, and deep. You're facing cross stream, the current belting you in the side, and you realize that you must turn back to safer water.

You try to maneuver, but a step is impossible. With each movement the flowing water threatens to break your balance and sweep you downstream. Your back foot begins to slip from its firm hold on the bottom. Grimacing, twisting, using unheard-of leg muscles, you attempt to work your foot against a solid rock or dig a hole in the streambed for support.

The current assails. You slip some more, but finally your foot lodges in a firm niche and you are on two feet again. You suddenly notice that you are sweating copiously. Five, maybe ten minutes have elapsed and you haven't moved more than an inch.

You look downstream and sweat even harder. There's that foaming mess of rocks and whitewater that you used to like because it washed food into your best trout pool. The jagged rocks, sucking currents, haystack waves . . .

You were in trouble there in the end. You didn't do anything right, and most likely would have been swept down the cataract. You had a good chance to save yourself from a fall, but from the looks of things, you just didn't know how. And what would you have done had you fallen? Would you have tried to swim or float or dive or what? There would be an excellent chance of surviving the dunking if you reacted with proper moves. If you reacted wrongly there would be an excellent chance of dying.

Let's look at one more scene.

The weeded banks of the stream rise and close together to form a rolling prairie. You and your dog are strolling along, perhaps scouting hunting coverts or maybe just limbering up a few kinky muscles. You pass a rocky gully, shaded from the midday sun, and your dog trots into it to explore. Seconds later you hear a buzzing rattle, then a yelp. Your dog has been bitten by a rattlesnake.

Well, your dog is in trouble this time and it's up to you to save him. If your dog means as much to you as mine does to me, your mouth is dry and your throat tight.

But what do you do? Do you have a snakebite kit along? And do you know how to use it to its full efficiency?

If you don't have a kit along, you can get by with makeshift procedures in an emergency. But are you familiar with them? The first few minutes after a snakebite are crucial. You had better work fast to do what you can and get that dog to a vet.

How painful it is to be in charge and not know what you're supposed to do.

Indoor types reading this are bound to raise their eyebrows and blurt, "By God! You outdoor blokes must live in constant fear. Snakes, drowning, starving—why not stay home and play chess or something else that's safe?"

But any outdoorsman who has logged a fair piece of time afield will tell you that there's nothing to fear in the out-of-doors. There are things to watch for, yes, and things to be alert to; bad habits to prevent and safety to heed. There are many things you need to know, but there is no need to be afraid.

Then why the scary scenarios? First I regale you with sweaty scenes, and then say there's nothing to fear?

Exactly. Those scenes weren't meant to frighten you, they were meant to start you thinking. Emergencies won't confront you every time you set foot outdoors, but they *may* present themselves someday. And if they do, will you be ready to meet the challenge?

There are lots of potential hazards in the outdoors. Some of them are natural dangers, but most are man-related, mishaps that stem from man-made outdoor pastimes such as hunting, fishing, boating and camping. Yes, there are a wide variety of dangers that can beset you, an out-doorsman, but fortunately there are redeeming factors that need to be scrutinized before you can have a true perspective on outdoor emergencies.

First, and before you decide to give up all outdoor recreation, realize that many hazards await you everywhere, outdoors or in. Some of the familiar arguments on this are: "You are in more danger crossing a busy street than hiking in the wilderness." "There's a higher probability of you killing yourself from a fall down your own stairs than while tramping about the woods." "You are more likely to be killed by a horse, cow or bull—or from a bee sting while planting begonias in your back yard—than you are by any wild animal you meet while camping or hunting."

Each of these points, although somewhat overworked, is valid. Unusual danger does not lurk in the outback, but there is some, just as there are hazards in sports, business and life in general.

Second, a high percentage of all outdoor troubles can be avoided. This is vitally important to remember. With a firm knowledge of safety and emergency prevention, plus a healthy dose of common sense, you can literally sidestep most potential trouble. A snake can't bite you if you recognize and avoid its habitat; an avalanche can't bury you if you spot a potential slide and steer clear of it; a bear encountered on the trail probably won't attack you if you make the right moves, and so on. This all reverts to knowledge of what and what not to do; the meat of this emergency/survival guide.

Last, and somewhat reassuring, is that once emergencies occur—once you are caught in the snowslide, or attacked by a bear or snake—the end is not necessarily in sight. Here again knowledge will help you, save you, by dictating the proper moves. That knowledge is also a major part of this book.

Now that you are able to view outdoor mishaps realistically without fearing them, let's focus on this thing we call an emergency, and see just what sort of a beast we're dealing with; its appearance, structure and physiology.

First, I suppose, we should define the term. Traditionally, outdoor "survival" has been dealt with only in limited form, covering the same sort of thing we saw in the opening scene of this chapter—a lost man fighting for bare subsistence in the wilds. Occasionally, books vary the theme slightly and include other gut-level predicaments such as being adrift at sea in a raft or being stranded in a wild land after a plane crash. This Robinson Crusoe stuff is not without merit—and, indeed, is covered in depth in these pages—but there is a lot more to safe outdoor recreation than knowing which plants are edible and how to start a fire with two sticks.

There are the far more frequent dangers, less dramatic perhaps than spending 20 days on a life raft, but just as much a threat to your health and well-being. There are the minor emergencies—a fishhook in your arm, a blister on your heel, a belligerent moose blocking your trail—that are far more common, and which are capable of blossoming into serious problems unless handled properly. And there are countless other domestic mishaps—falling down in a deep stretch of trout stream, riding out a storm while boating, avoiding catastrophe while canoeing or rafting, rescuing a man overboard, extricating a mired vehicle, treating assorted injuries—and many, many more perils you can encounter in the outback. All of these need to be included in a discussion of "survival."

These types of emergencies can happen on any outdoor excursion, not just on far-off wilderness treks. By my reckoning, more mishaps are encountered while hunting, fishing or camping near home than far away.

A recent survey by an automobile safety group showed that a striking 90 percent of all auto accidents occurred within two miles of the victim's home. I think there's a parallel here to outdoor accidents. Most occur a reasonably short distance from home, partially because that is where the average nimrod spends most of his time, and largely because we tend to grow careless in familiar bailiwicks.

You most likely are the cause of your own problems. Most mishaps will be the result of your own lack of prudence or sense. It's not an easy notion to accept, but it's an important one.

Granted, there are those rare times when fate stacks up against you and smacks you with an earthquake, hits you with a cannonading boulder or drops a landslide on your camp. These things do happen, but not often.

"But wait a minute," you say. "How about the poor guys who are just walking along, minding their own business, when a snake reaches out and poisons them? That's the damn snake's fault. Right?"

Well, maybe. But if a hunter is walking along shady rock ledges during a hot day, is it really an accident if he's bitten by a snake? He should know better than to frequent prime snake habitat, and had he been alert and used a little sense, he could have easily skirted the snake pit and avoided trouble.

Similarly, if a skier glides out on a sagging snow cornice, is it really an Act of God that he tumbles down a snowslide? Most people would say it was not. It was the skier's fault for not using common sense. The point here is not to quibble over the academic question of who's right or wrong, but to illustrate the fact that you can find the root of most of your outdoor troubles by looking in a mirror—at yourself.

That is not to say that all emergencies will be your own doing. There are times when you are placed in a dire situation by the ineptness or carelessness of someone else. A friend of mine had his 12-foot cartop boat anchored off a wooded point while fishing for bass. An overengined boat skippered by a fool roared around the point at a wholly unsafe speed and broadsided my friend's boat, throwing him overboard with wounds that crippled him for life. Another friend took a load of buckshot in the arm after a careless partner accidentally discharged a shell. The list of these accidents is endless: one hunter mistaking another for an elk, a fisherman catching a buddy in the ear with treble hooks, a camper parting with his ax in midswing and a fellow camper catching it in midsection. These sorts of disasters are largely those which you have no way of preventing. The outcome depends on how well you handle the situation once it occurs.

There's one more emergency producing catalyst you should be aware of and educated against: misinformation—remedies, corollaries and misleading clichés that have been handed down as fact by dubious sources. A golden example, perhaps, is the old wheeze about moss growing only on the north side of trees. This not-so-sage bit of advice has led more than one befuddled tyro in a circle through the woods. Fortunately, most outdoorsmen today know that moss grows on any side of a tree that offers favorable combinations of moisture and light. It's not uncommon to see a tree carpeted with moss on all sides, south as well as north.

Another common notion is that frostbitten hands should be rubbed with snow, or immersed in kerosene. Just why anyone would assume that cold snow or kerosene would help a frozen hand is beyond me, but it was (and is, in some cases) a procedure resorted to by many. That, of course, is exactly what you should not do. Nor should you rub a frost-bitten limb as is commonly believed. The hand should be warmed gently, as per the instructions given in the first aid section of this book (Chapter 19).

You've no doubt heard the advice: "When lost, follow a stream to civilization." That adage has been bandied about a bit too loosely, for it is not an unshakable maxim. Sometimes it pays to follow a stream if you are lost, but not always. There is an important consideration here that is not obvious to everyone.

In settled country this advice is usually sound. But in a wilderness area, you could trudge along a stream and find yourself getting deeper into the woods. As you'll see upon reading the "Lost!" chapter (Chapter 11), there are often far better alternatives to stream chasing when you need to find your way back.

Another tacky piece of advice usually reads like this: "Generally speaking, foods eaten by birds are safe for human consumption." (That's a direct quote actually, but I'm not saying from whom.) My question: "Generally speaking"? How do you know if the bird you see gulping down red berries is within the realm of the spoken generality? What do you do when you discover, too late, the bird was eating the berries of evening nightshade, a deadly poisonous fruit for humans? Or how about the avian species that can digest poison ivy with no ill effects, or dine on plant morsels purgative or nauseating to the human digestive tract?

An even tackier guideline that I read once and have heard more than a few times is that almost all food eaten by a wild animal is safe! This one is really off base. Ruminants—animals possessing multi-chambered stomachs (rumens) much different from our own—can eat and digest roughage you couldn't even chew. Or consider scavengers, which eat decaying, fetid materials that would wreak all sorts of havoc with human innards. And what do you say about coprophagous animals—those which are capable of eating their own fecal waste for added nutrition?

There are a host of other myths that can get you killed or hurt. To name only a few of the common ones:

When water is scarce, ration it according to the distance you have to travel.

Salt water can be drunk in small amounts if mixed with freshwater, and will sate a thirst.

Urine is drinkable.

Feces is edible.

The more clothes you wear, the warmer you'll be.

When you need a fire, all you have to do is rub two sticks together.

If you fall asleep in freezing weather, you will freeze to death in your sleep.

The temperature must be below freezing for you to die of heat loss.

This is just a light handful taken from a heavy sack. Most of these tired bromides and many others are discussed throughout the pages of this book. Be aware of them, and take them for what they are: dangerous myths.

Finally, it should be said that no one book or even series of books can cover the entire spectrum of outdoor calamities, and this one doesn't pretend to. The aim here is to isolate the common emergencies, explain how to prevent them and how to cope with them. Also included are rudimentary survival skills—reading the weather, starting fires, building shelters, finding food and water—a rundown on the mental and physical equipment that will enable you to avoid and overcome hazards.

If this book has done its job, after you put it down you'll know a lot more about staying alive than you did when you first picked it up, and you'll enjoy the outdoors a little more because of it.

2

General Emergency Procedures

Driving home one drizzly spring day after a futile trout fishing trip, my partner and I stopped our discussion short when the radio announcer droned out a report of weekend drownings in the area. The list seemed endless: two high school boys drowned when their canoe capsized near a dam spillway. A young couple trying to raft the high, torrential Blackfoot River ripped their raft apart on a branchy tree trunk that lay at the foot of the rapids—the man dragged himself to shore, but his wife wasn't so lucky. The last fatality occurred when two fishermen spilled their canoe on a deep, fast stretch of the Clark Fork River. One could swim, the other couldn't. Neither wore a life jacket. The swimmer made it to safety, the other man drowned.

After listening to these grisly drowning cases, my friend, who had only recently moved to Montana, turned and asked if there were always that many river deaths during high water. I had to answer that, sadly, there were. Every year, when the mountain snow melts and the rains fall, the larger streams and rivers swell. Rivers like the Blackfoot and the Madison—both clear, strong trout waters in the summer and fall—become roaring torrents of chocolate brown runoff. They also become graveyards for careless, adventure-seeking rafters and canoeists.

What makes these disasters even more tragic is knowing that almost all the deaths are needless. Almost without exception, the "accidents" were not accidents at all. Rather, they were consequences of foolishness. Look at the tragedies mentioned on the radio: the high school boys drowned when they paddled beyond the warning signs of the dam spillway. They invited trouble. In a later news interview, the drowned woman's husband said that he and his wife had never before rafted a river;

had, in fact, never been in any type of watercraft at all. They rented a raft and, because they had heard that the Blackfoot was a wild run in spring, launched their craft in the gushing, boulder-strewn water.

The last case was a classic. The drowned man couldn't swim—and knew he couldn't swim—yet was not wearing a life jacket. Just why he didn't wear one is anybody's guess. Perhaps he didn't want to admit to his partner his lack of swimming prowess. Perhaps he felt foolish or childish with a life jacket draped around his neck and chest. Perhaps he simply found safety jackets uncomfortable. No matter the reason, it wasn't reason enough.

All these examples point to a basic requisite for preventing and coping with emergencies: common sense.

This may seem like obvious or even unnecessary advice, but a brief look around will dictate otherwise. For example, we've all seen or read about Yellowstone Park visitors hand-feeding roadside bears. Sometimes "hand-feeding" becomes a very appropriate word, when a presumptuous bear fails to distinguish between a chunk of Aunt Martha's chocolate cake and Aunt Martha's fingers. Common sense doesn't seem to abound in such cases.

Where do you get this sense? Some people seem to be born with it. Most of us, however, must learn to acquire horse sense by blending patience with prudence.

Has impatience ever gotten you into difficulty? Perhaps you have become overanxious while unpacking your tackle at streamside and slammed the trunk door on your pet flyrod. Perhaps you neglected to stop and take compass and map bearings while hiking in uncomfortable weather, preferring to get to your destination without delay, and became lost in the process. Perhaps you didn't take the trouble to secure your boat to shore at night and awakened to find it splintered against a rock pile or lost completely. Take an honest look at any mishaps you've experienced. More than likely, impatience played a major role in causing your "accident." The surest way to prevent emergencies is to closely consider and examine an endeavor before setting out to do it.

Alertness and Awareness

Being cautious and patient in the outdoors is the first step to preventing emergencies. But a truly safe and competent outdoorsman must be able to go a step farther. He must be alert to his surroundings, knowledgeable in the way of the woods, and able to develop reliable conclusions from his observations.

I have a hunting, fishing and backpacking partner who is one of the keenest observers I have ever seen. Absolutely nothing escapes his eyes. One day, for example, while walking through an unfamiliar area, he turned and said: "This slope must have an interesting fire history." I looked up the slope and agreed. The mountainside was covered with blotches of western larch—a tree that grows readily in burned over western woods. Scattered throughout were various mosses and liverworts which also find a fire-cleared habitat favorable. Dotting the forest floor in lavender patches were fireweed plants—classic indicators of disturbed, burned sites. My partner had observed these clues without conscious effort. Because of his tremendous enthusiasm and interest in nature, he has developed a sharp awareness of his surroundings. It's not likely that he will ever be surprised by a blizzard or heavy rainstorm. Nor is he likely to starve in the outdoors as long as any edible plants or animals are present. His unfailing alertness and woods know-how not only increase his enjoyment of the outdoors, they increase his safety tenfold.

You can learn alertness, just as you can learn caution. You can learn to interpret the woods and weather by closely observing the outdoors in which you work or play. Chapters 3 and 19 will discuss the importance of practicing emergency techniques, but let me mention here that the fastest way of developing an acute "woods sense" is by conscious practice *in the outdoors*. Become familiar with the ways of natural systems. Know which plants and animals exist in the areas you hunt, fish or camp. Know the potential dangers.

It doesn't take an extraordinarily long time to develop knowledge and alertness to a modest level. The observant friend I mentioned earlier is in his early twenties, and is living proof that you don't have to be a white-bearded woods veteran to accumulate outdoor savvy.

There are a number of ways to learn about outdoor life. You can consult literally hundreds of excellent books on ecology and natural science, ranging from sophisticated scientific stuff to general information. A treasure trove of know-how can be tapped from conversations with scientists, rangers, naturalists and experienced woodsmen. There are even high-caliber college courses in wildlife biology, forestry, geology and zoology, from which you can learn a great deal of applicable outdoor lore. Best of all, you can combine these learning methods with knowledge gained from your own excursions. The results of such an education serve you in many ways—especially by keeping you out of trouble.

Personal Prevention

There is one person who can do more than anyone else to ensure your safety: *You.*

No one knows your strengths and weaknesses, your pleasures and fears better. And only you can tell if your body is tired, your feet cold or your head fuzzy. Trouble often arises in the outdoors when individuals fail to cater to their idiosyncrasies, or worse, try to cover them up.

Many a desk-bound worker, soft of muscle and low of endurance, has ventured carelessly into strenuous outdoor activity and suffered tragic consequences—very often from heart attack. Doctors tell me that, most of the time, the heart attack could have been avoided had the individual recognized his condition and rested before fatigue and strain set in.

My uncle, Joe Kieffer, is on the downward slope of his sixties. However, his age hasn't dampened his enthusiasm for things natural and wild. If anything, the opposite is true. But he refuses to be rushed or pushed beyond comfort when on the trail. Last year we were hiking in Tennessee's Cherokee National Forest. The trail cut up a steep mountain slope in long tedious switchbacks. About half way up my uncle stopped and called to me (I was a few yards ahead): "Hey boy, my heart's pounding like a drum. I'm going to rest for a few minutes. Go ahead if you want to."

I backed down the trail, shaking my head in mock disgust.

"I dunno, Unc," I prodded, "you must be getting old, resting at every corner."

"That's right," he answered, dabbing sweat from his neck, "and I intend to get a lot older—which is what I wouldn't do if I tried to keep up with you."

If you are out of shape or have an ailment or phobia, don't ignore it or pretend otherwise. Take whatever precautions you feel are necessary. Don't be embarrassed if you harbor strong fears of high places, dense woods, wild animals, darkness, being alone, or whatever. As you become more familiar with the outdoors and accumulate experience, many of the fears will dissipate. But until they do, recognize them, or they could force you into making an irrational decision, which in turn could generate an emergency. If you have even a mild sort of claustrophobia (fear of small places), you could become uncontrollably panicked in deep woods or high grass. Or, if you suffer from acrophobia (fear of heights), you could black out while standing on a precarious rock ledge. Don't allow yourself to be in a situation where you may lose self-control. Without a rational mind working for you, you become vulnerable to a wide variety of outdoor hazards.

Your Body's Signs

The human body reacts to environmental change with physiological responses—sometimes delicately, sometimes harshly. You can avoid many difficulties by being sensitive to the warning signals your body flashes. Here are some basic troubles that can confront anyone who ventures outdoors.

Fatigue

All of us, at one time or another, have experienced exhaustion and muscle fatigue, perhaps by backpacking with an overweight pack, wading too long in a deep, bucking river current, or hunting nonstop in rugged terrain. No matter what activity you pursue, don't allow yourself to become fatigued. In most cases there is simply no excuse for it. When fatigued, your muscles behave like weak rubber, your senses become dulled; you become apathetic and unable to make judicious decisions. You lose safe control of your mind and body. In short, you are literally begging for an emergency.

The signs of fatigue are easy to spot. Heavy breathing—to the point of all-out wheezing—is a sign that your muscles are not receiving the amount of oxygen necessary for fuel processing. When this happens, lactic acid accumulates and fatigue sets in. Normal muscle use is impaired. The fatigued muscles ache and may shake perceptibly. When you recognize these symptoms, stop! Sit down and rest. Breathe freely, and don't try to suppress your deep panting.

Muscles regain their strength rapidly, and a 15-minute break returns up to 90 percent of your muscle power. However, as you continue along, your slightly sapped muscles will succumb to fatigue more easily, so it pays to slow your walking and increase your rest stops.

When children are along on a trip, watch them carefully for signs of fatigue. Most don't recognize exhaustion, and will run until they drop.

Hypothermia

Hypothermia is one of the leading killers of outdoorsmen, yet a surprising number of people know nothing about it. Hypothermia occurs when the body loses heat faster than it can be replaced. It is not, however, limited to cold-weather situations. Hypothermia can occur even in mild climes: You may be drenched from a rain in 50 degree weather and be unable to retain body heat, or on a warm day you may lose body heat rapidly while standing in swimming trunks on a windswept ridge. Anywhere you encounter wind, cold or wetness, you can encounter hypothermia.

Like fatigue, hypothermia is easy to recognize in its early stages. Also like fatigue, failure to respond to the warnings can take you to a point of physical and mental helplessness, where you can no longer control your actions. If you recognize symptoms of hypothermia, act immediately. This cannot be overemphasized.

The first sign of heat loss is shivering—your body's way of creating heat. Shivering consumes high amounts of energy and weakens your resistance to stress. If you begin to shiver, if only once or twice, immediately call to mind the possibility of hypothermia. If the shivering persists, you are losing heat rapidly. Begin to treat yourself at once. If you are wet, dry yourself if possible. Water—rain, snow or sweat—evaporates surface heat at incredible speed, virtually refrigerating you. Add dry clothing if available. Build a fire; boil coffee, tea or even plain water to drink for vital heat. Do anything necessary to stop shivering and gain warmth. If the shivering stops, your body has restored essential heat.

There is no good reason to pass the shivering stage before detecting heat loss, but there are additional warnings that indicate advanced stages of hypothermia: shivering becomes constant and uncontrollable, making it difficult to operate the limbs and perform ordinary tasks; spoken words become tangled—you mumble and lose control of tongue and lips; shivering begins to lessen—your muscles feel boardlike and rigid, your senses are dull, your thinking fuzzy. You become apathetic at this stage, and can no longer help yourself. You will die if on your own. However, if another person recognizes these symptoms, and acts immediately to restore your body heat, you still can be saved. When body temperature drops more than 12 degrees you become irrational. Environmental awareness ceases and you float into a stupor. Your breathing and heartbeat slow. Survival is still possible if body heat can be restored, providing your condition becomes obvious to companions. If they are familiar with hypothermia treatment, you still have a chance. If not, you will lose consciousness. Your heartbeat will flutter erratically. Your brain, heart and lungs will begin to malfunction. And finally, when your temperature dips below 78 degrees, you will die.

Dehydration

The average outdoorsman is not in direct danger of dying from dehydration. Chances are water would be ingested before the problem became severe enough to cause death. But I include it here because, like fatigue and hypothermia, dehydration produces dangerous side effects —physiological responses that dull your judgment and movements and make you susceptible to other dangers. A hiker, dizzy from undetected water loss, may trip and fall down a steep trail. A person driving across a hot, dry area may be losing water rapidly without knowing it and black out at the wheel. The most dangerous problem with dehydration is that the symptoms—unlike fatigue and hypothermia—are not easily recognized. You can be severely short of water, yet not feel more than usually thirsty. You can be dizzy, plagued by a headache, nauseated— all signs of dehydration—and not be aware of your need for water. Again the danger is not that you will dry up and die. It is the loss of body control that can get you in trouble. There are, however, some clues that indicate lack of water.

First, of course, you will feel thirsty. Not exceptionally parched, just thirsty. You should drink water whenever you feel dry. You needn't gulp down a gallon; just take a few swallows at regular intervals throughout the day.

If you are thirsty, but drink no water, another sign of early dehydration will be the color of your urine. Dark yellow urine indicates deficient water. If your skin is flushed, your mood irritable and impatient, your condition nauseous, you are feeling the effects of one to five percent dehydration. If water is available, you'll need no further symptoms to persuade you to drink. But don't wait this long to notice your water needs. It may lead to other troubles.

Water is such a vital concern, an entire later chapter is devoted to finding and conserving it. But remember that dehydration can sneak up on you if you aren't careful and rob you of your normal good sense.

Heat Stroke and Exhaustion

Another hazard to your health and judgment is heat-caused body malfunctions. First, let's look at heat exhaustion. Less severe than heatstroke, it is still important to anyone who finds recreation in hot climates.

Heat exhaustion usually is caused by overexertion in hot temperatures, particularly when coupled with high humidity. Heat regulatory systems in the body break down and overheating occurs. Blood circulation is disrupted, causing an insufficient flow of blood. You feel faint and tired, and sweat profusely. Your face may become flushed initially, but will pale. Nausea will grip you. You may vomit. Your breath becomes short, your vision blurred. The signs need not be more obvious. Immediately find shade—or make shade by using a tarp, shirt or newspaper—anything that will block out the sun. If sufficient water is available, drink liberally, then pour water over your head, neck and chest. If a companion is handy, have him fan you if no breeze is blowing to aid in evaporation of surface water.

All of this sweating removes sodium or salt from your system, so you'll need to ingest extra amounts to make up for the loss. Plain table salt, mixed lightly with food or water, will compensate for the deficiency.

Heatstroke is more serious. The body's cooling system is overworked and fails completely. Usually this is caused by heavy sweating in hot, humid weather, particularly when there is no wind. Ill or elderly individuals are especially prone to experience heat dangers, and they should watch carefully for the symptoms.

Unlike heat exhaustion, heatstroke is not accompanied by sweating. It is in fact this lack of sweating that serves as the telltale sign that heatstroke is present rather than heat exhaustion. It is also vital that heatstroke be recognized and treated well before the cessation of sweating.

Usually initial sweating is accompanied by weakness, headache and cramps. These signs should be regarded seriously, for they are harbingers of a full-blown stroke. Don't wait for further prodding; treat the symptoms immediately.

If sweating stops, and the victim takes on a pallid, clammy countenance, the stroke has advanced into dire stages. He will become delirious and fall into a coma. Irreversible brain damage or death will follow if treatment isn't given soon. Total immersion in cool water is the best remedy.

You can avoid heat dangers in the first place by going slow in uncomfortably warm weather, particularly if you're unaccustomed to heat and hard work. A broadbrimmed hat that shades the head and neck will keep you cooler, as will frequent gulps from the canteen. If you're heading into hot, dry areas, pack along extra water—more than you think you'll need. Again, watch carefully for heat exhaustion and heatstroke symptoms and treat them immediately.

Pain

Your body's most obvious danger signal is pain. A stinging sore heel may be an omen of a later blister. Tender, throbbing skin may indicate initial stages of sunburn. Aching eye muscles may suggest eye fatigue, or oncoming snowblindness. Nobody likes pain, but small pains—when tended to quickly—can goad you into preventing much greater later suffering. You alone must recognize and interpret your pains; obviously, no one else can do it for you.

Don't try to be tough and ignore minor discomforts. Recognize them for what they are worth. An aching leg may indicate only that your muscles are getting some unconditioned use, but a throbbing headache may mean initial heatstroke or dehydration. You needn't become a hypochondriac, but listen when your body tries to tell you something. After all, it is on your side.

Choosing Companions

I flatly refuse to risk my neck by accompanying an unsafe person in the outdoors. I've had too many close calls with inept, incautious partners to bend my luck any farther. Several years ago a man I knew and liked approached me and suggested a fishing trip. I had never fished with him before, but had heard him speak often of fishing and hunting adventures. I accepted his invitation, but it took only two hours of partnership to realize my mistake.

Joe, as we will uncreatively call him, had a spooky habit of side casting half-ounce bass plugs, glistening with treble hooks, in careless swinging throws. After ducking a number of casts, I politely suggested he be more careful. He said he *was* careful and continued swinging his lures in my direction. He finished a beer and tossed the can overboard—to my astonishment. He clattered his tacklebox against the aluminum boat floor when he changed lures. He made jerky movements without warning, rocking the boat harshly. He sped his boat through stump-infested channels and backwaters with careless abandon. The day had scarcely begun when I was ready to quit. My attention was not focused on bass fishing, but on staying alive.

A poor companion can ruin your fun, but he can do much more than that. He can ruin your life, or end it. A careless partner who points the business end of his gun at you; a boater who speeds in shallow water with no regard for your safety; a backpacker who whips you in the face with a recoiling branch—all are hazards to your health. Avoid them. Instead, seek out individuals who match your level of interest, enthusiasm and caution. If you enjoy leisurely backpacking, stopping often to observe wildflowers, animals and scenery, don't hit the trail with a partner who delights in walking as many miles as a day allows. Chances are you will both become irritable. You will get sore legs trying to keep up with him, and he will become impatient waiting for you. And if you know a person to be reckless and short-tempered in daily life, you can bet he will be more so in the woods. Don't risk your safety with him.

On Going Alone

The standard warning in safety and emergency guides is an emphatic: "Don't go alone! Always have a partner in case of trouble." I'm going to stray from that well-worn path and offer a different view. Going alone —if you are thoroughly versed in outdoor safety and survival and follow a few guidelines—is vastly safer than accompanying an incautious companion. Put another way, the idea of "any companion is better than no companion" is bunk. A good, safe partner is pure pleasure and delight. A poor, unsafe one is painful and unhealthy. You are much better off, in the latter instance, completely on your own, provided you have the necessary knowledge. I don't suggest that a newcomer to the outdoors buy shiny new equipment and strike off into the brush. Not at all. But once that newcomer is familiar with map and compass, emergency prevention and action, and basic woods lore, he has nothing to fear in the outdoors. I'm speaking now of practical knowledge—not just knowing that purslane is edible, but being able to identify it; familiar not only with the theory of orientation, but able to plot and follow a course through the woods. At this level of proficiency you can find unmatched satisfaction in an intimate relationship with the land. You discover true independence. The pace of your walk, the tempo of your casting, the depth of your observation—all cater exclusively to your whims. But you must still follow one rule: let at least one reliable person know where you are going and when you will return. Even if the outing is on a trout stream close to home or in nearby woods, inform someone of your whereabouts. Incidentally, if you say you are going to a certain area, inform your contact if there is a change in plans. Failure to do this can mean a search party is combing an area you said you were going to be, and not the area where you are lost or in trouble.

Once you possess the essential knowledge of emergency prevention and action, and the security of having somebody know of your whereabouts, you may find the ultimate companion within yourself.

3

Preparing for the Unexpected

Several years ago I went to the woods with a man who excelled in primitive survival skills. Starting with nothing more than his bare hands, ingenuity and bits of rock, twigs, branches and vines, he eked out a comfortable living in the forest. He started a fire faster with bow and drill than some can with matches. With bone and rock he quickly chipped out a crude knife that functioned surprisingly well. He straightened reeds and willow stems into arrows, and fastened glass-sharp rock arrowheads onto the shaft with string he spun from vine. The bow he carved delicately from serviceberry wood, planing the limbs evenly with his rock knife. He turned the limbs slowly over a fire, weakening the wood temporarily so it could be fitted around a circular rock to harden into stiff recurves. The bowstring was meticulously spun and woven and tested. By snapping off the lower boughs of spruce and fir, he garnered materials for his shelter. A nearby creek furnished water. Before evening shaded the forest, he had engineered a comfortable camp without the aid of civilized equipment.

I was awed and impressed. I said half seriously that he probably didn't spend much for equipment in a year—he just made it all himself. He replied: "It isn't until you go without equipment that you really appreciate how much it is worth. I had it easy here. The weather is warm, water is handy, and we had breakfast this morning. Not very pressing circumstances. If it was cold, or very hot, or if my leg was broken, or if I hadn't eaten in days, then it would be a real survival test. One I'm not sure I would want to try without any basic gear."

The more I learn about the outdoors the more I agree. It's true that you can fashion your tools and needs from raw materials, but in many cases there is no need. You can carry basic gear with you—items that will keep minor troubles from turning into major crises.

Preparing for trouble may seem like a pessimist's task, but it isn't. Ignoring emergencies doesn't prevent them; it usually promotes them. It doesn't take much time to pack an emergency rucksack, check for necessary RV or boat safety equipment or round up an effective first aid kit. I hope you'll never need to build an emergency shelter, put out an inboard fire, or treat yourself for snakebite, but if the situation arises, the equipment is priceless.

Of course, to help you, emergency gear must be with you. Your doctor-approved first aid kit isn't much help if it's in the car while you're bleeding in the woods. To keep gear handy, many woodsmen sew a small pouch of essentials to the inside of their coats or drill compartments into their gunstocks. I have a special inner pocket in my down parka that always contains matches, strong fishing line and other necessities. If it's cold enough to be wearing the parka, it won't hurt to have matches and other emergency gear handy, just in case. But obviously, this has limitations. Gunstock kits and jacket pouches are fine for what they're worth, but they are not enough.

For carrying gear on your person, wear a pack. This can be a small rucksack worn on your back, or a belt pack that fits around your hips and buttocks. The pack needn't be large or noticeably heavy, and when equipped with basic gear, it should be snug fitting and comfortable, allowing you free movement of arms and torso.

For vehicles, be they canoes or motor homes, have a compact emergency kit stashed in an allotted place. Be sure the kit is easily accessible.

Essential Emergency Gear

You'll need a wide range of materials to have a truly adequate emergency kit, but it's surprising how much fits into a small pack.

First, include a map of your area. Topographic maps are best and can be obtained from a number of places. (See Chapter 11.) If topos aren't available, settle for detailed county maps. Road maps, if nothing else can be found, are better than nothing. To supplement the map, pack a compass. There are many types, but the lensatic and orienteering (see Chapter 11 illustrations) are best for most usage. Carry one in a pocket and have another one in your pack.

A spool of monofilament fishing line, at least 60-pound test, takes up a small space and can be used for lashings, snares and, of course, emergency fishing. Other assorted gear includes two knives, one in your pocket or on your belt, and another in your pack (sheath knife for belt, space-saving folding knife for your pack); flashlight with spare batteries; fishing hooks, sizes 1 and 2; signaling mirror; loud clear whistle; halazone tablets for purifying water; insect repellent; extra clothing (see section in this chapter on clothing); notebook and pencil; and food. Best foods are dried fruits, commercial food sticks (tasteless but nutritional), beef jerky and pemmican. The latter can be purchased commercially or made by following the instructions given in the chapter on food (see Chapter 13). Also carry a small aluminum foil salt package for spicing emergency foods and replacing sodium lost through exercise.

To ensure a fire when one is necessary, carry matches in a waterproof match safe. Metal containers are difficult to use in severe cold or if rusted. Plastic is sturdy and effective. Have one match container in your pocket, another larger one in your pack. As an extra precaution, carry a Metal Match—a small stick of special metal that produces sparks when grated against a knife or rock. The Metal Match is waterproof and will last for hundreds of fires. Candles are also handy to have for building fires, especially when working with damp wood. You can buy short, stubby candles that fit nicely into your pack, or cut regular table candles into two-inch sections. Commercial fire-starting tablets can be purchased in place of candles if you like. The tablets burn more intensely than candles, but don't last as long.

For shelter, take along an 8×8- or 10×10-foot canvas or nylon tarp or space blanket equipped with corner and side grommets. These fold up neatly into the bottom of your pack, and are cheap insurance should you need to spend a night in the woods.

To take care of your water needs, carry a full-quart water canteen. If you'll be traveling in a waterless area, add a 4×4-foot sheet of clear plastic. The plastic can be used to make a solar still that manufactures water, and also serves as a supplement to a tarp shelter.

If you wear eyeglasses and are dependent on them, carry a spare pair in your pack. Tend to any other personal needs as well. There are no stores in the backcountry.

First Aid Kit

A first aid kit should also be in your pack and, indeed, it is one of the most important items. Don't throw a first aid kit together hastily or settle for a cheap store-bought one. There are some good premade kits on the market, but check them carefully to be sure they cater to outdoor needs. Whether you buy a kit or make your own, familiarize yourself with the contents and know how to use each item.

The basic kit will contain:

Aspirin or Tylenol	To relieve mild pain;
or	ease shock.
Empirin, codeine or Darvon	Stronger pain killers; latter two require doctor's prescription.
Lomotil tablets	For diarrhea.
Burn ointment	
Merthiolate or similar antiseptic	For cuts, wounds.
Insect bite lotion (calamine)	
Personal medication, such as allergy or heart pills	

For Dressing Wounds
Assorted Band-Aids
Eyepads 2×2″ (two)
Gauze pads
Clean handkerchief
Butterfly strips
Adhesive tape (small roll)
Gauze roller bandages

Other Items

Scissors	For cutting bandages and adhesives.
Tweezers	For removing thorns and splinters.
Folding cup	
Safety pins	For holding bandages, splints.
Moleskin	For blisters.
Small bar of soap	

A snakebite kit should be added, complete with scalpel and suction cups. Antivenin serum is available through doctor's prescription, but entails the use of hypodermic injections. A lot of controversy revolves around the worth of antivenin in the hands of laymen, with each doctor having his own opinion. On trips that take you into snake country far from professional help, it may be wise to pack serum. However, talk to your doctor and seek his advice.

The first aid kit should be bolstered if you're planning a long trip or one that takes you far in the outback. Increase the number of bandages, gauze and adhesive. Add a thermometer to aid in diagnosing illness.

Mosquitoes and black flies can be exceptionally plentiful in wilderness areas, so pack extra insect repellent and bite cream.

If your plans include water craft, you may want to include Dramamine, Marezine or Bucladin for relief of seasickness. Dramamine and Marezine have the sometimes unwanted side effect of making you drowsy, while Bucladin does not. Again, see your doctor or druggist for details.

Other Equipment

Sunglasses

One piece of equipment that every outdoorsman should own is a pair of sunglasses. The glasses reduce glare and minimize eye fatigue. They also serve double duty by protecting your eyes from unseen branches or bits of dirt and sand. The best glasses for field sports have gray-tinted glass lenses, also known as "photosuns." These glasses offer variable shading. In bright light, the lenses darken, while in shade the glass changes tint to let in more light. For boaters, fishermen and other water sportsmen, polarized glasses are the best bet. Water glare is efficiently removed even when viewed through a boat windshield—something the photosun model cannot do.

No matter what style you buy, check to make sure they fit perfectly. Get large lenses; they cover more of the eye and do not allow glare leaks to flash in from the side. The glasses should fit comfortably without sliding down your nose, and the earpiece should extend well past your ear. For the best fit, have the frames adjusted by a professional.

Firearms

Some survival guides recommend carrying sidearms, .22 rifles or special "survival" pistols that shoot both shotshells and bullets. Except for hunting trips, where guns are already basic gear, the weight and space of a pistol or rifle doesn't really justify packing it. You have to be pretty handy with a sidearm to hit a small target at even modest range. In most cases, if game is close enough for the average outdoorsman to hit with a pistol, it's probably close enough to be clubbed or strangled by hand. However, if you can sling a pistol effectively, or if it gives you added assurance (however false) to tote one, the choice is yours. Just don't be fooled into believing sidearms are great emergency gear.

I have never used the iron framed, stockless .22 rifles designed for backpacking and survival purposes. Again, I hesitate to suggest one, although in average hands a rifle is much more effective than a handgun.

Most models break down into two small sections for easy packing. If you see a need for a small caliber rifle and want to invest the money, check one out at a local gun shop. However, stand warned that guns are overrated as necessary survival gear.

Specialized Emergency Equipment

Wilderness Gear

For traveling in areas well removed from civilization, extra emergency gear is mandatory. Besides the basic emergency pack described earlier (which should be along on all trips, regardless of distance) add 50 feet of nylon or manila rope (quarter-inch and three-eighths-inch respectively); copper wire for constructing snares; an ax, the lighter cruiser model or a full-size pole ax, depending on available space; some flare and smoke candle signaling devices; two hacksaw blades, taped, for emergency saws; extra fishing hooks and a pair of spoon-type lures; a medium-size pan for cooking emergency foods; a sewing kit, complete with a variety of needles and strong thread; and increased emergency food rations.

Another form of emergency "equipment" for wilderness treks is tetanus immunization. Everyone should be adequately immunized against tetanus infection, whether in the outback or not, but on extended excursions it is doubly important to have up-to-date protection. If you cut a finger on a tin can lid, or even worse, amputate it with a careless ax stroke, you are vunerable to infection. Tetanus protection is fast, painless and inexpensive. There's no excuse for not having it.

Fishing Gear

Fishing is by no stretch of the definition a dangerous pastime, but since it involves being on, in, or around water, there is always the possibility of drowning. An easy way to combat this danger is by adding a floating jacket to your duffel. These jackets are neat looking, comfortable and, most important, they float you like a balloon. In warmer weather, when flotation coats are uncomfortable, boat fishermen should carry the standard tie or snap keyhole life jackets. Wading fishermen in warm weather should at least have a chest sash for sealing their waders—should they fall, the locked-in air helps them float.

Boating

When a vehicle is used for outdoor sports, the amount of essential emergency gear doubles. This is absorbed, however, by the extra cargo load the craft can carry. In boating, the first safety items are life preservers. Any Coast Guard approved model is sufficient, but the recommended type is a tie-on vest. Floating coats, as mentioned for fishermen, work nicely and offer a less cumbersome fit. One readily accessible preserver should be carried for each person on board.

If your boat has a gas-burning engine, you'll need a workable fire extinguisher. There are different types of extinguishers, but the kind required for boats are labeled "Class B." Class B extinguishers handle gas, oil and grease fires, and usually contain carbon dioxide foam or dry powder. Carbon dioxide tanks should be weighed when new and reweighed every few months to check for leakage. If the tank loses more than ten percent of its original weight, have it checked professionally to be sure it is safe.

To remove the water that invariably collects on boat floors, you will need a bilge bailer. For larger boats such as cabin cruisers, you may want elaborate electric pumps. For fishing craft or small pleasure boats, the top half of a gallon plastic jug (with handle and cap attached) may suffice as a hand bailer.

Assorted other items include spare oars or paddles; extra line; a portable radio to announce storm or emergency alerts; anchors—one for small fishing craft, two or more for larger boats (you may have to ride out a storm at anchor); a boat compass that can give clear readings on a bobbing sea; a boat hook; distress signal flares and smoke bombs; an ample supply of fresh drinking water (especially at sea); spare engine parts; spare fastenings—especially sheer pins for outboards; and a complete set of tools, including screwdrivers, pliers, wrenches, ball peen hammer and specialized implements. Binoculars are handy for checking distant points and searching for rescue craft. A ring buoy is valuable for larger boats in case of a man overboard. Rafters and canoeists should carry quick-dry repair kits to patch up rips and punctures. Premade kits are available at marinas and outdoor discount houses.

One other item that is truly lifesaving for powerboaters—most notably bass boaters—is a mechanical kill switch that immediately shuts off the engine if you are thrown overboard, preventing a disastrous run-in with the props or a smack on the head from the moving boat. The driver attaches a line from the kill switch to himself, and if he is thrown overboard, the jerk on the line shuts off the engine. Installation of one of these devices is simple and requires no drilling or wiring. The small price of this item, about $7, makes it a sensible and reasonable investment.

Hunting

Most hunters can get along nicely with the basic emergency pack described earlier. Since hunting is usually a late-season affair, it is wise to pack some extra cold-weather clothing, which will be discussed in detail later in this chapter.

Since hunters frequent areas where it is easy to become lost, a roll of bright red tape helps find the way back. The tape is used to mark trees, rocks and other trailside objects, making backtracking simple. Of course, the tape should be removed as you work your way back.

It never hurts to stuff some extra cartridges or shotshells in your pack before a hunt. A polished Magnum without ammo can't shoot game or signal for help. It doesn't even make an effective club. Play it safe and carry extra ammunition.

Backpacking and Hiking

Of pure necessity, backpackers must carry enough merchandise on their backs to survive for the duration of their trip. Not much extra emergency gear is required, but a few items are often overlooked.

If you're hiking in bear country—and that takes in a wide range—a good way to keep bears from poking around your camp at night is to suspend your food in a distant tree. For this, carry a 50-foot length of small diameter rope and pack your food items in nylon stuff sacks. The sacks are inexpensive and come in a wide range of sizes.

It pays to fashion a small kit of repair materials for your pack. A broken strap or broken strap-ring attachment can be a problem if you are deep in the backcountry. The kit should include black electrician's tape for repairing straps, a spare strap, ring clips for strap attachments and a few inch-long cotter pins in case a strap pin is lost.

RV Camping

Camping is such a broad-level pastime today, it is impossible to cover the whole gamut from tent-trailers to motor homes. Scores of books have been written on each individual facet. Here is a smattering of suggestions for emergency needs.

For RVers, a lot of minor emergencies revolve around malfunctioning equipment. You could be crossing a desert, pop a fan belt, and suddenly break down, becoming stranded in a dangerously hot, isolated terrain. Or a windshield wiper blade may come apart during the height of a Midwest rainstorm. The list is endless. Nobody can anticipate all possible troubles, but assuming your vehicle is properly maintained and in good running order, most breakdowns result from minor causes. Particularly common are broken fan belts, corroded battery cables, burned out electric fuses, flat tires, leaking radiators and, of course, lack of fuel. It pays to stock your tool box (which should always be along, and well equipped) with fuses, battery cable cleaners, an extra cable, spare belts for each one on the engine and a can of liquid metal for patching minor radiator leaks. (Serves for minor gas tank leaks also—temporarily.) You must have a quality spare tire and rim at all times. If you pop a tire and use your only spare, don't take any chances. Have the flat repaired, if possible, or buy a new tire to have mounted on the rim. Incidentally, if you tote a heavy load (pickup camper and larger), purchase only high-quality six-ply or eight-ply tires. Rubber with lower ratings cannot withstand the abuse given to a heavily used camper.

It never hurts to carry a five-gallon can of gasoline along in case you run out short of your destination. Don't carry the gas in the cheap tin cans used for around-the-house gas storage. Buy a heavy-duty five-gallon can with a self-locking, screw-on top. If possible, strap the can on the outside of the vehicle, either on top if you have carrying racks, or high on the back of the camper.

If you depend on propane or butane gas for fueling your heater, refrigerator and other appliances, pack along extra bottled gas on extended trips—especially in cold weather.

Another area of trouble for RVers is getting stuck in sand, mud or snow. The best way to prepare for this is to study a backroad cautiously before riding over it. Even then you may find yourself suddenly buried to the bumper. Basic removal gear includes shovel, chains, heavy-duty jack, strong rope, a pair of foot-long planks, and fine-mesh wire screening for supporting a jack on sand. If you have a winch on your vehicle, you will also want a deadman—an iron bar that is planted in the ground or between two sturdy objects to brace the winch line.

Clothing

Almost every emergency guide provides lengthy advice on building survival snares and starting fires without matches, but few even touch on the vital importance of outfitting yourself with proper clothing. In a severe climate, you wouldn't last long enough to build a snare or start a fire if your clothing is inadequate. The wrong fabric in cold weather can make you wet from perspiration and susceptible to hypothermia. In hot weather, improper clothing can induce heatstroke. Viewed in this light, the gear you wear becomes as important as anything you pack.

A good maxim for packing clothes is: expect the worst possible conditions an area can shell out and pack accordingly. I've been fishing in southern Florida when temperatures dropped 30 degrees in a couple of hours. Similarly, days that dawn crisp and icy sometimes end in squelching heat. You can't stuff an entire wardrobe into an emergency pack, but you can fit in a garment or two that will increase your comfort range.

Remember that nights are generally cooler the farther north you go. An August day in northern Wisconsin or Michigan may be in the 80s, but nighttime temperatures may dip into the 50s. Also, figure a three degree temperature decrease for every 1,000 feet you climb in altitude. If you climb 5,000 feet to fish a glacial lake, the temperature at the lake will be 15 degrees lower than where you started. When temperatures are in the high 80s or 90s, the change isn't very noticeable. But hike from 70 degrees to 55 and the difference becomes obvious.

Winds also play an important part in fluctuating temperatures. A sheltered valley may be basking in 80 degree calm; but the mountain ridge you're climbing to may be ten degrees cooler if it is being belted with wind. The wind factor is especially important in cold weather. If you know a destined area to be periodically windy, take it into account when you dress. A wind-chill chart is shown on page 31. Familiarize yourself with the danger levels and notice how easily they can be produced by combining cold air with even a moderate wind.

Cold Weather Clothing

The big thing to remember when dressing for cold conditions is that your clothing must create dead air space between your skin and the outside air. This locks in the heat your body generates, forming a microclimate of warmth. However, if air space was all that was required to keep you warm, you could conceivably don four layers of any material and be comfortable.

Obviously, this isn't true. You must also be sure to have sufficient ventilation to prevent sweat from soaking your clothes and reducing their insulating quality. Let's say, for example, you begin a day's deer hunt by dressing heavily—a cotton undershirt, a heavy flannel shirt and a heavy wool coat. The temperature is a brisk ten degrees and you feel the chill as you leave your cabin. As you begin hunting up the ridge, the cold leaves you. Your body heat has become trapped between the layers of clothing. You continue to climb and you begin to perspire. The garment closest to your skin absorbs the sweat and becomes wet. You pause for rest, or to glass an adjacent slope for game. Maybe you open your outer coat to let in a little air. As the cold air circulates the sweat-moistened undergarment, it cools you rapidly. You begin to shiver. You zip up your coat and begin walking to regain warmth. Dressed the way you are, you could be in trouble. Your undergarment is cotton, a fabric that sucks up moisture quickly, but loses it slowly. If you stop, you will become chilled. If you continue exercising, you will only soak up more sweat. As the cotton becomes wet, it loses its insulating qualities rapidly. By the time you reach a deer wintering area five miles away, you are literally drenched and a prime candidate for hypothermia. Your next layer of clothing is becoming wet. The cold air evaporates part of the moisture, making you even colder. The only way you can stay warm now is to remove the wet clothing and hope the wool jacket will insulate you sufficiently until you make it home. The heavy clothing, although excellent when it was dry, failed to work because it didn't allow proper air circulation. In cold weather, this is a major consideration.

What then, would be a safe way to dress? Let's start from bare skin and build an effective outfit for a deer hunter in very cold weather.

First, start with a fishnet undershirt. The netting allows air to circulate freely and makes the layer of wool less irritable to the skin. Next slip on a loose-fitting wool pullover, or lacking that, a buttoned wool shirt. Over this goes a light wool jacket—the checkered kind generally worn by television lumberjacks—and the entire bundle is covered with a comfortable, light coat, preferably wool. This rig will keep you warm when you start out in the morning chill. As you travel, you will begin to heat up. Before you start sweating, stop and remove the inner wool jacket. This should fit into your emergency pack. Follow this procedure to fit your comfort needs: peeling off a layer of wool if you become warm, adding a layer if you become cold. For moderate temperatures you can eliminate the first wool jacket, merely covering your fishnet undershirt and wool shirt with a light coat. For more severe conditions the outer garment should be heavier and more wind resistant. You'll have to vary the procedure somewhat to fit your own needs.

A word here about fabrics. As indicated, for cold weather, cotton is out. Wool is the best choice for insulating shirts. Since the outfit described above was for a deer hunter, who must move silently through the woods, I dressed him in a wool overcoat. In cold weather, when silence isn't essential, I would unhesitantly swap the wool overcoat for a quality goose-down parka. In my opinion, nothing beats down when it's cold. Down is lofty and creates maximum air space for insulation. Also, if the weather warms and the parka must be shed, it rolls into a remarkably small bundle and fits easily into a pack. I bought my alpine-style down coat six years ago, and even though it's been mistreated in almost every way possible, from being dunked in a river to being smoked over countless campfires, it still keeps me warm in the coldest winter weather.

For pants, again avoid cottons. If they become wet from snow or perspiration, they will freeze cardboard-stiff. Wool is the best bet. If you need extra protection, or if wool irritates your skin, a ⅛-inch mesh pair of long johns will work nicely. There are also a number of wool-synthetic blends on the market. These aren't as scratchy as pure wool and offer satisfactory insulation.

Socks for cold weather should also be wool—or a wool-synthetic mix for tenderfeet. Two pairs of loose-fitting socks should be worn. No more, no less. The first sock should be light, athletic wool. The outer sock should be a heavier, coarser style. Carry an extra pair of socks in your emergency pack when the weather is cold. Wet socks and cold temperatures are the surest formula for frostbitten toes.

Anyone venturing into below-freezing weather should wear a warm hat. Your head is the primary radiator of body heat, and if you wear warm headgear you cut down significantly on escaped heat. This in turn allows more circulation in the extremities, keeping your hands and feet warmer. Thus the old adage, "To warm your feet, put on your hat." Wool pullover hats are good for still, cold days. Your head stays warm but enough air circulates under the hat to prevent heavy sweating. However, the hats are almost worthless in a stiff wind. The cold air stings through the gaps in the wool knit and heat is lost rapidly. A nylon hood worn over the wool hat keeps out wind, but it also restricts mobility. A better choice is a leather cap, fur-lined, with pull-down ear flaps. Another good hat, not often mentioned in outdoor guides, is the beret. These hats are comfortable and light, yet insulate well. They can be pulled down over the ears to ward off moderate winds.

For long trips in cold weather, fur-lined mittens are a must item. When resting, sitting on a hunting stand or watching an ice-fishing tip-up, mittens are the only way to keep hands warm. The mittens should fit loosely to allow maximum warmth. For more dextrous work, wear fur-lined, buckskin gloves. The leather keeps out wind and snow while the fur lining provides insulation.

When dressing for cold weather, remember the wind-chill factor. Here is a wind chart along with a brief guide for estimating wind speed:

WIND-CHILL CHART

Actual Temperature (°F.)

0	50	40	30	20	10	0	−10	−20	−30	−40

Wind Speed (mph) — Equivalent Temperature (°F.)

Wind Speed (mph)	50	40	30	20	10	0	−10	−20	−30	−40
0	50	40	30	20	10	0	−10	−20	−30	−40
5	48	37	27	16	6	−5	−15	−26	−36	−47
10	40	28	16	4	−9	−21	−33	−46	−58	−70
15	36	22	9	−5	−18	−32	−45	−58	−72	−85
20	32	18	4	−10	−25	−39	−53	−67	−82	−96
25	30	16	0	−15	−29	−44	−59	−74	−88	−104
30	28	13	−2	−18	−33	−48	−63	−79	−94	−109
35	27	11	−4	−20	−35	−51	−67	−82	−98	−113
40	26	10	−6	−21	−37	−53	−69	−85	−100	−116
Danger:	Little					Moderate		Great		

To estimate wind speed, use the following table:

5mph—Light breeze can be felt; grass and leaves rustle.

10mph—Leaves and small branches are moved; lake water ripples.

15mph—Tree branches are moved; dust or snow swirls; heavy ripples on lakes.

20mph—Snow piles in drifts; small trees sway; light waves form on water.

25mph—Large tree branches move; waves on water.

30mph—Large trees sway; loose snow swirls in clouds.

35mph—Leaves and twigs snap off trees; walking is difficult.

40mph—Branches break; trees lash wildly; whitecap waves crash; walking is difficult against wind.

Hot Weather Clothing

You needn't be as choosy when selecting hot weather clothing. Ordinary cotton shirts and pants work fine under most conditions. One prerequisite is that they fit loosely. Baggy duds aid in sweat evaporation and keep you cool. If you begin to sweat heavily, open your shirt for better ventilation, but think twice before removing it completely. Exposed skin heats rapidly under direct sunlight, dissipating body water and salt, making you susceptible to dehydration or heat dangers. You also run the risk of sunburn. It's better in many instances to keep on a light, partly opened cotton shirt. Similarly, it sometimes pays to wear light, full-length cotton trousers instead of shorts or cut-offs.

When buying clothes with hot weather in mind, choose light colors. They reflect scorching sunrays. Dark colors, on the other hand, absorb heat intensely, and can make you much hotter than you would be otherwise.

Two pairs of socks are necessary if any hiking is to be done. The inner pair absorbs sweat while the outer pair stays dry. The inner socks should be removed and dried when wet, because wet socks invite blisters. The socks should be light wool or synthetic blends. If your day is spent on a boat, or in any other way that does not require much walking, one pair of socks will suffice.

No matter what outdoor sport you pursue in hot weather, a hat will help you stay cool. The style is up to you, but the most functional types have broad brims that shade your head and neck. Your hat can also work overtime as a fan, drinking basin, water dish for your dog, or signal device. White is the best color because of its superb reflecting power.

A hot weather item often overlooked is the old-fashioned bandanna. This triangular length of cloth can be tucked partly under your hat, forming a veil for the back of your neck that wards off sunburn and keeps you cooler. To double the cooling effect, soak the neckerchief in water. As the water evaporates, the cloth cools; a delightful relief from burning sun.

Wet Weather Gear

Present-day outdoorsmen are confronted by an astonishing selection of raingear, some effective, some not worth discussing. A popular rain shield is the poncho, a large rectangle of waterproof nylon or plastic with a hole in the center for your head. Despite the large number in use, I think ponchos take a back seat to better raingear. Ponchos are clumsy and dangerous. Most leak with every move you make, and even if you do keep still, the waterproof fabric creates a literal steam bath inside, wetting your clothes with perspiration. On the trail, ponchos tend to catch on branches and twigs. If you fall, it will be flat on your face because ponchos bind you like a straightjacket. And don't wear one in a boat if you like dry legs. They function fairly well if you're on horse-back or similarly fixed in position, but that's about it.

Two-piece rainsuits are a better choice. Buy the better quality treated nylon ones; cheap plastic rips and splits the first time it is worn. It also heats easily.

Rainsuits are fine for fishing from a boat or sitting in a duckblind, but for more strenuous exercise a better ventilated outfit is needed. When hiking or hunting in a mild rain, I wear a light nylon windbreaker on top and rainsuit pants on bottom. The windbreaker allows more airflow than a standard rainsuit top.

A hat is necessary to keep your head dry and prevent water from dripping down your collar. A nylon hood keeps rain off nicely, but cuts down ventilation and restricts movement. For sitting still or exercising mildly, a hood is your best bet. If you're moving along, opt for a broad-brimmed hat.

Footgear

Footgear has taken such gargantuan strides in recent years, one almost has to speak a different language to discuss the various products intel-ligently. I suppose all the hoopla raised over boots is justified if you plan on walking the entire Appalachian Trail or down the Continental Divide, but for the average outdoorsman, boot selection need not be complicated.

The type of boot you wear depends entirely on the type of recreation you enjoy. A boater, for example, cannot expect to use the same shoe as a backpacker—at least not in most cases.

For hunting and hiking in all but very cold and wet weather, a "bird-shooter" or common hiking boot style is best. The boots are entirely leather, except for the soles, which are knobby or pleated Vibram.

Most people find the high-top-style boots more comfortable, especially in hilly country. The boots can be waterproofed with sealer preparations for traveling in light snow or wet conditions. I favor the clip-type speed laces over eyelets; speed laces require occasional tightening, but make up for this minor inconvenience by allowing you to lace quickly. Threading a bootlace through a dozen or so eyelets can be frustrating if you are in a hurry. These boots can be purchased in a price range of $20 to over $100. You can generally find a suitable model for $35 to $55. For rugged hiking, you may want steel plate reinforcers inside the toe and heel, and sponge cushioning around your ankles and boot tops. The list of additional features is immense—much like the price of a boot adorned with them. However, a good workable boot, without unneeded frills, is a reasonable and worthwhile expense.

For hunting, hiking or shore fishing in wet rain or snow, all-leather boots become limited in worth. Extremely wet conditions allow water to soak through even the best waterproofing mixture. You need to switch to a half rubber pac. The lower half of the pac is waterproof and rubber, the upper half leather. Pacs are strong and comfortable, and most important, they keep you dry. The boot shouldn't be excessively high. Tops that reach your lower calf are enough. In cold weather, they can be fitted with felt or sheepskin liners. In fact, pacs are my favorite footwear for ice fishing when used with a liner. They also work well for snowmobiling.

Plain sneakers will suffice in mild weather when boating or fishing. Good board-gripping soles and quality shoe material are the only requirements. Whether you wear high-top or low-top sneakers is purely up to comfort, because extra ankle support is not needed for most boating. A word here on safety: don't wear pacs, cowboy boots or other heavy shoes in a boat. I can testify that water filled pacs can pull you under if you fall overboard. You may think you can remove them quickly, but don't bet a penny on it. And by all means don't bet your life on it! Wear sneakers or other low-cut boating shoes and be safe.

For canoeing in mild weather, my favorite footgear is buckskin moccasins. Moccasins are light and comfortable, and shed water well. They don't fill up and weigh you down if you spill in a rapids. They are easy to make, but expensive to buy. If you can get your hands on a quality pair, you'll have one of the finest and most useful products ever invented.

Mental Preparation

The equipment you need to pack or wear for emergencies has been discussed in some detail. But the most important preparation of all is that of your mind.

I have seen normally rational and efficient men turn into fools when a crisis arose. I have seen and heard of people dying or being severely hurt because they made irrational moves. And I have felt panic swell up within myself and threaten to drown sensibility and self-control. It's easy to say not to panic in times of emergency; it's easy to tell someone to stay cool and collected. Damned easy. But if you see your child being swept down a frothy rapids, you are gripped with a panic unlike any other. Most people would dive in after the youngster and probably drown for their effort. Later someone would inevitably say that they were foolish for jumping in and probably could have saved the child had they kept cool. Of course, that is probably true. But you can't tell somebody to be calm in such an instance. The individual would need to have prepared himself in advance to operate calmly in the face of tragedy. Even then, it isn't easy.

You have to condition yourself to handle emergencies. You have to literally practice for them. Some people do this subconsciously. They practice without overtly trying. For others, however, training must be a conscious effort.

Lifeguards, park rangers, rescue men and other people routinely confronted with disaster must go through extended formal training to become efficient in handling emergencies. It's not unrealistic then to expect an outdoorsman to prepare himself as well. By practicing under simulated conditions, you begin to accept the fact that emergencies happen and you condition your mind to deal with them rationally.

The actual method of practice varies greatly. For first aid techniques, you should practice on another person. Practice the various ways of splinting, carrying and reviving an injured person. For other types of emergencies, the practice can be less direct. For instance, when you fish or hunt you inevitably pass by plants. Take a moment to identify the various species. Carry along a picture key if you're not up on your botany. See that low, woody shrub? That's serviceberry. The berries are not only edible, but taste good as well. Notice that spatterdock floating on the water? The roots are edible. In a pinch, you could live on this easy-to-find species. If you think these things to yourself, they become usable knowledge quickly. If you become lost and run out of food, you are less likely to utter your last gasp under a stand of serviceberry or near a weed-choked lake. Don't wait until an emergency to try to remember which species are edible and how to identify them. Most likely, your mind will become a confused jumble, and you'll end up eating a quart of poison ivy berries.

The following chapters cover assorted hazards and their solutions. Read them carefully, but don't stop there. Practice, both mentally and physically, the techniques described. The confidence, control and essential skills you will gain are without question the best emergency equipment on the market!

PART II

Preventing and Surviving Common Emergencies

4

Nature's Dangers

Animals

I've listed animals first not because they pose the greatest threat to outdoorsmen, but because wild beasts instill a deathly fear in many inexperienced nimrods—sometimes to a point that borders on the ridiculous.

A few days ago a friend called and asked if I could direct him to a scenic camping area. He had virtually no outdoor experience, but had become interested enough in the outdoors to want to spend five days camping and lingering in the woods.

"I want a spot," he said, "where no other people are around, and where I don't have to worry about dangerous animals."

That expression "dangerous animals" is an interesting one. Most animals can cause physical harm if pressed into fighting. If you grab a tiny pine squirrel, for example, chances are it will issue a painful and bloody bite. Yet a pine squirrel can hardly be considered "dangerous" in the usual sense of the word. What I'm saying, essentially, is that all wildlife is potentially dangerous, but must be provoked into action. In most cases, you must do considerable provoking to spur a confrontation. With a couple of exceptions to be mentioned later, wild animals have acquired an enormous fear of man and will make every effort available to avoid him.

Despite all of this, you may still encounter an animal on the trail or find one poking around your camp. Most times you need do nothing more than make your presence known to send the beast scurrying. A black bear will run away as fast—probably faster—than a white-tailed deer or a cottontail rabbit; though a run-in with a bruin triggers an

Black bears are widely distributed, but few will give you trouble if you keep a clean camp.

adrenaline rush unlike any other. Some animals, because of common abundance or behavioral characteristics, are potentially more dangerous than others. They won't attack you without reason, but they do deserve special attention.

Bears

Bears are foremost in the minds of most people. Bear stories are notorious anywhere there's a campfire, and like most word-of-mouth communications, they are exaggerated and embellished with each telling. It is a fact, though, that bears can be pesky and occasionally dangerous.

Black bears, the most common of the North American bruins, are found in the swampy tangles of the South, throughout the forests of the Northeast and Upper Midwest and in timbered areas of the West. Blacks abound throughout Canada and Alaska, excepting the Arctic climate zones. In short, most wooded, wild sections of this continent fall under the label "bear country." With the exception of panhandling national park types (which are among the most dangerous of all bears), most black bears are shy and retiring in daylight. It's difficult in many areas to see one even if you undertake a search. But nighttime is another story. This is when bears emerge from their daylight recluse and prowl for food. A camp littered with odoriferous foodstuffs is irresistible to an ever-hungry bruin, particularly one somewhat accustomed to humans and their tasty grub. Thus, heavily used canoe routes and well-worn backpacking trails often have recurring bear problems.

On the other hand, you could be in total wilderness and just as easily draw an unwanted bear into camp by being careless. At the very least, a raiding bear could scare the wits out of you, or ruin a substantial portion of your gear or food; at worst it could maul you badly or even kill you, if you get in its way.

The bright side of this is that you can avoid bears for the most part by following a few precautions. Keep your camp clean at night. Place all food items in a stuff sack and suspend it from a high tree branch 50 yards or so from camp. Some black bears can climb trees, so you must hang the sack away from the trunk, preferably on a branch thick enough to hold the food, but too thin to support a 100-pound-plus bear.

Never bring food into a tent. This includes candy bars, bubble gum or any other seemingly innocuous edible food. Sweet-smelling perfume, cologne or deodorant also attracts bears at times. Avoid using them while in the woods. (They also draw insects.) Wash pots and pans thoroughly after cooking, and don't store them in the tent. If sufficient space is available, place cooking gear in the stuff sack with your food and hang them together. If you've spilled bacon grease or fish oil on your clothing, don't wear the soiled garments inside the tent. Tie them outside instead.

Bears have an affinity for trash that borders on mania. Smelly refuse should be burned clean in a fire, then either buried or hung in a plastic bag to be carried out later.

Hang your foodstuffs at night. Drawing below shows the most bearproof method, utilizing two ropes.

Occasionally, writings on bear precautions include instructions for making a "bear alarm" consisting of a row of tin cans or pots and pans placed around the grub supply. In theory, the noise from the clanging tin not only alerts you, but scares the bear as well.

Actually, the noise may confuse the bear into running over you or your tent in attempted hasty escape. Or, if the bruin is an experienced pilferer, it will be unimpressed by your racket, and continue with its prospecting. Don't bother with an alarm when the same effort could be better spent hanging the food out of reach. With the chow away from camp and beyond the reach of food thieves, you can sleep contentedly, without listening nervously for a tin-can alarm. Follow this advice and you should have no trouble with camp-pirating bears.

Then there are "those other bears"—grizzlies—a different breed entirely. Truly awesome creatures, grizzlies are pound for pound among the most powerful and dangerous animals on earth. It is said that woodsmen camping in grizzly country learn to sleep with an alert ear for the telltale crunch of a platter-size foot and with one eye open for signs of a hulking shadow. While I've never mastered the trick myself (I can't keep from falling into a sound sleep), I can vouch for the slight tug of apprehension that pulls on your mind as you crawl into a sleeping bag and let the night sounds toy with your imagination—especially after hearing the dozen or so standard grizzly yarns that pop up at every backcountry campfire. Unfortunately for adventure seekers, and happily for less courageous individuals, more dangerous grizzlies roam in human

You're not likely to run into a grizzly, even where they are abundant. But take no chances. Watch your backcountry manners when in silvertip habitat. (*Photo: National Park Service*)

imagination than in all the great outdoors. Your odds of running into a silvertip are worse than your chances of winning the Irish Sweepstakes. (Well, almost.) In Yellowstone Park, for example, which has one of the most concentrated grizzly populations in the lower 48, your chances of being injured by a grizzly are one out of 600,000, according to a study done by grizzly biologists, John and Frank Craighead.

Not only that, but very few places have a grizzly population at all. As mentioned, Yellowstone Park sports a sizable, though diminishing, number. So does Glacier Park in northwestern Montana. The wilderness regions of western Montana and Idaho contain scattered grizzly bears, and a few bears exist outside Yellowstone Park in Wyoming proper. Alaska, British Columbia and Alberta contain the bulk of the remaining bears. If you are in areas outside these places, don't concern yourself with a grizzly encounter. If you are in known grizzly habitat, you needn't travel or camp in constant fear, but you should use your good sense to avoid trouble.

Given half a chance, even the mighty grizzly will generally outdo itself to avoid you. But you must do your part to let it know of your presence. Some authorities advise wearing bells or other noisemakers on your pack or belt. Others suggest loud conversation or even singing. I enjoy woods silence and wildlife watching too much to outfit with bells or engage in clangorous discourse, but I will unhesitatingly sacrifice these pleasures to whistle or yell loudly when it's obvious that I'm sharing a woodlot or mountainside with a grizzly. Fresh tracks, droppings, trails, audible grunts, growls or "whoofs" (characteristic of a surprised grizzly) are all clues—or rather, glaring signs—that you should proceed with caution.

Don't travel at night in known grizzly habitat; your chances of encountering a bruin increase dramatically. In fact, if a stretch of riverbank or berry patch is famous for high-density grizzly activity, avoid it entirely, day or night. You owe it to the bears as well as yourself. Their habitat is limited, while yours is vast.

When camping, follow the same procedures of food hanging and general clean camp manners described for black bears—only follow them more rigorously. A black bear in camp sometimes can be frightened off with clanging pans or loud shouts. Try this on a grizzly, however, and you may find yourself smothered by a quarter-ton or more of muscle, teeth and claws. The idea is to give the bears no good reason in the first place for inspecting your bivouac.

Grizzlies have been labeled short-tempered, irascible and quick to attack without provocation. These descriptions are not wholly accurate. A grizzly is an aggressive animal; no doubt one which pretty much gets its way in the wild. When surprised, threatened or cornered, it will sometimes attack and sometimes retreat. No one to my knowledge can make a positive statement saying it will do either. "Sometimes" and "probably" are common words when grizzlies are discussed. If you want to test a grizzly's temper, do any of the following—but bolster your life insurance first:

Surprise a grizzly in heavy woods or from a short distance.

Somehow get yourself between a mother bear and her offspring, or for that matter, just get reasonably near the young bears.

Cause a bear to feel cornered or threatened, even if it actually is not.

Keep a messy camp, or eat dinner in your tent.

Inspect the carcass of a chewed-on animal that's covered with dirt and rubble. (A possible grizzly meat cache.)

On the other hand, if you want to avoid grizzly trouble, never be caught red-handed doing any of the above.

Even if you've taken all the recommended precautions, what if you still bump noses with a bear—either black or grizzly?

First is the ever-present emergency advice: Don't panic. Next, heed the words of Charles Jonkel, an internationally known biologist who has worked extensively with grizzlies, blacks and polar bears.

Jonkel suggests a slow retreat when a bear is at least a few yards distant.

"Keep a low profile while retreating," he advises, "and, if possible, get out of view as you move away."

If the bear shows aggression at your moves, stand absolutely still. You couldn't outdistance him on foot under any conditions, much less in his own territory—running is useless and may even provoke an attack. Talking in a clear, soft voice has calmed down an occasional bear, and may be worth a try. Don't shout or scream, however, for either may spur on onslaught.

If you have enough distance between yourself and the bear to make it safely to a tree, by all means do so. Shed your pack before making your break for the tree; it not only makes you obviously lighter, but may deter the bear long enough for you to scamper to safety.

Although a remote possibility, you could find yourself being charged by a bear, and have no means of escape or defense available. You are pretty much at the bear's mercy, but "playing dead" may save you from death or a bad mauling. Drop to the ground, pull your knees to your chest and clasp your hands behind your neck. In this position, the bear has less of a chance of disemboweling you, or biting into the vulnerable neck and lower head region. If you are wearing a pack, keep it on to protect your back and spine. Try to lie still under the animal's attack, and make every effort to refrain from screaming. You may suffer only a few swats or bites before the bear decides it has rendered you harmless, and leaves.

It's impossible to tell for sure if a bear is going to charge or retreat, but there are a few signs that may give you a clue as to what a bear will do—and, accordingly, what you should do. A bear with ears laid flat and jaws popping is not a content critter. Sometimes the quiet talking mentioned earlier will soothe the bruin's ruffles enough to avoid further trouble. If the ears pop up in an upright position, and the jaws cease to clatter, try a slow, cautious retreat. In no way challenge an angry bear or attempt to bluff it. Most likely you will trigger an attack. According to biologist Jonkel, a bear that dips its head low along its front leg is giving in to you and has no desire for conflict. But Jonkel stresses that there is no pat formula for predicting behavior; don't think you have the bear "figured out" and abandon caution.

Finally, this discussion of bear attacks and maulings is not to be over-dramatized. Use your head and you needn't worry about bear troubles. Jonkel, for example, in 16 years of studying North American bears, has handled over 1,500 individual bruins—blacks, grizzlies and polar bears. Despite constant presence in bear country and much contact, he has been charged only once by a free-roaming bear, when he inadvertently surprised a black sow in a patch of heavy timber. He escaped uninjured.

Snakes

Snakes are critters worth avoiding. Though poisonous snakebites are rare—and fatal bites rarer still—the potential danger does exist and it never hurts to be careful.

There are basically four types of poisonous snakes in the United States: rattlers, copperheads, water moccasins (cottonmouths) and coral snakes. Each delivers a bite capable of maiming or killing its victim. The combined range of these snakes covers every state except Maine, Alaska and Hawaii—reason enough to become acquainted with snake precautions.

But first, some good news. You can traverse snake country regularly and never have a run-in with a serpent. Although they occur in 47 states, snakes are found mostly in patches. And where poisonous snakes are plentiful, their shy, withdrawn nature prevents you from seeing them. Herpetologists stress the fact that most snakes shun—rather than seek—your company.

Coral snakes hurl the deadliest bites, but confrontations with humans are rare. Unlike the long-fanged rattlers, copperheads and moccasins, coral snakes chew more than they bite. Even light clothing can serve as protection against them. Most people venomized by coral snakes are bitten while handling the creatures. Thus, if you avoid teasing or fond-ling snakes—particularly those having alternating bands of red, yellow and black (as do corals)—you can dismiss the likelihood of being bitten by a coral.

Cottonmouths (water moccasins) are found mostly in the South, and usually near water. They are more aggressive than most other snakes, and issue painful, incapacitating bites. Fishermen, especially, should be

The four poisonous North American snakes: The rattlesnake (top left); cotton-mouth or water moccasin (top right); coral snake (bottom left), and the copperhead (bottom right). (*Photos: Charles E. Most, U.S. Sport Fisheries and Wildlife; Luther Goldman, U.S. Sport Fisheries and Wildlife; Wallace Hughes,* Florida Wildlife *Magazine.*)

cautious when casting on southern waters. Moccasins sometimes drape themselves over a tree limb extended over water, and have been known on occasion to drop into a passing boat. When wading along shore, check ahead of your step, and move through branches carefully. Before grabbing hastily for a lure hung in shore brush or water weeds, look closely to be sure no snakes are present.

If you're hunting in moccasion-infested swamps or river bottoms, wear high leather boots or "snake leggings"—knee-high guards strapped above your boots (available from most large mail-order houses). At night, sleep away from the water's edge. A zip-up tent with sewn-in floor is virtually snake-proof. If you're sleeping without a tent, rig a mosquito net around your bag; no snake can enter it, and you have protection from insects as well.

Copperheads and rattlesnakes are widely distributed, and pose the greatest threat to outdoorsmen. Though usually shyer and less aggressive than cottonmouths, the 15 species and dozens of subspecies of "rattlers" put them in the path of hunters, fishermen and campers around the country. But do your part to stay clear of them, and you can coexist peacefully.

In snake country, be conscious of where you place your hands and feet. Don't step over fallen logs without looking first at the other side. It's better to step atop the log before going over. If you hear an angry buzz, you can jump back down safely. Snakes bed down under rocks, logs, ledges and leaf piles. They frequent caves, crevices and burrows. Avoid poking around these features. Never stick your hand into an animal burrow or cave. Snakes slide into these backwards, with their heads nearest the entrance. By the same token, it's a dangerous practice to kneel down and peer into a hole or crack: you may be slapped in the face with a pair of venomous fangs. Children especially are susceptible to this sort of thing. Warn them thoroughly of the danger before you take them into the woods.

Snakes are cold-blooded creatures whose body temperature fluctuates with environmental temperatures. They seek warmth when it's cold, and coolness when it's hot. On hot, sunny days, avoid shady brush piles or lowlands. If you want to rest in the shade, inspect the ground carefully for snakes. Conversely, on cool days or during early morning, shy away from sun-bathed rocks or slopes, and move cautiously when on sun-struck ridges.

A snake can strike without coiling, though not as accurately or with as much range. If you're close to a snake, and it bends its neck in a sibilant curve, don't make the deadly mistake of thinking it can't hit you. Indeed it can! A snake will coil if given time, but at close range it can sling a blurring bite with neck muscles alone.

Don't expect to be always warned of a snake's presence by loud rattling. Sometimes a rattler will buzz like a mill saw, other times it will strike first, and then rattle. If you do hear a chattering rattle, freeze immediately. The snake may be underfoot, and any motion on your part could trigger an attack. If you are several feet from the snake, jump back quickly. Even the largest snake can strike no more than three feet. (Figure roughly half the snake's length for striking distance.) When inside a snake's shooting range, freeze absolutely still. Chances are the reptile will coil, buzz and depart while you remain motionless.

If you kill a rattler for some reason, be wary of its head. A profuse number of stories illustrate the ability of a snake to bite long after it is dead; the tenacious nerves in the reptile's body operate the jaw muscles well after it has been dispatched. It's best to decapitate the snake, and bury the head or cover it with a log or rock.

Insects and Arachnids

While you're nervously scanning the ground for snakes and whistling to warn away bears, the most dangerous and pesky of all wildlife will no doubt be buzzing, crawling, swirling and swarming about you: insects and arachnids. Writers on this subject like to point out that more people die from insect bites than from snakes and bears combined. In fact, in one sample year snakebites claimed 138 lives while stinging insects killed 300. Add the deaths caused by disease-carrying mosquitoes, ticks, fleas and flies, and the seemingly innocuous forms of smaller life rise to the top of the danger list. Even so, you needn't stay home because of them. Flying insects can be thwarted, and run-ins with the few poisonous arachnids are rare.

Mosquitoes, blackflies, deerflies and no-see-ums are some of the few forms of life that truly want your blood. Each of these organisms needs blood to complete its reproductive cycle, and will make every merciless effort to get it.

Mosquitoes are the most common of the lot, and perhaps the most tireless in their quest for blood. They carry such diseases as malaria, yellow fever and encephalitis, depending on the sex and species of the mosquito. Not all mosquitoes carry communicable diseases, but it's impossible to tell whether the critter that's biting you is "clean" or not. Recently, an encephalitis (sleeping sickness) outbreak occurred in parts of the South and Midwest. Scores of people contracted it, and a number died. Mosquitoes were the transmitters.

Blackflies and deerflies don't stick you with a proboscis in the manner of mosquitoes, but instead bite and gouge viciously, often drawing blood. A cloud of these pests swarming around your head and biting every available patch of skin is worse than Chinese water torture. They can easily drive an unprepared man away from a stream or out of the woods.

No-see-ums are the sneakiest of the bunch. They are, as implied, nearly invisible, but the pin-sharp bites they deliver are most obvious. They slice into your skin, brush on a layer of thinner to prevent natural coagulation of the cut, and suck up a meal of blood. The accumulated effect of dozens of no-see-ums is a painful burning sensation.

All of these insects can be squelched by more or less the same methods. One of the best ways is to simply avoid them. Each type needs water for reproduction, though water in different forms. Mosquitoes breed in stagnant pools, swamps and ditches; no-see-ums sprout from moving streams, and backflies require cold turbulent rapids. It pays to avoid these insect-breeding grounds. If a breeze is blowing, camp on the upwind side of such places. (Camping downwind blows the insects to you.) Stay on high, breezy ground, preferably on dry land and removed

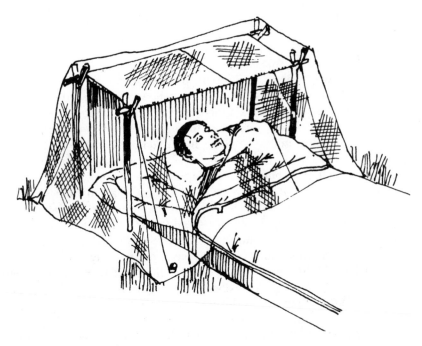

Mosquito net rigged over your head allows fresh air in, but keeps mosquitoes, blackflies, no-see-ums—even snakes—on the outside.

from your enemy's breeding waters. Shun high, damp grass—it attracts and holds mosquitoes and flies. Drape mosquito netting over your sleeping bag, or keep your tent screen zipped tightly. Open it only to crawl in and out, and spray the inside of the tent with repellent before going to sleep. Don't overfumigate to the point of asphyxiating yourself, and don't spray bug repellent directly on the tent material. This may cause undesirable reactions within the fabric.

Outside the tent, stay protected with fresh coats of repellent. The most potent stuff is a compound known as N,N-diethyl-meta-toluamide—DEET for short. Many popular brands, including Cutter's, 6-12, and Deep Woods Off, contain effective amounts of DEET. Also, wear loose clothing tied shut at wrist and ankle openings. If bugs are really bad, you'll need a headnet, homemade or commercial. Use regular mosquito netting or bobbinet if you decide to make your own. Commercial models are available in a variety of styles. Some even have an elastic opening to allow pipe smokers to indulge in their habit.

Smoking is sometimes touted as an effective mosquito and fly repellent. I'm generally puffing on a pipe or cigar, and have found both to be more effective in repelling friends than flies. But, assuredly, the right quantities of smoke will do the trick. Smudge fires, for example, will help thin the air of insects, particularly in emergencies when more desirable methods aren't possible. Build your fires 20 feet or so upwind from your camping or resting spot. Pile on green wood or wet vegetation to create heavy smoke.

Stinging insects pose a different problem, and to some people, a deadly one. Bees, hornets, wasps and yellowjackets are the main culprits in question. Each has a stinger and exudes a venom that is irritating to many individuals, fatal to a few. If you have been stung before, with no adverse reactions, it doesn't mean you are immune to the venom. Upon repeated stings, you may become sensitized to the point of having a bad reaction. Vomiting, nausea, diarrhea, cramps, labored breathing—all are signs of a reaction known technically as anaphylactic shock. The shock can occur immediately after the sting, or be delayed until several days later. Any discomfort should be reported to a physician as quickly as possible. A commercially made kit which contains treatments for anaphylactic shock may be worth having, especially if you are known to react badly to stings or are on an expedition far from medical help.

Unlike mosquitoes and blackflies, the stinging insects aren't out to get you. They attack only when disturbed or threatened. Consequently, you can eliminate a lot of unnecessary stings simply by steering clear of hives, nests or feeding areas, particularly fragrant flower patches. If a bee, wasp or hornet lands on you, or buzzes about your head, don't swat it or attempt to brush it aside. After finding you inedible, it will most likely leave on its own.

One way to keep insects from landing in the first place is to refrain from using cologne, perfume, hair tonic or other fragrant attractants. Another way is to outfit in the proper clothing. Avoid shirts bearing flowered prints and bright colors; they make you one big flower in the eyes of a bee. I'm told that black clothing angers bees in the same fashion red supposedly provokes bulls, hence it pays to refrain from donning dark colors. Dull white, green, doeskin and khaki are the safest tones to wear. (Mosquitoes are also attracted to dark colors. A white shirt supposedly repels them; thus you can cut down on mosquito bites and bee stings with the same garb.)

Many stinging insects alight on small clovers and other ground plants in search of nectar. Therefore, a barefoot outdoorsman is asking for trouble—and a swollen foot. Wear shoes when tramping about; boot leather is impervious to stings.

Occasionally, you'll surprise a nest of insects, either purposely by poking around a hive, or accidentally by stepping on or near a ground nest. It's an unfortunate move. You may be attacked by a swarm of angry inhabitants, most notably wasps, hornets and yellowjackets. A nest can hold thousands of these beasts, and a full-fledged attack, although rare, can be a matter of life or death. Head out quickly and take to water if there is no other alternative. Unlike comic-strip cartoons, real-life insects won't follow you for long.

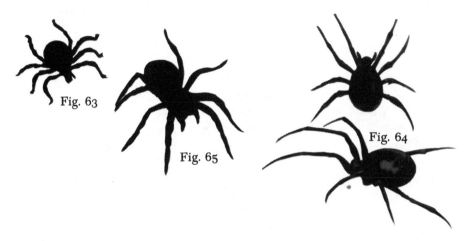

The dangerous arachnids: Ticks (Fig. 63), the brown recluse spider (Fig. 65), the black widow (Fig. 64). (*Photo: American National Red Cross*)

Arachnids—spiders, ticks, mites and scorpions—scare people more than insects do, though they are actually less bothersome. Spiders especially seem to cause a lot of unnecessary screaming and fretting. Most are harmless, and all are shy. The black widow spider is a notorious poison variety, but it is more common in graveyard fiction than in the wilds. They are predominantly southern in range, and frequent shady, moist haunts. You're likely to encounter them in dilapidated shacks in and around swamp country.

The brown recluse spider also slings a dangerous bite, but, as its name implies, is reclusive in nature. You hardly ever encounter them, but the main danger lies in their affinity for dark places. They may crawl into waders, boots, packs, woodpiles and cabin corners. Most bites occur when you accidentally brush against one occupying such places.

Tarantula (Fig. 66) and scorpion (Fig. 67). (*Photo: American National Red Cross*)

It never hurts to shake out boots or waders before slipping into them, and always look ahead of your hands when probing in corners or wood-piles. (A good way to prevent snakebite as well.)

The tarantula is another critter blown totally out of proportion by novelists and television writers. They can indeed deliver a painful bite, and are snakelike in reflexes. When threatened, a tarantula will raise up in a sparring position and gnash its vampirelike chelicerae fangs—truly a vicious sight. But it will not seek you out and attack. Most tarantula bites are the result of teasing and prodding. If you leave tarantulas alone, they will generally cause you no trouble.

Scorpions are a bit more formidable. They possess a whiplike tail, complete with stinger and venom, and do not hesitate to strike when threatened. Unless you are hit by a rare eight-inch variety, you won't die from a scorpion sting, though the pain may make you want to. Don't worry about meeting them on the trail; they are inactive during the day. The danger lies in their habit of seeking darkness in a boot-bottom or heap of clothing. Shake your boots and clothing in the morning before getting dressed and you'll avoid stings.

Much more common than poisonous spiders or scorpions are the itchy ticks and mites. Ticks are flat-bodied creatures which depend on the blood of mammals for food. They occur worldwide, and transmit several diseases, most notably tularemia and Rocky Mountain spotted fever. You pick up unwanted ticks in wooded or brushy areas and in and around rocks and caves. Most wild mammals are infested with parasites, and ticks can be an undesirable by-product of a freshly killed animal. Because of their flat bodies and light frames, ticks can crawl around your skin for hours without your being aware. Most search for two or more hours before selecting a part of your anatomy they like—assuredly a part you won't want them around. After choosing a feeding site, they burrow into your skin, immersing their palpi and heads completely to suck up a pouchful of your blood. The longer they feed, the more chance you have of contracting a disease. (Not all ticks are disease carriers.) A feeding tick will sometimes make you itch. Rather than scratching frantically, inspect the irritated spot and probe for the tick. Don't attempt to pull it out; the head will break off under the skin and possibly become infected. Instead, hold a hot match head or cigarette to the beast's rump. It will pull out quicky. Alcohol or kerosene rubbed over the tick will give the same result.

As everyone knows, ticks also pester dogs. They can literally sap a pup to death. Inspect your dog and yourself every night for ticks, especially if you feel itchy or your dog is doing an unusual amount of scratching. Remove dog ticks in the same manner as for humans.

Chiggers are minute tormenters that keep southern sportsmen from becoming too complacent. These red devils burrow into your skin to lay their eggs, and create an itching unlike any other. Chigger-infested skin has countless red dots, not unlike a rash.

The best defense against chiggers (also called jiggers, chigoes and red bugs) is a hearty dose of insect repellent, especially around openings in clothings. Don't handle Spanish moss—the long, beardlike lichens that hang from southern trees—because chiggers thrive in them. Avoid camping or picnicking in heavily mossed woods or in thick grass. If you're heading South for an outdoor excursion, consider bringing along a bottle of calamine lotion, just in case you aren't entirely successful in eliminating chiggers.

Wolves

For some inane reason, a number of beginning outdoorsmen harbor a fear of wolves. Considering that few places have any wolves at all; even where wolves exist, it takes seasoned effort or blind luck to spot one; and wolves never attack people anyway, at least not on this continent, it is foolish to fear them. Count yourself exceptionally lucky if you see one outside a zoo. And if you're camped in an area wild enough to harbor a population, don't be alarmed by their night-howling. Enjoy it; it's the wildest lullaby ever composed.

Coyotes

A fear of wolves is foolish, a fear of coyotes is downright ridiculous. These wild canids are among the wariest critters to be found. The pains they take to avoid human contact is simply amazing, and inarguably effective. If you cornered one somehow it could be dangerous, like any other animal, but barring that, coyotes are not a problem.

Wolverines

While we're dismissing needless fears, let's consider the wolverine, or injun devil as it is sometimes called. Scarce animals in most parts, wolverines are like wolves in that you're lucky to even see one. They pose no physical threat by way of viciousness or attacks, but can wreck a camp in short order. The same camp methods described for thwarting bears will work for injun devils.

Porcupines

Not many people live in fear of porcupines, but they are worth mentioning because they can be pesky. Everybody knows that porcupines sport long, sharp quills for defense purposes. The only way you can get quilled is by prodding or handling a porky; they will never attack you. Of course, they cannot throw their quills as is sometimes written. You must touch the animal or be within striking range of its tail to pick up quills. Dogs are more apt to pick up a face full of quills than you are, and the result is a painful session of quill pulling. The best ways of accomplishing this task are described in the first aid chapter (Chapter 19).

The major concern with porcupines is not in their quills, but in their relentless quest for salt-soaked equipment. Canoe paddles, pack straps, ax handles, tent ropes, toilet seats—anything that holds a trace of salt from human perspiration is liable to be gnawed to pieces by a porky. Cover or hang such items out of reach, but remember that quill pigs can climb trees adeptly.

Some hunters fashion makeshift canvas-covered outdoor racks for their guns when hunting out of a spike camp. It never hurts to rub a little linseed oil or gun oil on your gunstock before turning in, should, God forbid, a porky decide to sample your polished Circassian stock. Linseed oil rubbed on any material will prevent porcupine damage.

Other Rodents

Mice, rats, chipmunks and squirrels can be pesky and damaging. A clean camp generally holds little attraction for them. Permanent log cabin structures have the most trouble with rodents, which gnaw on furniture, make nests out of mattresses, and eat through sacked grub supplies. Storing food items in metal or tin containers, setting mouse or rat traps and keeping the place clean will cut down on such problems.

Antlered Animals

Antlered animals are rarely bothersome; the exception being semitame park animals which seek handouts or poke fearlessly through camp. Occasionally, a rutting buck deer or bull moose will charge a human, but this is rare.

In general, it pays to give moose a wide berth, for they are large, powerful creatures, and occasionally short of temper. As with many animals, if you bother the newborn, mama will do her best to defend them. A belligerent ma moose is a formidable adversary. Leave the little ones of all species alone.

Bigfoot

Also known as Sasquatch, this beast is purported to be seven feet tall and resembles what may be best described as a cross between a gorilla and a man. No one has documented its existence, though allegedly realistic pictures have been taken. Sasquatch is said to roam in the Pacific Northwest, most notably in the Cascades and the surrounding country or up through British Columbia. I mention this not for a joke, but because I've met a few people who are genuinely afraid of running into a bigfoot creature. Since expeditions have spent considerable time and money trying to locate Sasquatch, and since no one has brought in a carcass, alive or dead, for scientific inspection, it is reasonably safe to assume that a run-in with a bigfoot would be rare—if the animals exist at all. Worry more about driving safely to and from your home than about running into Sasquatch; the odds are hugely in favor of a driving accident.

Sea Animals

Sharks have become a national conversation topic. A best-selling novel, and subsequent movie relating the story of a man-eating white shark have brought sharks to a level of unprecedented attention. Newspapers are suddenly dotted with stories of shark attacks; beach-goers won't enter the water, and coastal resort owners are losing customers. Last summer, on a television interview, a Lake Michigan lifeguard said many people were afraid to enter the lake for fear of shark attack! Things are obviously getting out of hand.

It's certainly true that a full-size shark of any species can be dangerous, but consider the odds of an encounter, much less an attack. Most of the deadly sharks—makos, whites, threshers, blues—spend their time in deep water and offshore feeding lanes. If you're a diver, you may want to think twice about diving in open ocean, especially if sharks are a known local problem. Few outdoorsmen, however, will be swimming in such places. Most encounters occur along shallow reefs.

A shark cruising these waters is most likely on the prowl for food fish. One may swing around to inspect a diver or snorkeler, but conflicts are few. Most shallow water sharks are not generally aggressive toward man. Fishing off the Naples Pier in Florida, I have watched sand sharks mill through groups of splashing swimmers, sometimes moving within a few feet of an unsuspecting person. No one there, to my knowledge, has ever been hurt by one.

Occasionally, however, a large tiger or hammerhead shark will be in the same water as a diver, snorkeler, off-boat swimmer or wading fisherman. Consequently it doesn't hurt to take a few precautions. If you're spearfishing, realize that the blood and struggles of a skewered fish will attract local sharks. Spear your fish, then quickly deposit it in a nearby boat while you search for another. Whether spearfishing or wading, never wear a belt stringer full of fish. You literally become a moving blood-trail for a shark, which may not, in the excitement of pursuing a meal, discern between you and the fish.

Water that is excessively dark from sediment is dangerous. Visibility is limited, and a nearby shark might rely on its sound senses rather than its eyes to find prey. Your movements may register as food, and the results you can guess.

Sound is important in shark waters. Avoid splashing on the surface;

struggling fish do the same, and sharks are conditioned to move in at the cue.

If one does approach you, make no erratic moves. If you have anything in your hands, use it to prod the shark away. If it moves in wide, elliptical circles, it is only curious. But if the circles tighten, and the shark moves quickly and jerkedly, get out of the water if possible. Otherwise, swim steadily underwater toward whatever safety you can find—usually in the direction of land. If the shark makes actual passes at you, try shouting as loudly as possible. As a last resort (well, not necessarily a *last* resort), swim straight toward the shark in an aggressive manner. Hopefully you will frighten it out of its appetite. This procedure is for underwater use only. Swimming on the surface, with all the accompanying splashing and gurgling, may serve only to provoke an attack.

Barracudas are not the culprits they are generally made out to be. A small number of attacks have been recorded over the years, fewer still have been documented. Most barracuda run-ins occur when a section of human anatomy is mistaken for prey. Occasionally a 'cuda will strike at the flash of a belt buckle, or a flick of white from a swimmer's hand or foot. Such accidents usually occur in turbid water, where visibility is limited and the fish strikes in a flash at anything resembling a baitfish. Staying out of muddy water is a great way to prevent both 'cuda and shark encounters.

Octopuses have killed many men in movies, but few in actuality. They are reclusive creatures and are simply not interested in you. When threatened they exude a harmless cloud of blue-black ink. Their suction-cup arms will not reach out and hopelessly entangle you.

There is at least one poisonous variety of blue-ringed octopus, a tiny, beautifully colored creature inhabiting the seas of the lower hemisphere,

Stingray. (*Photo: American National Red Cross*)

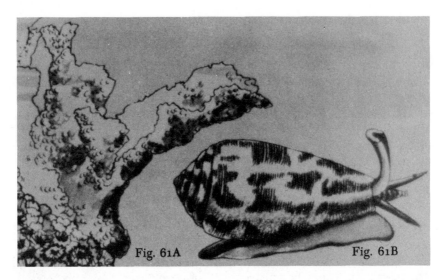

Among the numerous hazardous sea animals are the stinging coral (Fig. 61A), and the poisonous cone shell (Fig. 61B). The venom of the latter has caused occasional deaths. (*Photo: American National Red Cross*)

most notably around Australia. Its poison is potent stuff, capable of bringing death in a matter of minutes. There is, however, one redeeming fact: these beasts are rare, and encounters with humans are even rarer. Unless you dive extensively in southern seas, chances are you'll never see a blue-ringed octopus outside an aquarium.

Stingrays are more interested in avoiding you than anything else, but are capable of a scorpionlike sting which is painful and sometimes dangerous. Wading fishermen occasionally step on a ray, semi-buried in bottom sand. Such an encounter doesn't necessarily mean a sting. The ray will do its best to leave in a hurry, and only if you brush against the tail are you likely to be stung.

The sea has a number of stinging, burning bottom-dwellers that can painfully warn a wader or diver to watch where he places his hands and feet. The list varies with locale and climate, and is too broad to be covered in depth here. Before departing for a saltwater trip, bone up on local varieties and learn what to avoid. Sea urchins, sea biscuits and anemones are common nuisances for waders and swimmers. Urchins, which resemble oval porcupines with extra-large quills, are especially noisome. Step on one of these and your foot will burn for hours. It always pays to wear sneakers when wading; you never know what you'll step on.

Moray eels are a concern of many people, divers mostly, but are not offensively aggressive. Their habit of lying in dark places with jaws agape is truly scary, even though their mouths are open only to aid in breathing. Trouble arises when diversr poke around dark holes and

pockets searching for shells and such. Sticking your hand into underwater burrows and caves is a good way to get bitten by a five-foot eel.
Watch where you put your hands and feet, and eels should give you
little trouble.

Last in this discussion are jellyfish and man-of-wars—amorphous blobs
of pelagic animal which have stinging tentacles capable of causing much
discomfort and pain. You'll see these drifting aimlessly in the water. Do
not pick them up for inspection. When swimming, avoid brushing against
them and wear a wet suit if jellyfish or man-of-wars are abundant.

Plants

Aside from eating poisonous plants, there is little danger in North
American flora. The notable exceptions, of course, are poison ivy, poison
oak and poison sumac. Contact with any of these can result in an irritating rash, and for sensitive sorts, medical attention may be necessary.

Poison ivy is a low-growing ground shrub or climbing vine that is easy
to identify. It has glossy, sometimes toothed leaves arranged in sets of
three. Poison oak is a shrub bearing three-set, hairy-bottomed leaves
which are oval with wavy edges. Like poison ivy and sumac, the toxic
oak has clusters of white berries. Poison sumac grows in dense cover,

Jellyfish (Fig. 60A) and Portuguese man-of-war (Fig. 60B). (*Photo: American
National Red Cross*)

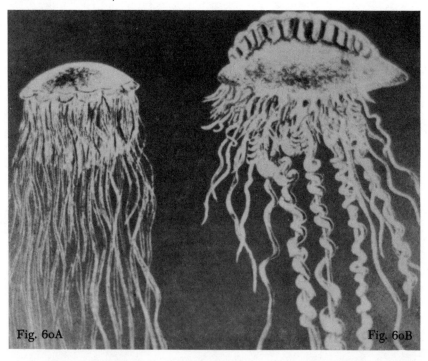

Fig. 60A   Fig. 60B

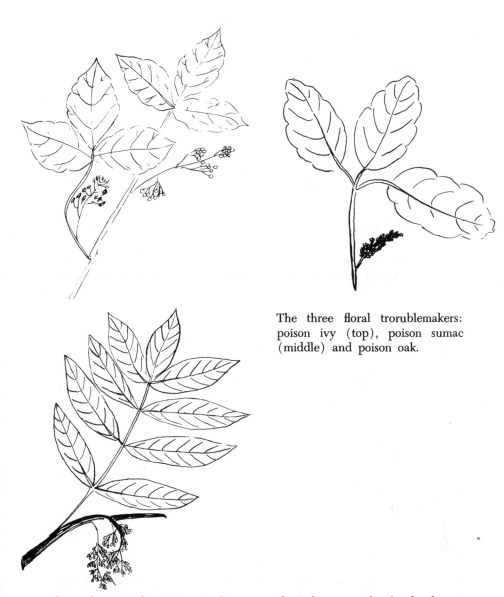

The three floral troublemakers: poison ivy (top), poison sumac (middle) and poison oak.

where, fortunately, it is out of easy reach. It has smooth, slender leaves which grow alternately from a woody stem. The poison variety is easily distinguished from harmless red sumac by its smooth leaf edges and white, drooping berries.

Each of these plants contains a resinous alkaloid that can make you itch upon the slightest contact. You don't have to actually touch the plant yourself to pick up the toxin. A blanket, or piece of clothing that brushes any part of the plant and picks up resin can infect you. Similarly, resin on a dog or other person can be transmitted to you and others. The stuff dies hard and strong soap or alcohol is needed to remove it completely.

If you do become infected, don't scratch the rash; you'll only spread it. Never touch your eyes or face if you have resin on your hands. It can burn them painfully. All parts of poison sumac, oak and ivy are toxic; so be sure not to burn the dry stalks or leaves in your campfire. The resulting smoke is noxious, and dangerous if inhaled.

Some people claim to be immune to poison plants, but the potency of the resin varies with season and conditions. If you are hot and sweaty, you're more likely to react unfavorably. Sometimes you will brush against a poison plant and have no reaction at all, but it doesn't necessarily mean you are immune. The next encounter could cause you to itch violently. Always take pains to avoid these plants; don't camp where they are abundant, and check around your sleeping bag or resting area for signs of them—poison ivy and oak make lousy mattresses. In general, avoid plants with white berries and leaves of three and you'll save a lot of scratching.

Another plant to avoid brushing against is stinging nettle. Although edible and tasty when boiled, this plant has stiff, acid-containing hairs that are irritating to bare skin. (Nettle is illustrated in the edible plants section of this book. See Chapter 13.)

Whenever you're in cactus country, scan the ground before sitting down. A seat full of cactus needles is not funny, though an onlooker may think so as you try to remove them. A pair of tweezers is a good item to have handy in such an instance, since it's impossible to pluck out the needles with your fingernails.

Other Hazards

Quicksand

The word conjures up images of a devilish, sucking bog that waits silently for unsuspecting outdoorsmen. If class B movies are based on even a nugget of fact, it would appear that a step into quicksand is the last step you'll ever take. As it is, budget movies are rarely in line with science, which tends to be less impressive and dramatic. In actuality, quicksand is not an inexplicable phenomenon; for that matter, it is not even complicated to understand.

Any sand can become quick when held in suspension by water, and that's all quicksand is: a layer of sand floating on water. Usually, underground water infiltrates the sand from springs and rock fissures. When the water pressure equals the weight of the overlying sand, the sand becomes quick. This occurs most often in hilly terrains, particularly in what geomorphologists call karst topography—land that is heavy in easily eroded limestone and crisscrossed with underground springs and streams. Karst regions have numerous caves and sinkholes, such as the Mammoth Cave area of Kentucky and parts of Tennessee, North Carolina and Virginia. But quicksand is not limited to those areas. Any hilly country with sandy lakeshores, streambanks and streambeds is liable to have patches of quicksand.

Quicksand appears as normal dry sand at the surface, and if you are light, or walk fast enough, you can walk right over floating sand without knowing it. If you are heavy, or slow moving, you may sink in where a more nimble person has passed. When in an area having all the signs of potential quicksand—particularly if you're hiking along a sandy hill-country lakeshore or streambed—carry a walking staff to probe the sand ahead of your feet.

But what if you suddenly find yourself sinking to the knees in crumbly sand? Will you be sucked into the earth in a devilish slurp?

Not at all. Quicksand has no pulling forces whatever, and in fact can float you better than water. If you struggle violently, a vacuum will be created under the mired part of your body (most likely your feet) and will pull you down, thus the impression of a sucking force. But if you move slowly and smoothly, you will float easily, and nothing will draw you under. Follow these steps for extricating yourself from the annoying stuff:

First, the constant emergency advice is, don't panic. Keep cool and use your head. The sand cannot pull you under unless you create a vacuum by struggling.

Shed extra weight—pack, rifle, tacklebox—the minute you become mired. If someone is near, call for help; otherwise save your breath and energy.

When you're free of extra weight, fall spread-eagle onto your back, as if backfloating in water. Patiently and smoothly try to free your legs, one at a time. Avoid thrashing or making jerky movements.

Once your legs are floating free, "swim" your way to the nearest solid ground by rolling and squirming alligator-fashion across the surface. If you become tired, rest. Progress is liable to be slow, but a cool head and persistence will get you out. If a companion is nearby, have him throw you a rope or extend a sturdy branch or pole to expedite the procedure.

Luckily, kids and dogs are light enough to usually scamper over quicksand without breaking through, so you needn't overly trouble yourself with thoughts of them falling in. But it never hurts to educate youngsters in the proper procedure for survival in quicksand—just in case.

Mud Mires

Mud mires are much like quicksand, the obvious difference being that mud, not sand, is the culprit. It's a scary feeling to sink steadily and helplessly into a soft marsh or swamp, particularly when the mud passes your waist with no signs of slowing. As a kid, I lost lots of shoes to marsh muck when strained pulling freed a foot from the shoe as well as the mud, but I always managed to squirm out of the mire safely.

The same principles suggested for quicksand apply to mire: Shed excess weight and "swim" through the muck as best you can, without thrashing or struggling. If help is near, stay absolutely still until it arrives. Remember the vacuum concept: struggling only pulls you deeper.

Snow

In mountain country, winter travelers need to be alert for avalanche danger. Any snow-covered slope with a steep gradient can slide, particularly if it is barren of vegetation (an indication that a slide probably occurred there before). Hence, a good snowslide precaution is keeping away from the base of steep slopes, especially during late winter and early spring, when avalanche danger is at its peak.

Snow cornices—crests of drifted snow overhanging a ridge or cliff—are also dangerous. Don't walk or ski along them; the weight of a man is sometimes enough to trigger a slide. Radio reports often advise of avalanche conditions, and it is prudent to heed the warnings by staying out of potentially dangerous areas. But if you are caught by moving snow, all is not lost. Try to stay atop the snow by swimming an exaggerated backstroke. If backswimming fails, and you suddenly find yourself buried, do your best to stay calm. Your first move should be to punch out an air pocket around your head to aid in breathing. Next, orient yourself in the snow until you know which direction leads to the top. Tamp the snow beneath your feet so it is capable of supporting you, then begin digging upward through the drift with your hands.

Less serious, but at best chilly and irritating, is suddenly plunging to the withers in a deep snow drift. This happens sometimes when you travel in snow country without the aid of snowshoes. The early-morning snow is often crusted enough to hold you without webs, but as the sun goes to work, the crust gives way. I was once walking without snowshoes across firm morning snow, when my partner ahead of me suddenly broke through up to his neck. While trying to extricate him, I became buried to the chest. By crawling and swimming, we managed to work our way to a shaded area with snow crusted enough to support us.

Another snow danger is "white blindness," caused from overexposure to glaring bright snow. Snow blindness, while only temporary (a few hours to a couple of days, depending on severity), is painful and under some conditions extremely dangerous. Quality sunglasses are the best prevention, and every winter wanderer should be adorned with a pair. If you lack sunglasses, a bit of charcoal from burnt wood rubbed under both eyes will reduce glare. Better yet are "glasses" made from cardboard, bark or rawhide. See Chapter 18 for details on making these.

Ice

Ice is truly dangerous stuff. In a wilderness situation, crashing through thin ice and into frigid water can mean cold death if a fire isn't started quickly. And there's always the horrid possibility of breaking through into deep water and not being able to find your way out through the entrance hole.

The sure way to avoid these disasters is by staying off ice that isn't positively safe. Some people—particularly fishermen—court danger by running onto ice without testing it first. Worse yet, I have often seen fishermen venture onto ice that they *knew* was unsafe. When I lived in the Midwest, it was common to see fishermen spreading wooden planks across thin ice for support while they jigged for perch and bluegills. Each year a number of anglers fell through, and some didn't come up for a couple of days.

Clear lake ice must be at least two inches thick before it will support one person. Maybe I'm overcautious, but I won't venture out until I have four solid inches of frozen water beneath me. And even then I'm cautious. Bay ice may be solid, but more open water ice may not. Then, too, springs can occur anywhere, and they create large circles of weak ice. Slushy, dirty ice is weaker than the clear blue variety. Four inches of it may not be safe.

Rivers and streams are more dangerous. Currents under ice can form weak spots anywhere, and you can never be sure of safety. Ice in mid-stream is generally thinner than that near the banks, and the inside of

A pole outstretched in front of you distributes body weight over a wider area and lessens the likelihood of breaking through weak ice.

stream bends is safer than the outside. Rocks, logs, and other obstructions are generally surrounded by weak ice. Keep your distance from them. On both lakes and streams, snow covered ice is weaker than bare ice because of the insulation snow provides. What may appear to be solid ice may be nothing more than slush covered with a crust of snow.

In spring, "candle" or "trapper's ice" looks sturdy when it is actually not. It occurs when melting ice forms vertical needles to the surface—solid on top, but egg-shell weak below. A man's weight shatters it easily.

It pays to carry a long, light pole whenever you're on possibly unsafe ice. Should you break through, the pole held horizontally will keep you from plunging away from your entrance hole. Also, if the ice begins to crack and buckle, you can use the pole to distribute your weight over a larger area. Lie down spread-eagle with the pole held tightly against the ice. By crawling and inching forward (or backwards if land or firm ice is there), you may be able to make it without a dunking. Always carry a pole when traversing stream ice; you can never tell when you may approach a weak spot. If you do encounter cracking ice, and do not have a pole, follow the same spread-eagle procedure. Distributing your weight evenly may be enough to see you through your crisis.

If you decide you must drive your vehicle across a frozen lake, have the sense to check first to see if the ice can support your weight. Just because cars and snowmobiles are on the ice, you can't necessarily wheel your half-ton pickup across with no mishaps. Figure that it takes six inches of ice or more to hold your snowmobile; seven inches for a car; eight inches for a light truck, and ten inches or more for rigs tipping the scales at over two tons.

Clean ice is in itself a hazard, regardless of thickness. As everyone knows, the stuff is slick, easy to slip on, and miserably hard to fall against. If you do much ice fishing, you may want to invest in a pair of ice-creepers. These are spiked sole coverings that slip over your boot, or half of it, depending on the model. Creepers are inexpensive, and not only make ice hiking easier, but may save you a few broken bones as well.

Crevasses

In high country, particularly in glacial high country, you occasionally run across deep fissures in snowfields or ice packs. Few people traverse actual glaciers, but those who do should be aware of the deep cracks that run at right angles to the glacier flow. In heavily crevassed areas, members of a party should link together with strong rope. Should one hapless person plunge into a fissure, he can be hauled out easily by the others.

Open crevasses are generally easy to avoid, but often they are covered with a crusty skim of snow, thus becoming dangerous traps. By probing ahead with a walking staff, you can detect extremely weak patches. Should you decide to cross a snowbridge over a crevasse, do so gingerly, one person at a time. If on horseback dismount and *lead* the horse over. Traveling alone in such country is dangerous. If you fall in a crevasse, you may drop only a few feet before hitting bottom, but without help will have no way of extricating yourself.

Another occasional hazard in mountain areas lies in wide rock fissures. While these are crevices rather than crevasses, they essentially pose the same problem.

Once while sprinting across a huge, upended slab of igneous rock, running on a slight upslope, I suddenly came to a breathless stop that nearly threw me forward. A few feet ahead gaped a rock crevice clearly three feet wide, dark and deep. A few pebbles dropped into the fissure to determine the depth did nothing more than clatter from wall to wall in a fading staccato. A head-over-heels plunge into the crevice would have, at best, resulted in broken bones.

The danger is exemplified when a thin layer of snow covers the ground. As precautionary strategy, avoid areas that are known to be heavily creviced, and never travel alone in high, rocky country when a thin skim of snow is on the ground.

Lightning

Great bolts of lightning crackling in the sky are beautiful to watch, but as everyone knows, they can be deadly. However, like many of the dangers we have discussed, your chance of succumbing to a heavenly electrical spear is extremely small. Lightning claims roughly 200 lives annually in this country, an infinitesimal fraction of the total population.

It's common knowledge that lightning often (though not always) strikes the highest object from the ground. It's also well known that standing under a singularly tall tree is a prime way to get zapped. However, don't get carried away with this notion. It isn't necessarily dangerous to be under *a* tree.

An even-height stand of trees is in fact a safe place to be during a storm. I've seen people at a near panic because they were caught in the woods during a storm, even when there was no basis for this fear. Avoid tall trees (relative to the surrounding cover) and you have already narrowed the odds of being struck by 80 percent or more.

You must be far away from tall trees to be really safe. Anyone who wanders the woods has noticed how a group of four or five trees will all bear spiral lightning scars. The reason why is plain—lightning rebounds off one object to another. Usually the largest tree is struck first, then the bolt bounces to an adjacent tree and then to another, until its energy is sapped. If you are near a tall object, you may be hit by such a deflected bolt.

This idea of "tall" objects bears looking at. In a mature forest, "tall" may mean a tree stretching 100 feet or more into the sky. On the other hand, in an alpine situation, a scrub fir scarcely three feet high becomes "tall." If you're standing in a grass field or meadow during a storm, *you* are the highest thing in sight, and the likeliest to be zonked with a lightning bolt. Ditto for a boat on water.

Water is the most dangerous place you can be in a storm. Get to land as quickly as possible. The low, level profile and efficient conductivity of water makes it a prime place to be struck. If you're in a boat and can make it to land, do so immediately. Don't hold fishing rods or other conductors that enlarge your susceptibility as a target.

If you are on flat ground or in a boat, don't stand. Crouch down in the lowest spot you can find, away from fences, power lines and other conductors. According to lightning safety charts, a rundown on the best places to be during a storm looks something like this:

> Cars, trucks or any similar metallic cages provide complete protection from lightning. Even if the vehicle is struck, you are safe inside.
>
> Houses, sheds and other complete buildings are very safe places to be. Electricity grounds down the walls of the structure. However, stay away from metal door or window frames; refrain from using electric appliances—including the telephone—and don't handle water faucets or metal pipes.
>
> An even-aged forest, where all trees are roughly the same height, is a good place to be, though not as safe as a vehicle or building.
>
> A boat equipped with grounded lightning rods or masts is completely safe. Small fishing boats with no grounding, on the other hand, are dangerous.
>
> High altitudes are hit the worst by lightning. If you're in the high country, stay low and off exposed slopes. Caves and rock tunnels are excellent places to be during a storm. Stay near low cover.
>
> A lone tree is a terrible object to hide under. You are better off crouching in a ditch and getting drenched if circumstances require it.
>
> Water is the greatest danger zone. By no means swim when a storm front is moving in.

5

Fishing Dangers

Fishing is one of the safest avocations a man can pursue, at least as far as statistics are concerned. The average weekend angler tossing poppers over bluegill beds, bouncing jigs off a walleye bar or combing underwater structure for bass is a pretty good insurance risk. In fact, those fishermen are probably closer to danger while driving to their fishing waters or fueling their boats. Once these preliminary details are completed, and all concentration swings to the gentle art of angling, the likelihood of an accident drops like a fat lady on a campstool. Assuming you don't bring trouble on yourself by sitting on a mess of treble hooks, sticking your hand into the maw of a well-dentured fish, or committing any number of other wrong moves, the odds are highly in favor of having an enjoyable, but safe day.

There is a comparatively small number of hazards that an incautious angler can find himself caught in, and we will look at them in this chapter. But first a general look at some basic safety advice.

The classic (and somewhat overplayed in cartoons) fishing malady has an angler catching himself or a buddy in the seat of the pants with a hook. There's no doubt that this sort of thing happens often, and an ill-placed hook has ruined more than a few fishing trips. If you are impaled by a hook, follow the directions given in Chapter 19 for removing it. If you're not hooked, and don't want to be, note the following:

> Watch your partner's casting arc, and make sure you aren't at a point tangent to that arc. If he is careless with his lure-slinging, warn him to be more careful. If that fails, **threaten** him to be more careful.
>
> Keep an eye on your own casting form, particularly if you're flycasting in a wind. Change positions or casting arms to suit the conditions.

Don't keep lures lying loose on the seat. After an exciting fish battle, you may unthinkingly sit on the lure, and its well-honed hooks.

This is an important one: Don't try to remove the hooks from a "green" fish—one that is still fighting spiritedly. You may reach down into the mouth of a bass at the same instant the bass decides to shake its head, and get a handful of hooks for the effort. There are few things more excruciating than having a barbed hook buried in your hand while a large, thrashing fish is attached to another hook on the same lure. To avoid such an experience, play your fish until it tires, then land it quickly and smoothly, being ever wary of hooks.

Landing fish is one of the major trouble areas for fishermen, especially for saltwater anglers. Not only are there sharp hooks to avoid, but also an assortment of teeth, fins and razor-edged gill rakers. I remember well the first time I boated a snook. I slid my fingers under the gill slats in the same manner I'd hoist a salmon or trout I wanted to keep, and ended up cutting a finger badly. I learned the hard way that snook have a thin, glass-sharp patch of transparent material in the middle of each gill cover, quite capable of deeply slicing an unsuspecting fisherman's hand.

Treat all saltwater fish with respect when you handle them. Most have at least one way of painfully warning you to be more careful.

The most obvious danger zone is a mouth full of portentous teeth. Toothy fish are bluefish, wahoo, weakfish, mackerel, sharks and barracudas, to name the more popular species. Don't attempt to remove hooks from one of these fish while it's still green, and use needle-nosed pliers or hook disgorgers once the fish settles down. Never reach your hand into the maw of a toothed fish, no matter how passive the fish may seem.

Next on the agenda for saltwater fish hazards are formidable gill rakers. One thing you learn early as a beginning saltwater angler is to keep your hands out of a fish's gills unless you know in advance that the species can be safely landed that way. If you're wetting a line in salt water, don't gill-handle channel bass (also called redfish), snook or striped bass. Also be wary of groupers, which have coarse gills that need to be handled with care.

A number of species have sharp fins and spines, and you should watch for them. The popular and tasty snapper is better gripped from the underside than the back. The jack crevalle has a pair of spiny protrusions near its anus that you'd be wise to avoid. Clamp your hands over the gill covers to render a jack motionless while removing hooks.

Few fishermen have the opportunity to land a billfish, but those who do proceed with great caution. The fish is grabbed by the bill with gloved hands, and held off to one side of the angler, never directly in front where a sudden lunge by the large fish could skewer the fisherman like a martini olive. The fish is held firmly by the bill until it tires. Then, if it is to be brought aboard, it is stunned with a billy club.

Sharks warrant special mention, too, for they are possibly the most dangerous of all fish to land. They have a spooky habit of appearing to be dead, then suddenly they burst to life with frantic thrashings and clacking jaws. For this reason, never bring a shark into a boat, alive or dead.

If you hook a shark and want to release it, cut the line near the terminal tackle. If you plan to kill or keep the fish, lasso its tail and drag it backward through the water, or hit it with a "bang" stick—a stick having a cylinder on one end capable of discharging a high-powered center-fire cartridge. The loaded stick is jabbed against the shark's head for the *coup de grace*.

Never "tail" a live shark, or for that matter attempt to hold it in any way. Sharks are cartilaginous rather than bony, which means they are capable of incredibly lithe body contortions. A shark held by the tail can twist up and chomp your hand if it has the urge to do so.

Freshwater fish are much easier to get along with; just a few have dangerous characteristics. The most obvious are the toothed species, including gars, pickerel, pike and muskellunge. Steer clear of the gaping jaws, remove lures with pliers, and handle the big specimens with caution. Use a net to land the larger fish. For the smaller ones, use a firm grip on the outside rear of the gill covers. If you're using a single hooked lure, you can shake off a small "snake" pike by gripping the lure solidly and giving it a quick flip. That way you avoid the hassles of hook and fish tangling in the net mesh, and you lose comparatively little casting time. But don't try the lure-shake with a very large fish or when using a multi-trebled-hooked lure.

A number of freshwater fish have sharp spines that can prick a careless angler, though rarely is such an accident severe. Catfish and bullheads are noted for their ability to "fin" an angler, and their slightly toxic mucus covering sometimes causes a punctured hand to swell and ache. Perch and walleyes also have sharp dorsal fins, and they often stiffen them in defense while you're attempting to remove a lure. These pose no real problem, though, unless you accidentally jam your hand against an erect spine.

Almost without exception, freshwater fish should be landed by hand or with a net rather than a gaff hook. A thrashing bass can be paralyzed by placing your thumb against the inside of its lower jaw, gripping the jaw tightly and at the same time pushing out and under. You can remove the hooks while the bass remains motionless. Other species can be collared around the gills, hoisted by a hand inserted into the gills (but do this only with fish you intend to keep, for such a hold damages the gills mortally), or lifted from the water by placing your hand lightly under the belly and lifting evenly. The pressure against the innards has a pacifying effect on the fish, which will lie quietly in your hand until you remove the hooks. I've had 20-pound-plus lake trout behave as docilely as an infant when handled this way.

Gaffs, in my opinion, have little place in fresh water. Unless wielded by an expert, the big sharp hooks can be dangerous, and more than a few fishermen have gaffed themselves or a partner while clumsily stabbing at a fish. Most fish are just as easily, in fact more easily, landed with a net.

Gaffs in salt water are another story, and are often the most effective landing tool. But care should still be taken to avoid injury. The gaffer should stand ready as the fish is drawn near, waiting for a sure shot rather than taking careless swings. The gaff is brought down and across, and the fish is swung into the boat in one clean movement. An alternate method is to place the hook in the water, point up, and wait for the fish to swim over it. A jerk on the gaff impales the fish and the motion is continued to pull it aboard. If the fish is a large one, or one to be released, the gaff is inserted through the lower jaw, and the fish pinned against the side of the boat while the hooks are removed.

When not in use, the gaff should be placed where no one can step or fall on it, and the hook point should be covered with some sort of sheath-like material such as leather or hard rubber.

Wading

A trout fishing friend of mine, watching me inch slowly and carefully across a waist-deep stretch of heavy water, remarked: "You know, your problem is you're afraid of water over your knees."

He was talking from a safe and comfortable seat on a shoreline rock, and his slight smile told me he was only needling, but later I reflected on his gibe and discovered it almost true. It's no secret that a fisherman can reap grave results from a fall in a swift, rocky trout stream, and a healthy respect for rough water seems a virtue rather than a fault. You bet I'm careful when negotiating a slick-bottomed, turbulent piece of water; anyone who plans on spending a long life fishing had better be!

A midstream slip can produce a variety of outcomes: you might simply get wet and irritable; you might collide with a rock on your way down, breaking arm, leg, head or flyrod; or you might be swept downriver and drowned. Viewed in this light, the subject of wading becomes serious. Wading properly, you narrow the odds of an accident, and maybe catch a few fish in the process. Wade without thinking, and you're asking for trouble.

In slow, shallow water with a sand or gravel bed, there's not much about wading you need to know. You just place one foot in front of the other with deliberate, slow steps, testing for a firm hold with one foot while settling your weight on the other. Simple.

But quality fishing streams rarely offer such piece-of-cake conditions. More common are slippery, irregular rock bottoms which trap ankles and offer ice-slick footholds compounded by swift currents that buck

John Faltus gains added balance by stretching out his arms like a tightrope walker . . .

and push, threatening to sweep your feet from beneath you. This is gamefish water, tricky to wade if you aren't careful. It calls for a more sophisticated wading technique than the basic test-and-step used on gentle streams.

Balance is your crucial ally, maintaining it the trick. In fast water you

and checks a slip by instantly plunging his fly rod into the stream, using its flex against the current as an added balance point.

can't risk even the momentary lack of balance created by picking one foot up and swinging it ahead of the other. Rather, you must more or less shuffle along, keeping a solid point of balance at all times and never allowing your feet to form a straight line parallel with the current.

The required footwork is analogous to that used by karate freestylers, who lay the bulk of their intricate maneuvers on a solid foundation of proper balance. A fisherman moving cross stream assumes a stance much like a fighting "T" stance. One foot is placed in front of the body, pointing ahead, while the other foot is set slightly back and at right angles to body direction. Connecting the front foot to the back makes a T. The angler places the foot nearest the current (the one on the upstream side) ahead, and the other foot behind.

The T stance allows humans, with normally two-pointed balance, to attain three points of balance—the maximum that can be achieved without getting down on all fours. In this firm stance, you shuffle across the stream, front foot moving ahead and planting, back foot sliding up behind. This way your feet never cross, and you never pick a foot completely from the bottom for more than a couple of seconds.

If the current pulls you down, or if a foot slips, use your fishing rod as yet another point of balance. By plunging the rod into the water, you use its natural flex against the current to your advantage. Flyrods, with their usual long length, are especially handy for preventing dunkings.

To make wading easier, the angler utilizes a makeshift wading staff, keeping the staff on the upstream side so that he can lean into the current.
When a casting position is reached, the staff can be used as a pivot point and third leg of balance.

Say you are wading upstream and across, when a foot slips or you somehow lose your balance. Instantly you thrash the rod into the water on the side you are falling toward. The push of rod against water often is enough to enable you to steady your footing.

Or you may be shuffling through a particularly fast stretch, where you need all the balance you can get. Then, hold the rod in one hand and stretch both arms out at your sides like a tightrope walker. The increase in balance is substantial, and may just be the ticket for preventing an unwanted bath.

If things really get hairy, and you find yourself in current too strong to stay upright without aid, push your rod butt-first into the water on your upstream side, using it as you would a wading staff. The rod won't break, and you'll have an added, and crucial, point of balance.

Anglers frequenting turbulent, tough-to-wade rivers should go one better than using their rods for the extra balance point—they should use a true wading staff. Most commercial models are light, inexpensive and effective. Staffs aren't essential on many waters, but on certain tough ones they become must items.

Something all stream fishermen should have are bottom-grabbing boot soles. The standard rubber cleating found on most waders is sufficient for sand and gravel, but doesn't cut it on slipperier stuff, such as moss-covered rock or irregular boulders. Slick bottoms call for felt or carpeted soles capable of planting a firm grip in the most treacherous places. You can buy commercial waders equipped with felt soles, but they are expensive and wear out easily. A more economical solution is to beg a few scraps of outdoor carpeting from the throw-out pile of your local carpet store, and glue the pieces to your wader boots with a sturdy waterproof cement. You'll notice the change in foothold first time you use the waders.

Another useful item is more of an insurance policy than a wading aid —floating vests. They are comfortable, stylish, and some even have multi-pockets for storing flies, leaders, bug dope and other tackle. They won't keep you from falling in, but they will keep you afloat if you do.

If you must go fishing without a floating vest, at least seal off the top of your waders with a wading sash. If you fall, the sash will do two things: prevent large amounts of water from pouring in, and keep the air in your waders from rushing out. The net effect is mild buoyancy—possibly enough to keep you afloat long enough to reach the safety of shallow water.

The best equipment of all for safe wading is your good sense. Plan your points of entry and exit carefully before you enter the water. Don't splash in carelessly—this is not only a good way to ruin your fishing, but a prime way to trip on a rock, twist an ankle or step over a sharp drop-off. Be deliberate and methodical in your steps. Take special care when traveling along a thin gravel bar that parallels deep, fast water. The gravel on the edges is often loosely packed, and a step there is liable to crumble beneath you, sliding you to the bottom of the hole.

If you do find yourself in such a predicament—riding a gravel slide—take short, quick backward steps, but try to remain in a nearly vertical position. Leaning back excessively pushes your feet outward, toward the hole. Like a rock-climber, keep your body straight and gravity will work to your advantage.

The best of all wading medicine is not to walk in places that are beyond your ability. The way to judge such water is to consider the depth, current speed and bottom consistency. These three factors team up to spell wadable water or that which is unwadable. For example, a fast stretch of waist-deep water may be within your ability if the bottom is smooth, but that same stretch is dangerous if the bottom is moss-covered rock. Or juggle the ingredients another way: A smooth bottom, roaring current and chest-high water combine to make for treacherous wading. Consider each of these factors before moving into a spot which you might not be able to get out of safely.

Getting out of tough water is much harder than getting in. Every trout fisherman has no doubt ventured into dubious water while trying for a better casting position, only to find himself unable to turn around and go back. Turning in fast water is one of the hardest things a wader has to do. In fact, in one particularly hairy run, it took me what seemed like 15 minutes to decide on a course of action and to execute it slowly and deliberately. Not only was I worried about my own safety, but also that of a few hundred bucks worth of camera gear hanging from my neck.

If you find yourself in such a predicament, make short half-pivot, half-step turns into the current; that is, so the front of your body faces upstream in mid-turn. Never turn your back to a swift current; you'll find it much more difficult to retain your balance. Keep your feet at about shoulder width apart and lean into the flow as you turn. Continue your pivot-and-step progress until you are facing slightly upstream of your shoreline exit. Then proceed to wade in that direction rather than directly cross stream.

If the time comes when you suddenly find yourself underwater, being sucked through rapids and rocks, how you react in the ensuing seconds could either make those seconds your last, or make the experience little more than something to tell around campfires.

If you're wearing a floating vest, tuck your knees to your chest, facing downstream, and ride with the current until you reach shallow water or are able to grab an overhanging branch with which you can pull yourself out. If your only protection is a wading sash, lay back into the water, with your feet pointing downstream, until the river deposits you in shallow water. *Do not* try to stand up in deep water. You'll only fill your waders that way, creating an anchor that will sink you to your doom.

An alternate method exists in fast but rock-free water. Instead of facing feetfirst downstream, float on your stomach with your head downcurrent, swimming on a down-and-across course toward shore.

Hip boots and chest waders without belts are more of a nuisance, but the same methods of surviving a spill apply. Avoid a vertical position in the water and you'll stay on top. With open chest waders, it helps to clasp them shut with a free hand while using your other hand to help negotiate the current. If that is impossible, bring your knees to your chest and clamp them there tightly with your arms while floating on your back. The waders are less apt to fill, and some air will be trapped to assist your buoyancy. When you bump against bottom, you're in water shallow enough to stand in. As you make it to shore, remember the possibility of hypothermia if the air and water are cold, and get into dry duds as soon as you can.

A few final words on wading. A number of anglers are discovering the fine big-trout potential of night fishing, and are taking to their favorite streams in the dark. Night wading presents a few more hazards because of the absolute lack of visibility. Planning an entrance into the water is difficult, and more than a few anglers have jumped into the river only to find it over their wader tops. The solution is to scout carefully during the day those waters you wish to fish in the dark.

When you're in the stream at night, don't venture into water above your waist, and probe carefully ahead of each step. Never night wade waters you aren't thoroughly familiar with, for a sizable potpourri of hazards awaits you. I remember a certain bend in Michigan's Au Sable that, along with harboring behemoth browns, contains a rare collection of currents which results in a true whirlpool. Locals tell me that more than one night angler has perished there, stumbling unknowingly into the hole, being submerged and rocketed round and round until life was blacked like the night water. No trout is worth the risk; if you don't know the water, fish from the bank instead.

6

Hunting Dangers

Guns don't always go off where and when you want them to, nor are they selective about what they hit. The muzzle, a piece of cold steel which directs the bullet or buckshot to whatever happens to be in line, should never be pointed at anything you don't want to kill—not for one second, intentionally or unintentionally.

Each year there are thousands of hunting accidents—a lot of them gun accidents—and each year dozens of men lose their lives afield. It's not the fault of the guns, but of the people handling them. Too often gun users are unfamiliar and uncomfortable with their firearms. And worse yet are hunters who consider themselves expert gun handlers, even though they only take a firearm in hand once or twice a year. Combined with an oft-found indifference to safety, these hunters are walking disasters.

You can often spot one of these types without even seeing him in action. Just hand him a rifle and watch: He grabs the weapon, inspects its stock and in so doing points the barrel at your face. He shoulders the arm, never bothering to check the action for assurance that it is unloaded. A real dolt might even aim at something and pull the trigger, not stopping to think that the rifle just might fire.

If this sort of a pilgrim wants to make a hunting date with you, make plans for a more important appointment that day, like sleeping late or putting up storm windows. It's almost a sure bet you'd spend most of the hunt dodging his rifle barrel anyway.

Not all gun accidents result from slob hunters, however. Even a normally safe and careful gun handler can make a mistake which may prove disastrous.

76

For example, just last fall a hunter and his dog had finished working a cover and were in the process of climbing a wire fence. The hunter leaned his shotgun against the fence and began to climb over. His dog, jumping against the fence, came down on the gun and somehow hit the trigger. By deadly coincidence the angle of the gun barrel, the time of this discharge and the position of the climbing hunter all meshed to meet at a fraction of a second in time, catching the hunter squarely with a charge of shot. Given those same circumstances, the leaning gun, the climbing hunter and the jumping dog, the possibility of a hunter being shot is probably less than one out of a thousand. But the only safe odds where guns are involved are those which are infallible. Anything less is dangerous.

That hunter could have shattered the odds by following the safe, albeit slightly time-consuming precaution of unloading his gun and sliding it under or through the fence barrel-first. Then all the jumping, slipping and accidental triggering in the world couldn't have hurt him.

Had there been two hunters, both guns should have been broken or unloaded and given to one man while the other climbed the fence. Once over, he would take the guns while the other hunter scaled the fence. Only after everyone in the party and the dogs had crossed the fence should the guns have been reloaded and the hunt continued. This rule

Never climb a fence while carrying a gun. In a two-man situation, one climbs over while the other holds the guns. The guns are handed over, then the remaining man crosses.

should not be broken, even in the excitement of a fruitful hunt, or if game is in sight.

As a hunter you may be interested in knowing exactly how hunting accidents come about; who's involved; the sort of conditions under which mishaps occur; and general statistics that provide an insight into hunting dangers and how they happen. For this let's look at the hunting data provided by one sample state. No attempt has been made to draw conclusions from the report—your analysis is as good as mine—but take note of the most prevalent accidents and their causes and you might be more alert for them next fall.

Wisconsin is fairly representative of the norm—moderately populated, heavily hunted, yet offering a wide variety of plentiful game. The following is paraphrased from the 1974 Hunting Accident Report issued by the Wisconsin Department of Natural Resources.

What Is a Hunting Accident?: A hunting accident is injury received from a firearm or bow and arrow, occurring outside the home while pursuing the activity of hunting. If you shoot yourself while climbing into the car on your way to a duck shoot, you register as a hunting accident. But if you're cleaning your gun the night before, and accidentally shoot your foot, you don't make the statistic sheet.

Number of Accidents: Wisconsin saw 178 hunting accidents in 1974. (There was a total of 795,336 hunters.) Sixty mishaps occurred during the regular deer season and 108 resulted during the small-game season. Five accidents befell bowhunters chasing deer, and five more were associated with bear hunting. From the total were ten fatalities, eight of them on deer hunts, two while chasing small game.

Age of Victims and Shooters: Thirty-six percent of the shooters were under 18. Out of the ten deaths, eight of the shooters were under 25 years old. Of the fatal victims, five were younger than 25 years. Of all casualties, 33 percent were under 18 years old.

Firearm Involved: Ninety-one mishaps involved shotguns, 61 rifles, 10 handguns and 5 bow and arrow. Sixty percent of the long gun accidents involved shotguns. Four of these scattergun injuries were fatal. Twenty-two deer-hunting accidents, including three deaths, were caused by unsafely directed shotgun slugs.

Cause of Accidents: Fifty percent involved hunter's judgment. Reasons included are: "victim moved into line of fire," "covered while swinging on game," "victim was out of sight" and "victim was mistaken for game." In 49 percent of the cases, the shooter was less than ten yards from the victim. Dense cover was a factor in a third of the casualties. Twenty-six percent of all injuries, including four mortal ones, were self-inflicted. Twelve resulted from stumbling and falling.

Hunting Partners: In 80 percent of the cases, the shooter and victim were members of the same party. (Watch your partner!) In nearly half of those accidents, the shooter had less than five years' hunting experi-

Don't let your partner get away with pointing his gun at you in this fashion. In more than three-quarters of all gun accidents, the shooter and victim are partners. Watch your own gun manners, but keep a constant eye on your companion.

ence. Exactly half of the shooters could plainly see their victims.

Types of Injuries: Of the total injuries, 43 percent involved legs and feet, 20 percent maimed head and neck. Seventy-two percent of the deer-hunting casualties and 67 percent of the rabbit- and squirrel-hunting injuries were to the arms, legs or feet.

Animal Being Hunted: Deer are the most dangerous animals to pursue, with 65 injuries resulting, 5 by bow, the remainder by firearm. Squirrel hunters racked up 27 accidents (and a few other hunters), pheasants were third with 22 injured hunters. Duck hunters had 8 accidents, and grouse shooters suffered 6.

When Accidents Occurred: Twenty-eight percent of the deer-hunting accidents occurred on opening day. Of all accidents, 67 percent happened to weekend hunters, with Saturday being slightly more dangerous than Sunday. Slightly more than half of the total mishaps occurred from noon to 5 P.M., and the next highest accident frequency was between 9 A.M. and noon.

That's a look at the statistics; now let's look at how to avoid becoming one.

Gun Safety: The list of gun-handling rules is not an original one, for safe gun toters have obeyed them and preached them for decades. You've no doubt read these rules, with slight stylistic variations, more than a couple of times before. But read them again and see if maybe there's a rule or two that you tend to fudge on. Then go back and reread

Always keep your gun pointing at nothing more than the atmosphere when you aren't pointing at game. An accidental discharge will kill only air that way.

those accident statistics. Chances are a violation of that rule cost at least one hunter life or limb.

In no particular order of importance, except for the first rule, which is the cardinal law of firearm handling, here's a rundown on safe and sensible gunsmanship.

Treat every gun **at all times** as if it were loaded. Check every firearm you pick up by first opening the action and looking and feeling inside the breech or chamber to see if it is loaded.

Keep your gun loaded only when you intend to use it. Unload the gun before bringing it into an automobile, house or camp.

Always carry your gun in a way that allows you control over muzzle direction, even if you trip or fall.

Never point a gun at anything you don't intend to shoot and kill. That means watching the muzzle to be certain it isn't pointing at a partner or dog. Always consider the possibility of an accidental discharge and keep the muzzle pointing so that it can only shoot atmosphere or ground.

Be positive that your target is what you want to shoot, and be alert to what's behind it. Before you squeeze the trigger, have a plain and clear vision of what you're aiming at. Never shoot at a sound, movement or color. Better to miss a buck than shoot your partner while he's blowing his nose with a white handkerchief you mistook for a deer tail.

Know what's in range of your gun besides your quarry—other hunters, livestock, houses, cars, etc.

Don't lean a gun or rifle against trees, fences or cars, where they can easily fall and discharge. It's better to lay the firearm on the ground, unloaded, if you must set it aside momentarily. Dirt can be wiped off later.

Be thoroughly familiar with your gun and its functions before you take it afield. Operating the safety should be reflexive, done without thought or conscious effort. Loading, unloading, and proper cleaning methods should be second nature.

When you become tired, quit. Fatigue dulls the reflexes and numbs alert thought—no way to be with a gun in your hand.

Never, never, never handle firearms while intoxicated or while drinking.

It's bad policy to leave a loaded gun unattended for even a few moments. Passersby may decide to examine the gun and may shoot themselves or someone else in the process. Children are especially vulnerable to this.

Don't attempt to climb a tree or fence with a gun in your hand.

Don't shoot at a flat, hard surface or the surface of water—both are conducive to ricochets.

Never shoot a gun with an obstruction in its barrel, however slight. Don't try to shoot the obstruction out; you might blow up the gun in the process. If you fall in snow or mud, unload, check the barrel immediately for clogging, and clean it thoroughly before shooting.

In the field, keep a close eye on your partner's position. Know where he is at all times, and never shoot in that direction. See to it that he observes this same courtesy with you.

Other Hunting Hazards

Guns aren't the only threat to a hunter's safety, as more than a few sportsmen have discovered. More common than gun accidents are hunters who become lost while excitedly tracking game, or who bog their vehicles down while attempting to negotiate roads that would mire a mule. These maladies are covered in other chapters, but there are a few safety concerns unique to hunters.

Dangerous Game

On this continent, there aren't many animals that can be called dangerous game when in their free-roaming range. Possible exceptions include members of the bear family and perhaps an occasional rut-crazed moose or elk, which may on rare occasion make an all-out charge. On the whole, however, hunters have little to fear from healthy wild animals.

But plant an ill-placed slug in any of a number of species, and a transformation occurs. You're dealing with a wounded animal, one less likely to behave according to its usual man-fear. This is true of some big-game species on this continent, and many which are found in safari countries of Africa. The best way to thwart this hazard is to do your absolute best in the first place to kill quickly and humanely. Use enough gun, and place your shot carefully into a vital area.

A wounded animal at close range should always be approached with caution. This applies as much to deer as it does to bears. The animal may charge you deliberately, or may run over you while trying to escape. In either case, it takes an alert hunter to safely end the animal's suffering without endangering himself.

Approach a downed animal slowly, with your gun held at ready. Approach it from its blind side and poke it testingly with your rifle barrel. If the animal appears to be dead, look at its eyes. If they're closed, the animal is unconscious but not dead, and if they're open and twitching, you're dealing with a critter that has not yet expired. But if the eyes are open and glassy, and a poke against them with your rifle barrel doesn't stimulate a twitch or blink, the animal is dead.

Many a hunter has rolled his "dead" deer over, straddled it to begin gutting, when suddenly the animal came to life with a staccato of jerks and jabs. Hooves are sharp enough to rip a man open, and antler tines can gore you as neatly as a Spanish bull. Don't take any chances around either piece of equipment. Be absolutely certain the animal is dead before you draw your knife.

About Gutting

Once, in Wisconsin's North Woods, I came upon a man gutting a fat eight-point buck. Attempting to cut through the tough breast area of the deer, the man sat on the buck's neck and inserted the knife at the base of its chest. He planted his feet like a rower preparing to lay back on the oars, grimaced, and with a loud grunt jerked back forcefully on the knife, pulling it toward himself with all his strength. I grimaced, too, but for a different reason. Had the blade ripped upward through the deer's hide, he would have rammed three inches of hunting knife into his belly. On another occasion, a hunting partner was careless while dressing a young buck, and lost a pint of blood from a badly sliced leg.

The idea is to gut the animal, not yourself. To do this safely and efficiently, you need a sharp knife. (See camping section—Chapter 7—for sharpening tips.) You need to push the knife away from your body when cutting, never inward. You need to watch where your fingers and legs are in relation to the knife blade, and you need to work methodically and smoothly.

Safe Outerwear

Most states have regulations on proper safety garb. It varies slightly, but the idea is the same; you need so many inches of fluorescent orange material to meet the minimum requirements. Tennessee requires big-game hunters to wear at least 500 inches of blaze orange, including a fluorescent cap. A number of Western states call for 400 inches. The rest vary, some being stricter, some more lenient. If you plan to hunt big game, check your local laws or the laws of the state you're traveling to for its specific requirements.

In areas that don't have such regulations, wear safe clothing anyway. Shy away from browns, whites and greens. These colors may sing "Deer!" to some overeager hunter who shoots first and finds out what he's shot later. Bowhunters are exceptions to the blaze-orange rule, simply because there aren't enough of them in the woods at one time to present a major hazard to one another. During early archery seasons, camouflage clothing is considered safe by authorities, but in areas that have overlapping bow and gun seasons, swap your cryptic garb for more obvious stuff when the guns infiltrate the woods.

Small-game hunters should wear at least some articles of bright clothing to make their presence known to partners. Bright caps are most effective, for they stand high on your head, above concealing cornstalks or weeds. Bright gloves are also useful, but use shooting gloves that fit tightly enough to allow trigger dexterity.

7

General Camp Safety

General Camp Safety

The first step for stacking the odds against a camping accident is to select your campsite judiciously. Scan a potential site thoroughly for falling hazards, such as a standing dead tree or large overhanging dead tree limbs which may topple suddenly. Don't camp at the base of a steep cliff or rock ledge; rain, wind or simple gravity may send a cannonading rock or boulder your way. And by all means never attach your tent's guy ropes to a precariously leaning rock or dead tree. A strong wind against your tent flaps could exert just enough force to pull the object down upon you.

Make sure your site is roughly level both for safety and comfort—it's impossible to enjoy a night's sleep with one end of your body appreciably lower than the other. (Not to mention the possibility of rolling downhill.) If possible, don't camp low—in gullies, ravines and depressions—for these areas accumulate bugs, water and cold. Never camp in a dry wash (dry streambed). Dry washes are common in arid areas, and often suddenly and dangerously gush with roily water—even if no rain has fallen near your campsite for weeks. (A distant storm could send a wall of water down the streambed.) By the same token, always stay above the high water line when camping near water of any kind. Look for signs of water flooding—rock, gravel or sand deposits, trammeled vegetation and river debris—to determine the boundaries of the primary flood plain, and camp well above it. If you bivouac on a sandbar or island, be certain your site is high enough to stay dry should the water rise during the night. Take special not of this when you're near a dam-regulated river or lake. Dam operators often make their adjustments in water level during the night, sometimes without sufficient warning.

Avoid camping in marshy areas, at least during the warm months when bugs and snakes are prevalent. If you must camp in a marsh, never cross a mud flat to pitch your tent; an incoming tide or rising waterline could seal off your exit.

If children are along on a trip, you may want to avoid any area with dangerous natural features, such as turbulent rapids, geyser basins, hot springs and abrupt ledges. Kids have an insatiable curiosity about natural death traps, and considerable skill in slipping out of your sight to explore them. If you have no choice but to camp in a dangerous (for children) area, take time to carefully instruct them of the hazards, and make risky places strictly out of bounds.

The next step in maintaining a safe camp depends upon a neat and orderly setup. All gear should be given a particular niche where it is out of the way yet easily accessible. While neatness is pleasant in city living, it is essential at camp. A site carelessly littered with debris and equipment is hazardous, particularly when it's dark.

All lines, most notably tent guys and clotheslines, should be marked in some manner to make them obvious both day and night. You can mark rope with luminous paint or bits of white cloth. Also mark all tent stakes. With the stakes and lines clearly obvious, you'll avoid strangling or tripping yourself or passersby. A good idea is to rig your clothesline slightly higher than the head of the tallest person in camp.

Keep potentially dangerous gear, particularly knives, axes and saws, off the ground and sheathed when not in use. Fishing rods should not be left on the ground or in the tent if rigged with a hook or lure. Not only are the rods liable to be broken that way, but you could be injured by stepping or falling on a hook.

Fires are an important part of camping and add much to a trip, but they can also be very dangerous. Build your fire on clean, level ground and clear away bordering forest litter that may catch a live spark. Whether you use rocks, logs or a metal grate to support your cooking utensils, make sure your cooking setup is steady and level. A leaning, precarious pot can easily dump your dinner or scald a bystander. Don't allow children to play near a fire or cooking stove. Once at a wilderness fishing camp I saw a small boy fall headlong into a large skillet of sizzling bacon fat, burning himself severely enough to warrant air removal to a hospital. There's plenty of room in the outdoors for play, but the area around the cooking fire belongs to the chef.

Survey your campsite thoroughly for hazards before dark. This bit of reconnaissance will prevent you from tripping over a rock you didn't know was there on a nighttime trip to the latrine. Look for deadfalls that lie across camp trails, precipitous ledges and holes or burrows that may catch and twist your ankles. Be especially alert for "jabbers"—dead twigs that protrude from tree trunks at head height. In the dark they are invisible eye-pokers capable of inflicting serious injury. Patrol around camp while it's still light and snap off all potential jabbers. (They make great kindling for your fire.)

You can see that it pays to make camp well before dark. Not only can you scout for natural hazards, but you have a better idea of what your campsite is really like. One wilderness campsite in Wyoming proved the wisdom of this advice. Well after nightfall a friend and I left a high-meadow trail to make camp. We found what appeared in the dark to be a perfect campsite: level and breezy, with an overstory of fir for wood and storm protection. We cooked a quick meal over our fire, laid out our sleeping bags on the dark, moist ground, and went to sleep. In the morning we discovered that apparently we weren't the only ones who thought our campsite comfy. The area happened to be a bedding ground for a large local elk herd. We had camped on a solid half-inch-thick mat of elk droppings.

Equipment Hazards

The most frequent threat to campers is not wild animals or environmental hazards, but dangerous misuse of equipment. A lot of campers are part-time outdoorsmen, lucky to get away two or three times a year. In this age of booming camping interest, there are many raw novices out trying their hand at camping for the first time. Consequently, many campers are afield with gear they don't really know how to use. As you can guess, the outcome is often unpleasant, and sometimes tragic.

Specific equipment dangers aside for now, there are a couple of initial steps to take for avoiding the bulk of gear mishaps. The first involves a common malaise: failure to read the operating instructions that accompany many items. Granted, these brief bits of journalism are often befuddling, and always uninterestingly written, but they at least provide a basic knowledge of how an item works. And most factory blurb sheets list warnings of how not to use the gear—reason enough to take a few minutes to absorb the sheet of directions. If nothing else, at least read the "caution" section to keep the gadget from blowing up in your face.

The next step requires familiarizing yourself with your equipment before you take to the woods. Pitch your new tent in your backyard, and maybe spend a weekend in it to get a better idea of life under canvas. Cook a meal or two on your gas stove; acquaint yourself with the features of your camper unit or the fit of a fully loaded backpack. That way you iron out gear usage problems and personal idiosyncrasies well in advance of your upcoming camping trip. It's much more convenient to experiment on the lawn, with the comfort, food and shelter of your house only footsteps away should something go wrong.

Lastly, remember that well cared-for equipment rarely breaks down or malfunctions. Keep your gear clean and maintained, and never allow it to suffer unneeded abuse. Modern technological wonders have created an array of waterproof, windproof, shockproof, dustproof and fireproof gadgets. Few items, however, are idiot-proof. Remember the old bromide: "Take care of your gear and it will take care of you," and you will seldom, if ever, experience an equipment-caused emergency.

With general warnings stated, let's take a closer look at some common trouble-making paraphernalia.

Axes

Axes are synonymous with the outdoors and camping. Somehow, the chore of splitting firewood or limbing a deadfall doesn't seem like work at all when done properly. Apparently this fondness for ax work isn't limited to a hardy few, for many people enjoy visions of themselves in woods clothes, swinging an ax and breathing clean air. The reality is something else, however, especially when a neophyte who hasn't bothered to learn the fundamentals of axmanship (perhaps thinking there's nothing to it) clumsily chops away at a log or tree, either cutting himself or experiencing a couple of near misses. There are a few basics to simple and safe axmanship, and the place to start is with the ax itself.

A good all-around ax for general camp use is the popular Hudson Bay model. It's light, equipped with a handle long enough to use with both hands but short enough to swing with one, and sports a single blade. Novice axmen are wise to avoid the heavier double-bit axes used by professional woodsmen. The double blades increase the danger margin, and the heavy head limits accuracy. A double-bit ax is a fine tool, without question, but not for most campers.

Before using an ax, make certain the head is snug against the handle. A loose axhead could slip loose in midswing and make a rather unpleasant projectile. To tighten a loose head, either wedge bits of shim tightly between the handle and head, or immerse the head and upper handle in water to swell the wood, coating the head liberally with petroleum jelly beforehand to prevent pitting and rust.

Check the handle for cracks or splits—it could splinter on stroke impact. If you're buying an ax new, inspect the grain pattern of the handle to make sure it flows evenly along the sides. Severe curves and twists in the grain normally indicate weak spots. Don't buy an ax with a completely painted handle. Not only does the paint hide the telltale grain, it also causes hand blisters.

Never use a dull ax, for it is much more dangerous than a sharp one. A blunt edge will bounce or deflect from a knot or tough spot in wood, but will cut your epidermis easily. A sharp edge, on the other hand, is more likely to sink in and bite where you aim it, making the work smoother and safer. Dull axes can be slicked into shape with a file and whetstone; the file smooths out the rough edge, the whetstone is rotated in a circular motion across the blade to add the finishing touches.

Now for the actual techniques of safe axmanship. Before you commence swinging, there are a few precautions you should take. First, if the ax has been in a cold place, the head should be warmed before it is used. A very cold blade can shatter when driven into hard wood. Next, check the full arc of your swing for obstacles that may catch or deflect the ax while in midstroke. Most notable are overhanging branches, test guys, clotheslines and kids. Clear them away or shift to a safer position. If you intend to chop down a tree—either live or standing dead—look carefully for dead branches that may jar loose from the impact of your ax. A large branch could seriously harm you.

Next comes the proper stance. Your feet should be spread wide and your body should be limber and relaxed. If you're chopping logs or splitting kindling with an overhead swing, the wide stance makes it less likely for a deflected ax to hit your foot or leg. Logs are stood on end if possible, and on a chopping block. Uneven wood should be leaned upright against another log on the side opposite you. Never follow the cheechako practice of holding the target log in place with your boot. There are few better ways to lose a bunch of toes. Similarly, never hold a log in place with one hand and swing the ax with the other. If you need to slice off sections from a thin piece of wood, lay it horizontally

The drawing on the left shows the proper way to split a log that can't be stood upright. The drawing on the right is something you should never try.

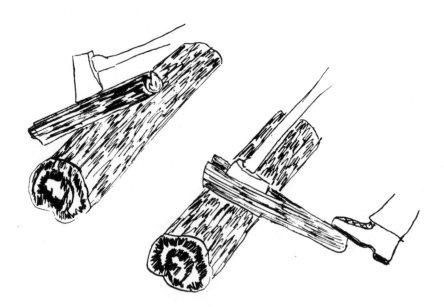

on the chopping block or lean it on the far side of a log and strike with just enough force to sink in the ax. Lift the ax—with the wood still attached—and bring down both together against the block or log to split the wood completely.

If you're chopping down a standing tree, first check the direction in which you want the tree to fall. If you're new at the game, inspect all directions the tree might fall, just in case you make an error in your calculations. Be certain the toppling tree will not damage property or people, and allow more room than you think you will need for a safety margin. It's normally not a good idea to fell a tree that's very near a camp or cabin unless you know well what you are doing. If the tree falls in the wrong direction, it could cause serious damage and injury to your camp and its members.

Remember that the natural leaning direction of the tree, prevailing winds and notch placement determine the path of a falling tree. Take all of these factors into consideration before you make the first ax cut. Make your notches roughly as wide as the tree's diameter and cut the lowest notch first (the side toward which the tree will fall). Once the tree begins to creak and fall, stand clear to one side. Never stand behind the tree, for the butt sometimes snaps up and back a few feet. If you must push the tree to aid its falling, do so from one side, and jump away when it begins to topple.

To "clean" the fallen trunk of limbs, stand on the side opposite the branches you want to cut. That way a glancing ax is more likely to sink into the trunk than your leg. Cut the limbs *with* the angle of their growth—that is, from the outside bend of the branch. Cutting into the fork of the branch will bind or deflect the ax.

Stand atop the trunk to cut it into manageable pieces. Spread your feet wide, and cut the wood between your feet with even strokes. Chip a wide notch on one side, then on the other to sever the log completely.

Many beginners make the mistake of thinking they must swing with all their strength to split or drop a tree. Actually, a firm, even stroke is better. It allows more accuracy and is less tiresome. If the ax is brought down evenly on an upright log, the wood will normally split nicely. When it's impossible to cut with the grain (such as with a standing tree or horizontal log), you get the most bite out of a swing by cutting at obtuse angles rather than a right angle. You sometimes see a novice axman take a vicious right angle cut at a tree or log, only to have the ax barely sink in or bounce right back at him. This happens because he is bucking the wood's supporting grains rather than using them to his advantage. A lighter stroke at a 45 degree angle into the wood is safer and much more efficient.

Here are a few more do's and don'ts for safe axmanship.

Be cautious of using an ax while standing on slick leaves, mud or snow. Make your strokes light and deliberate; a hard swing may throw you off balance. Never attempt to chop wood while standing on ice. The stuff is just too slick to be safe. If you want to use an ax to cut a hole in ice, kneel down and sit back on your legs while chopping with light swings.

When possible, keep your ax sheathed while traveling. Should you fall, the masked edge can't hurt you. If you're carrying an unsheathed ax, hold it by the handle directly under the head. If you start to fall, throw the ax to one side, but not downhill of your fall. (You may land on the upturned edge.)

Don't cut at wood knots. They are hard, and can chip or deflect your blade. Chop around knots instead.

Never leave axes or hatchets lying around camp unsheathed; they're too easy to step or fall on. Imbedding an ax into a chopping block is okay for short periods, but it's better to sheath the blade and store the ax when not in use.

Knives

A lot of people experience minor knife cuts while camping, and the majority of mishaps can be attributed to a dull knife or lack of good sense, or a combination of both. Like an ax, a knife is a much safer and more efficient tool when honed to a razor's edge. Cutting or whittling with a dull knife means you have to exert more force on the blade. It is easier for the dull blade to slip, cutting a hand or fingers in the process. A dull knife makes a jagged tear in skin tissue, destroying surrounding epidermal cells and drawing an onrush of blood, while the cut from a sharp knife is hair-thin and less damaging.

The only requirements for woodsmanlike knife sharpening are a good whetstone and a little know-how. To put an edge on a thoroughly dull knife, use a fairly coarse sharpening stone. If you have honing oil, a drop of it on the stone will help the procedure. Lacking oil, good old-fashioned spit will work. Lay the blade across the stone, with the edge pointing away from you and cant it forward so the angle formed by the blade and stone is somewhere between 10 and 15 degrees. Stroke the knife across the stone while exerting a little pressure and maintaining the 10 to 15 degree angle, as if shaving the stone. Repeat this procedure, first on one side of the blade, then on the other, until the edge sharpens noticeably. If you have a double-surface stone, flip it over to the harder, smoother side and moisten it with oil or saliva. Repeat the technique used on the coarse side, only apply less pressure to the blade. Keep the knife at a very low angle; ten degrees will produce the sharpest edge. When you're satisfied the knife is sharp, test it by shaving a few hairs from your arm. If it won't cut hair, go back to the whetstone.

When the knife is sharp, strop it against your boot or belt a few times (by drawing the blade backward and across) to eliminate the thin line of steel known as a wire edge.

Sharpening a knife.

Once you have a good, sharp cutting edge, the job of keeping your knife sharp is much easier. The trick is to never allow it to become really dull. Carry a small, hard carbonium stone with you in the field, and touch up your knife frequently. A sharp knife doesn't stay that way very long, especially in camp.

Even with a keen-edge knife, you must work with safety in mind. It's a fact of life that knives slip, so it's best to allow for that slippage by keeping your anatomy away from the front of the blade. Never put pressure on a blade if a part of your person is in the knife's path of travel. This would seem to be obvious, practically unnecessary advice, but anyone who has spent much time observing outdoorsmen handle their cutlery will understand my mention of it. Campers who cut rope by inserting their knife inside a loop, and drawing the blade forcibly toward themselves; or who rest knotty whittling wood against their chests or thighs to gain cutting leverage are common sights—as are, understandably, campers patched with Band-Aids. The best solution for this sort of thing is to make sure a slipping knife cuts nothing but atmosphere, and the best way to do *that* is to keep your body parts behind the blade.

Lastly, knives should never be allowed to lie around with the blade exposed. Pocketknives should be folded, and belt knives should be sheathed. The time-honored tradition of jabbing a knife into a log or stump may add a rustic touch to your campsite, but that exposed edge is a potential source of danger. Ditto for plunging a blade into the ground, which is not only unsafe, but dulls the blade as well. A resting knife is best placed in its sheath.

Chain Saws

Chain saws have become popular with many campers because of the ease and rapidity with which they handle formerly arduous chores. But like any power tool, chain saws can be dangerous. The best safety advice is to carefully read the manufacturer's information on use and maintenance before you start the saw up. Once it's going, treat the machine with the greatest respect. More specifically:

Keep your mind on your task. Daydreaming with a buzzing saw in your hands is a prime way to get cut. If you want to ponder your work, keep the saw at an idle, or better yet, turn it off completely.

Be careful when nearing the end of a cut. Your pressure on the saw plus gravity can cause the whirling chain to break through the last of the wood forcefully enough to travel a foot or more before you can stop it. Hence it pays to keep well back from your work and to anticipate the final slip by keeping your body—especially your legs—clear.

Never touch the moving chain. Also warn children to keep their distance. A moving chain has a mysterious allure for kids, who often want to touch it experimentally. Make them thoroughly aware of the danger.

Don't wear loose, hanging clothing such as scarves or stocking hats. They can tangle in the chain and draw you to the saw (or vice versa) before you realize what has happened.

Exercise some prudence when refueling. Don't spill fuel on the motor; it may be hot enough to cause combustion. And of course, you shouldn't smoke near inflammable fuels.

Chain saws exude noxious fumes which are capable of asphyxiating you if used where there is insufficient ventilation. They should not be used indoors.

Stoves

Stoves are not inherently dangerous items, but must be used with care. In small tents, such as the various two-man designs, stoves should never be used. The main danger lies in the lack of ventilation. All stoves emit some sort of noxious fume which is dangerous in an enclosed area.

Wood-burning stoves are great items, particularly for winter camping in large tents (with special asbestos portholes for the stovepipe), but should not be used for extended periods in a closed tent—no matter how large the tent may be. Gas stoves, on the other hand, should never be used indoors unless there is good ventilation.

There's another danger present with gasoline besides noxious fumes. The vapors are highly combustible and accumulate easily in stagnant indoor air. Striking a match in gasoline vapor is akin to tossing a lit cigarette into a gunpowder bin. As an added danger, white gas—the type used for many stoves and heaters—doesn't emit a gasoline odor, so you may unwittingly be sitting in the midst of a potential explosion. Because of all this, many experts recommend using gas stoves outdoors only.

Bottled gas—propane or butane—is popular with some campers, and again, can be dangerous if used in small enclosures. It's best to keep the stuff outdoors. However, bottled gas can be safely used in a large family-size tent if the windows and entrance are kept open. One writer described the smell of bottled gas as garlic-like, and that is probably the best description. Should you notice a garlicky smell in your tent, it's likely to be a gas leak. Remove the gas tank immediately and open all tent flaps to evacuate the fumes. Don't smoke or light a lantern (or make any fire or sparks whatever) until fresh air can permeate the tent.

Sleeping Bags

Sleeping bags can't cut you like an ax, or blow up in your face like a stove, but they can be a very subtle hazard. Periodically, even the shaggiest woodsman must have his sleeping bag cleaned. This is necessary both for sanitation and sanity. The most effective cleaning method for most bags is dry cleaning, but therein lies the danger.

Every now and then a camper makes the news by perishing in his newly cleaned sleeping bag. Evidently, the dry cleaning process leaves a dangerous gaseous residue in the fibers, and when an unsuspecting camper pulls the bag over his head for a cozy snooze, he is subjecting himself to an asphyxiating vapor. I don't know how many people die this way, but since it has caused deaths in the past, it is worth considering. The best medicine is to air your bag thoroughly after a cleaning. A day on the clothesline should make it safe to use.

8

Boating: Dangers and Safety

Usually the first thing boating writers point out in an article on safety and accident prevention is that boating is one of the safest of all outdoor sports. Be that as it may, there are still hundreds of boat-associated deaths each year, and even more nonfatal accidents. In 1974, for example, 1,400 lives were lost through boating mishaps. These deaths resulted from some of the 5,000 collisions and other accidents recorded by the U.S. Coast Guard. Add to that nearly 15,000 insurance claims for submerged-object damage, hundreds of engine fires and incalculable unreported accidents, and the cheery assertion that boating is incomparably safe comes into question. This is not to imply that boating is unsafe either, but the subject should be looked at realistically. As with any motor sport, the ignorant or careless participants can fall subject to a variety of dangers, or impose trouble on others.

There's a lot more to safe boating than first meets the eye. In fact, the subject is an enormous one. It would require an entire book or series of books to give comprehensive coverage, and no such attempt is made here. If boating is of major interest to you, check any of the dozens of excellent books found in libraries and stores. They will fill you in on the fine points of maintenance, handling and nautical skills. The following material is a condensed version of the varying aspects of boat safety. It's useful for any boater, but should be of special help to the casual water-farer—hunters, fishermen and other part-time skippers who use a boat as a vehicle for other forms of recreation and who are not necessarily interested in boating for boating's sake. These outdoorsmen are often the least nautical boaters, and are consequently prone to become webbed in boat-related difficulties.

In case you have a few boating seasons under your belt, and feel all this talk of safety boring and rudimentary, cogitate this nugget of fact: insurance firms handling boat coverage say their statistics reveal the most dangerous skipper is one with between 100 and 500 hours of experience at the helm. Restated, that means rank beginners and old pros are much safer (statistically) than a cocky dolt who has spent just enough time on the water to become overconfident, but not enough to learn proper and safe boat handling.

Even with that insight aside, it never hurts to brush up on safety basics, regardless of your experience.

General Boat Safety

Before delving into the specifics, let's take a general look at precautions—a do's and don'ts approach to the roots of boating safety. The following list is in no particular order of importance. All are equally worth considering.

As in any outdoor excursion, it's just good sense to inform a trustworthy friend or authority of your destination, the number of individuals in your party and your expected time of return. Should you become stranded for one reason or another, you have the assurance of knowing that someone is aware of your whereabouts. If you're in an unfamiliar area, where you have no acquaintances, file your boating plan with the operator of the marina from which you launch, a local warden, ranger or, if necessary, sheriff.

Always have modern, reliable emergency equipment onboard and accessible. The amount and types of gear depends entirely on the sort of craft you're running and the waters you are in.

A coho fisherman on the Great Lakes has different needs, for example, than an angler poling a skiff for tarpon in the Florida Keys. You have to vary with conditions. A rundown on emergency essentials is outlined in Chapter 3. Consult it for an idea of what you'll need, but remember that you may want to add or subtract from the list to suit your specific requirements.

Keep your boat and motor well maintained and operating smoothly. Cared-for equipment seldom fails its owner. Also run a clean ship.

Coils of rope, beverage cans, tools and other debris should never be left carelessly about the deck or floorboards. They present tripping hazards, or may themselves be kicked or bounced overboard. Keep the deck or floor free of excess bilge or other slick substances. Give your boat a thorough looking-over before starting out. You may discover something as seemingly insignificant as a loose gas tank fitting. That minor trouble, unnoticed and unattended, could cause your entire boat to burst into flames!

Left, proper installation of copper fuel line requires a section of flexible neoprene hose at end connected to engine to absorb vibration. Easy to get at shut-off valve is good, kink in hose is not—could cause fuel flow problems and eventually break.

Neoprene hoses in fuel distribution system should be checked periodically, middle, and, if spongy, replaced. Below, antisiphon valve installed in fuel tank withdrawal fitting is good insurance against fuel draining into boat if line break occurs. (*Photo: Tempo Products; courtesy, Jerry Martin Co.*)

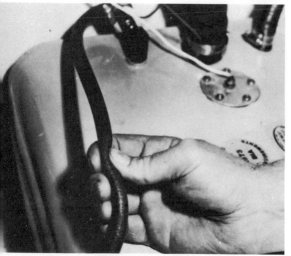

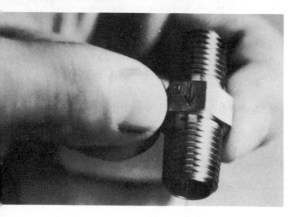

Know your boat's limitations, for it assuredly has some.

This aspect of safety is often overlooked by careless boaters, and the price paid for such a mistake is usually high, costing anywhere from a

Your boat should be loaded so that it sits properly in the water. The top boat is just about evenly balanced, the one in the center is bow heavy, and the bottom boat is dangerously stern heavy.

severe scare to a life. Your boat may be too small, or too large, for some conditions. View these limitations realistically and you'll prevent one of the most serious boating dangers—getting in water you can't handle.

A lot of boating mishaps occur because of overloading.

A properly loaded boat sits deep in the water, perhaps, but rides evenly, with a safe amount of freeboard all around. You may have to shift gear around to prevent one end or side from resting lower than the other. But there's no way to cheat on overall weight. If your boat is over-loaded, there's only one out: leave the least useful items behind. Remember also that you need more freeboard in rough water. (Freeboard is the distance from the water to the gunwales of your boat.)

Proper loading is important not only for gear, but for passengers. All boats have a maximum limit of passengers which should never be exceeded except in an absolute emergency.

Never overpower your craft with too much engine.

Many boats have the engine specifications and limitations written right on the transom or near the wheel. These specs should never be exceeded. Not only do you run the risk of swamping, but you can also weaken and damage the transom, which is built to withstand only a limited amount of thrust.

Weather affects all outdoorsmen, but it dictates to boaters. Anybody who launches a craft on water should know the rudiments of weather prediction; open water is a lousy place to be during a storm. Chapter 12 deals specifically with weather forecasting and interpretation. Study it closely and get off the water immediately if you recognize trouble ahead.

Whenever you're boating on big waters that are liable to get rough with a shift in wind, you increase your safety margin significantly by carrying a small auxiliary motor.

The spare engine needn't be large or elaborate. A small five or six horsepower is sufficient insurance that you won't be stranded far from shore. If you have a large boat, with a transom higher than the auxiliary engine's shaft, you'll need to purchase a commercially made bracket that attaches the engine low to the transom, submerging the propellers adequately. These are inexpensive and available at many marine dealers.

Bone up on your marlinspike seamanship.

Marlinspike seamanship is what crusty salts and nautical sorts call rope skills.

Rope is essential to boating of all kinds, but to be effective it must be strong and reliable. Inspect your lines periodically for signs of fraying or weakening. Look for cuts, deep abrasions or rotting. Replace rope that you suspect to be weak. The cost of new rope is cheap insurance against the possible damage that could be caused by a faulty line.

Whenever your boat is in the water, keep a lookout for other boaters.

You may be the epitome of safe and skillful skippers, but that won't stop an intoxicated or careless bloke from broadsiding you. Keep a suspicious eye on yourself at all times to be certain you are operating in a safe manner, but be extra suspicious of the other guy; docks and marinas are full of gory stories of boaters who weren't.

Become familiar with and obey boating's rules of the road.

If you're not up on your boating etiquette, now is a good time to learn.

Rules of the Road

At first glance, a heavily used waterway appears as though there is no order. Boats weave and web around each other, horns blast, and a newcomer to boating might suspect that nothing other than divine intervention prevents constant disaster. There appears to be a singular lack of logic in the boating world, but such is not the case. Rather than depend on painted highway lines and traffic lights, boaters employ a stringent set of running rules which keep things in order.

Before delving into specifics, let's clear up a few terms which may be confusing.

When two boats are on a path that could lead to collision, a "situation" exists. Composing the situation are a "burdened boat," and a "privileged boat." The privileged boat is the one having the right of way, and must hold its course and speed during a situation. The burdened boat is the one that must alter its course to prevent a collision.

In an overtaking situation, where one boat wants to pass the one ahead of it, the passing boat is the burdened craft. The boat which is to be passed, the privileged craft, must hold its course and speed. Usually the burdened boat wishes to pass on the starboard (right) side. To signal its intentions, it gives one short blast on the horn. (Canoes, rowboats and sailboats are not required to give signals.) The privileged boat returns the signal if the move is a safe one, and the boat passes. If the passing would be dangerous, the privileged boat replies with four blasts, signifying danger. The burdened boat must then slow or stop and wait until the privileged boat gives the go-ahead by returning the original signal.

In a head-to-head situation, where two boats are moving toward each other from opposite directions, both are burdened. Both boats signal with one blast and swing to the starboard, passing each other portside (left) to portside. There's a bit of latitude here, however, if the boats are not on a direct line to each other. When two boats are far enough from each other to hold their course and pass safely by each other on the starboard (right) side, they can do so after signaling their intentions with two blasts. But be sure of two things: one, that there is enough horizontal space between you and the oncoming boat to prevent the other boat from automatically steering to the left (the normal procedure); and two, that your signals are clearly understood and returned.

When two boats meet in a crossing situation, where one boat must pass in front of the other, the boat on the right has the right-of-way, just like cars on the road. But use your head if the vessel doesn't acknowledge your right-of-way. Stop or change your course; being in the right doesn't make a collision any more pleasant.

Along these same lines, use common sense in conjunction with water rules. Don't expect a giant river barge to bow the right-of-way to an aluminum cartopper. Rules of the road are guidelines, but at times they must be amended for safety's sake.

Other powerboat rules include:

> Keep to the right in channels, streams and rivers, much the same as you would while driving. Never anchor in a channel or where you will back up traffic or create a collision hazard.

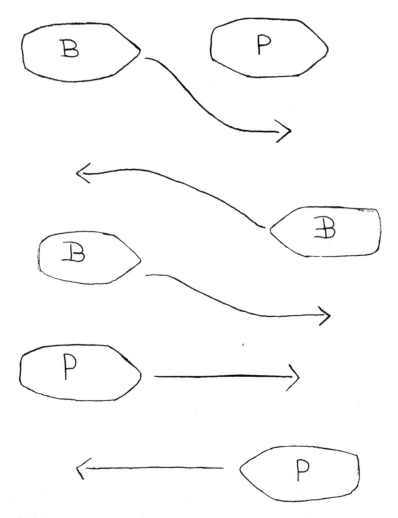

Here one boat wishes to pass the one in front. The passing boat is burdened and must signal and receive acknowledgment before overtaking.

When two boats are on a head-on course, both boats are burdened, and must swing to the starboard, passing portside to portside.

When enough room exists between passing boats, both boats become privileged, signaling and holding their course.

Give the right-of-way to all unpowered boats, including canoes, rowboats and sailboats. Pass far behind them or to one side, so as not to interfere with their course.

Signal with one long blast before entering a traffic lane, emerging from a dock or rounding a sharp bend.

Move slowly in adverse conditions such as fog, snow or rain. A safe speed is one in which you can stop the craft in half the distance of your visibility.

Be careful around smaller boats. You are responsible for your wake, which may swamp a smaller craft. Obey markers that warn against high speed travel, and stay out of all restricted areas, most notably swimming beaches. Watch also for floating red and white flags that signal divers are in an area. Give these a wide berth.

Some Common Boating Dangers

Drowning

Several thousand people drown each year, and about a thousand of them are boaters. Drowning accounts for roughly 70 percent of all boating deaths. Let's take a closer look at how these drownings come about, and how they can be avoided.

The high percentage of boat-oriented drownings are due to capsizing. In 1974, for example, 602 of the 1,400 boating deaths resulted from an overturned boat.

What causes capsizing? Mostly things we've looked at: taking a small boat on big waters; overloading a craft with gear and passengers; over-powering a boat with too much engine; and ignoring upcoming rough weather. Many boats tip because of improper handling in rough water, when a skipper unwittingly causes his boat to capsize by making a wrong move. (Rough-water handling will be looked at later in this chapter.) The remainder of overturned boats can be laid at the door of careless, thrill-seeking boaters who bronc-ride their boats.

People who fall out of boats are the second highest contributors to boating's "drowned" list. In 1974, 330 boaters drowned because they went overboard.

One major cause of overboard deaths is surprising. A significant number of drownings occur because people fall overboard while urinating! There are a couple of remedies for this. When you're near shore, and it's a simple matter to make land, complete your task on steady terra firma. Or, carry along a plastic cup to use as an intermediary between you and the water. Be sure to mark such a cup conspicuously.

Assuming that you suddenly find yourself overboard, either because your boat capsized or you fell, what do you do?

First, stay with your boat. This is for safety, not chivalry. A floating boat, even if capsized, is easier to spot in the water than a lone swimmer. And you can't sink if you're holding onto the hull of an unsinkable boat. If you fall overboard, and your craft is floating right-side up, make all attempts to get back aboard. This isn't difficult with a rowboat, but a slick-sided cruiser is another story. If you own a high-decked boat, keep a length of rope (long enough to hit the water but short enough to stay out of the props) fastened securely to a boat cleat and hanging overboard. If you fall out, you can use the rope to shimmy back on deck.

This setup is even more effective if you splice several loops along the length of the rope. The loops form a crude ladder, making it easier to climb aboard.

If for some reason you cannot get into your boat or it sinks, explodes, drifts away or in some other fashion becomes out of reach, you'll have to swim for your life, but not in the traditional, arm-flailing manner (unless shore is so close that you're sure you can make it that way). Rather, depend on a fairly new breakthrough in water survival known as "drownproofing."

The drownproofing method (sometimes called "survival swimming") can keep you afloat and alive for an indefinite period, even if you can't swim a stroke of the traditional breast-stroke technique. There's only one catch: there is no better medium for hypothermia than water. Cold water can suck the life out of you in a matter of minutes.

For example, if you fall overboard one blustery early spring day, when the water is near freezing, you would lose consciousness in under 15 minutes and die before three-quarters of an hour had elapsed. In 40 to 50 degree water, consciousness fades between a half-hour and an hour after immersion. You can last for one to two hours in 50 to 60 degree water, two to seven hours in 60 to 70 degree water and from three to twelve hours when the water is 70 to 80 degrees. After 80 degrees, water no longer becomes a threat to your body heat, and you can float for days without perishing, excluding other factors.

Drownproofing is essentially a way of using your body's natural buoyancy to stay afloat while conserving and maximizing energy. You float upright in the water, with your chin tucked against your chest, and your arms and legs dangling freely. The back of your head protrudes a few inches above the water surface, and you hold your breath in this position until you need fresh air. Then you slowly bring your arms in front of your head, crossing them so that both forearms touch. Lift one knee to your chest and begin exhaling through your nose while raising your face toward the surface. Push out with your hands and lift your head above the water, completing the exhale and inhaling fresh air through your mouth. Sweep your palms outward to remain above water long enough to complete the breath, then close your mouth, tuck your chin to your chest as before and drop back into the original position—letting your arms and legs dangle while relaxing your entire body as much as possible. You must drop your arms to your side immediately or you will begin to sink slightly. Study the accompanying illustrations to be sure you have a clear picture of the procedure in your mind.

From this basic floating position, you are ready to move into the swimming stroke if you need to. To do this, start from the basic floating position, then dip your head toward bottom, raise your hands to your forehead and bend your legs as if running, holding your rear foot as high as possible. This will swing you into a position diagonal with the

Drownproofing method.

surface. Next, reach your hands forward, to the surface, and just as they straighten kick frog-fashion with your legs. With the upward thrust, sweep your arms forward and out in a butterfly stroke, as if pulling yourself through the water. Make this stroke smoothly and forcefully, but don't thrash or jerk as you move, for you only waste precious energy that way. As you complete the forward movement, bend forward slightly, tucking your head and bringing your knees to your chest, exhaling as your body rises. This swings you back into a vertical position. As you near vertical, raise your head to the surface and push down and out with your palms to bob your head above water for a breath. From there you drop back to the original floating position and repeat the procedure. Consult the illustrations for clarification.

Practice this in a swimming pool or under safe conditions if you can. A short practice session is usually enough to get you acquainted with the method. This technique is being taught to one-year-old children by various safety groups, and the success has been remarkable. Teach drownproofing to your kids—it may be one of the most valuable lessons they ever receive.

Submerged Object Collision

Probably the most common boating hazard occurs when you inadvertently plow into a submerged or semi-submerged object. These "objects" take many forms, including tree stumps, rocks, driftwood and so on—all capable of punching a wide gash into your hull.

The best medicine is preventive rather than antidotal. Avoid busting into submerged hazards in the first place and things are much simpler. Keep a sharp eye on your course. Watch for floating driftwood, protruding rocks or stumps and other assorted snags and flotsam. On rivers, go slowly over water that ripples in every direction, for there may be a rock pile or wing dam a few inches subsurface. In waters known to contain lots of submerged stumps and trees, such as most man-made reservoirs, run at low speeds as a matter of habit—particularly near shore or in bays and backwaters. And always run at low speeds at night or in poor visibility.

If all of your caution is to no avail, and you come to a crashing union with an unseen object, your cause is not necessarily lost. If your boat is of a type which floats upright regardless of hull damage or water weight, you can either motor to shore or stay with the drifting craft until help arrives. Otherwise, you can sometimes make it to shore by buzzing along at high speed, planing the bow to prevent excess water from gushing aboard. Or, if the hole is a small one and clearly visible, stuff a rag or shirt into it to plug the leak while you head shoreward. Have all passengers don their life jackets in case the boat goes under before you make it to land.

Fire

Fires account for a large number of wrecked craft and more than a few injuries. As with most mishaps, boat fires usually occur because of a careless or ignorant operator: a guy who smokes while fueling or doesn't take the time to check fuel lines and inspect gas tanks. A careful skipper will observe the following fire-prevention rules religiously:

> Periodically tighten gas-line fittings, scrutinize fuel tanks for leaks and wear and run regular maintenance checks to keep the boat free of flammable bilge, oily rags and other combustibles.
> Since most fires occur because of or around fuel, be careful when refueling. Shut off all motors, electric appliances and stoves; don't smoke; hold the gas nozzle tightly against the fill pipe to prevent static electricity from throwing a deadly spark; don't fill the tank to the brim, since gas expands as it heats and may flood over; wipe up any spilled gas, and wait a few minutes before starting the engines after refueling to allow the highly flammable gas fumes to dissipate.

That's all it takes. Practice those rules and your odds of catching fire are minimal.

A word on extinguishing fires: Never throw water on an oil or gas fire. The oxygen in water mixes with the oil or gas and intensifies combustion.

Collision with Another Boat

Adherence to the rules of the water will steer you clear of potential collisions, but there's another type of collision that hasn't yet been discussed.

More than a few times I've seen or heard about a boater—usually a fisherman—who was broadsided by another boat while anchored or slowly drifting at night. Equip your boat with the large red blinkers raised high fore and aft, flashing constantly.

Running Aground

Not as serious as some of the boating hazards we've looked at, grounding a boat on a shoal or sandbar still ranks as a common boating mishap, if only because it happens so often.

The first impulse when stuck fast to the bottom is to throw the engines in reverse and lay on the gas. If your props are not in a position to be damaged, backing out may be the easiest solution. Have all passengers move astern to raise the bow, then back out steadily.

If that fails, and help is near, flag someone down and ask for assistance. Otherwise you have little choice but to wait for high tide if at sea, or for help if the water is not expected to rise in a reasonable while. Sometimes currents or winds can push you farther aground, and if that's the case, toss out a sturdy stern anchor to hold you in place until help arrives.

Handling a Boat in Rough Water

The best initial advice is *don't*. If at all possible, stay off the water when wind and waves are strong enough to toss your boat. But during

The boat at top is running with the wind, cutting down the odds of being flipped by a wave. The bottom boat is "broached" to the wind and waves, and is vulnerable to capsizing.

those times when for some reason you are caught in rough water, keep the following advice in mind.

The first step is to batten down all loose gear, so that it won't be flopping around during the height of the storm. Next, hand out life preservers to all passengers, and make sure they wear them at all times.

The safest course you can run in choppy seas is quartering into the waves. You'll bounce and bob plenty, but you eliminate the chance of the boat being flipped over by a bucking wave, which is what would happen if you ran sideways to the waves. If the boat is under power, throttle very slowly up and over each wave. This can be a little tricky, for too much throttle plunges you into oncoming waves and too little allows the wind and waves to "broach" your boat (turn it broadside to the waves). If you feel the boat broaching, increase the throttle to regain control. It is imperative that your boat does not swing broadside or nearly so—even for a moment. One large wave slapping the boat from the side is enough to flip the boat like a tiddlywink.

Fishermen in small aluminum boats are especially susceptible to broaching, particularly when running with little load and an elevated bow which swings side to side in the wind. If you're caught in rough water with such a boat, forget about making a destination unless it is on an upwind course. Concentrate on running straight with a steady throttle to prevent broaching.

If you're afloat in water you don't want to power through, there's another alternative: anchoring. If your anchor line is ten times the depth of the water or more, point the bow into the wind and drop the anchor. Make sure it is fastened tightly to a bow bit or cleat. Seat all passengers low to the deck to allow the boat to ride the waves easily.

In deep water, when your anchor line isn't long enough, throw out a sea anchor or a makeshift facsimile of one. These are cone-shaped canvas bags which drag through the water, weighing down the bow and preventing broaching. If you lack a sea anchor, tie a bucket, a pair of pants, a sweater or a heavy shirt to a line and cast it from the bow to provide the drag. If your makeshift anchor doesn't create enough drag, throw out additional drag lines until the bow holds steady.

Sometimes, for any number of emergency reasons, you must make shore as quickly as possible, even if that entails running a course in a broached position. This is a dangerous practice, and should be resorted to only when absolutely necessary, but in an emergency here is the right way to run abeam of the wind and waves.

Your course will be a zigzag path rather than a straight line, for it lets you run at least partially with the wind safely against you. First, angle upwind, with the wind blowing directly across the bow. Run in this direction for a few yards, then angle downwind, so the wind blasts across your stern. Travel a few more yards in this direction and then swing back to the first position into the wind. Repeat these small turns until you make your destination.

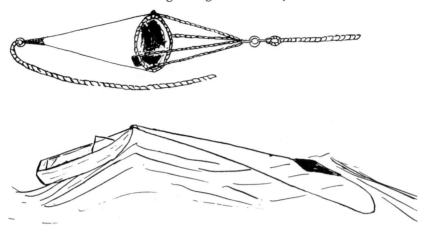

Using a sea anchor.

Running a zigzag pattern in rough water.

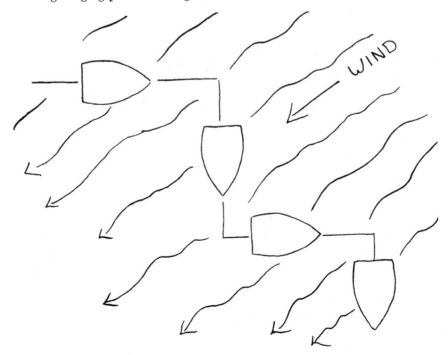

Rescue Techniques

We've talked a bit about preventing and handling mishaps that affect you as a boater, but now we move to those that affect other boaters. It could be a relative, a friend or a person you've never seen before and likely will never see again, but the rule of the sea prevails: never pass a vessel in distress; always stand by to help.

But heed that word "help." The first rule of first aid is "to do no harm," and that advice applies equally to rescue. Consider the following questions before you rush to scoop up a man overboard or pull passengers from a blazing ship.

Can you handle your craft well enough to avoid complicating the trouble by colliding with your rescue target?

Rescue can turn into disaster if you can't make your boat obey your wishes like a well-trained dog. You might knock a victim out with the bow, or accidentally catch him with the props.

Do you know what to do?

If not, stand by, but don't move in unless no other boats are around. With other people on the water, there is a good chance somebody will know what to do, and proceed to do it. Your fumbling will only complicate and muddle his efficiency.

Are you calm enough to work rationally?

This is an important question, but probably if you are level-headed enough to recognize the danger of panic in a time of stress, you can control the situation. People who lose their cool don't have to worry about being calm, because the thought will never occur to them. Most turn into statues or zombies—unmoving and incoherent.

If you decide to move in on a rescue, think about what you need to do (not always easy, however) and then work smoothly and calmly to do it.

Man Overboard

The first thing boating pundits tell you to do is yell "man overboard," so the crew (if you have one) can function as a unit. In addition to the man overboard cry, shout out which direction the victim lies; for example, "Man overboard, port [left] side!" Next, maneuver bow first toward the person, moving close enough to toss a life ring if you have one, or in its place a life jacket, boat cushion, beachball—anything that will keep him afloat. If a line is attached to the object, throw it past the victim, so he can grab the line and pull the float within reach. Loose objects

Approach a man in the water carefully, being ever watchful of your bow and props. Toss him a line, then kill the engine until he's aboard. (*Photo: U.S. Coast Guard*)

should be cast as near to the person as possible, without beaning him.

Circle around to the downwind or downstream side of the victim (to avoid drifting into him) and slowly move until you are alongside him. Shut off the motor immediately to avoid catching him with the props, and toss out a rescue line.

If the person is uninjured, pull him aboard. If he is hurt, and shore is near, it may be better to slowly tow him into shallow water where he can be carried to safety without aggravating his injuries. Common sense will dictate the best procedure for the situation. If the person isn't breathing, apply mouth-to-mouth resuscitation as described in Chapter 19. Tend to any first aid needs if qualified help isn't available.

Fire Rescue

If another ship is ablaze, be careful your craft doesn't catch fire during the rescue attempt. Stay upwind or upstream of the blazing boat, and board a burning craft only when the fire is small and you have equipment that can positively extinguish it. If the boat is hopelessly ablaze, maneuver near enough to toss lifelines to the passengers. Have them tie the lines securely around their chests before jumping overboard. If no oil or gas slicks are on the water, have each person don a life jacket if possible before jumping. But don't do this when there's a chance that surface fuel will cause the water to catch fire, or the floating rescuees may evaporate in a surface fire. If water fire is a possibility, have the people fasten themselves to a line and swim underwater as much as possible toward your boat.

Since children are in the most danger, pull them aboard first. If you're chivalrous, women come next, and men last. Once all the passengers are aboard your boat, move away from the blazing craft, and inform local authorities of the mishap as soon as possible.

Helping a Disabled Craft

When another boater is in trouble, and hails you down for help, it's often a simple chore to approach him from his downwind or downcurrent side (the water is calmer on that side), tie together, and loan him gasoline, fix a minor breakdown, or assist in whatever way you can. But if the boat is considerably larger than yours, and the water is even mildly rough, your craft can be damaged if you aren't careful. The yawing and bobbing of the larger boat could crush a gunwale or damage a hull. The trick here is to move the smaller boat to the lee side of the larger one, and fasten it loosely with a bow line.

If the boat is irreparable, you may have to tow it in. This is fairly simple under most conditions. Fasten the boats with six lengths of sturdy line, tying your (the tower's) end as near to midship as possible. Move out slowly, easing tension into the line rather than jerking it taut. Pull at steady speeds. In rough water be prepared to cut or cast off the line if your boat is severely crippled by the weight of the boat in tow. It's better to cut loose quickly and rescue the passengers on the disabled craft than to risk your life and boat trying to bring both boats safely ashore.

Rescue boat on the left side might be damaged by the yawing of the larger, disabled craft. A better procedure is to move to the disabled boat's lee side, as shown on the right.

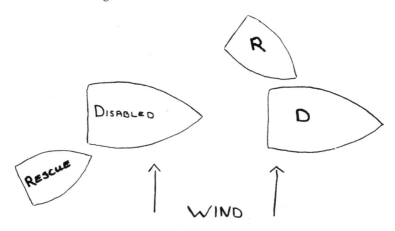

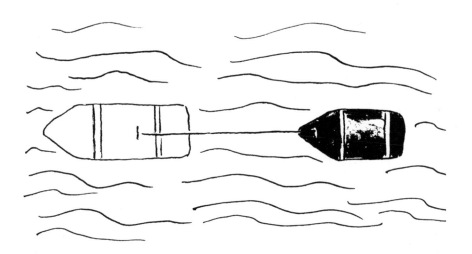

When towing a disabled craft, fasten your line as near to amidships as possible.

9

Canoeing and Rafting

There is excitement and euphoria in running a fast river, but there is also the lurking potential of horror. Whichever you find depends entirely on your judgments and skills, for the river flows uncaring and ceaseless. You must make your peace with it.

Those uninitiated to canoeing and rafting underestimate the complexities and sophistication involved. Perhaps they have paddled a canoe around a millpond or lazy stretch of river, where just about any technique or lack of it sufficed. Perhaps they have enjoyed an entertaining but adventureless raft ride down a gentle low-water stream. It doesn't take much learning to participate in that aspect of the sport, but fast-running water is an entirely different game—a more challenging and dangerous game, but to many, a far more enjoyable one.

Along with the increased pleasure of fast water, rides a corresponding increase in required skills and savvy. A knowledgeable rafter or canoeist possesses a finely wrought understanding of his craft and of rivers; of their manipulations and limitations, their good sides and bad.

But this is not to make a mystique out of the subject. Running whitewater is a skill like any other; one that requires learning, practice and more practice. You may not want to invest the time and training necessary to become an expert, but for safety's sake realize that there is more involved than first meets the eye.

Before you even approach whitewater, you'll need to know the fundamentals of paddling and oarsmanship. An excellent textbook for canoeing, rafting and kayaking is *Whitewater!*, by Norman Strung, Sam Curtis and Earl Perry. If you plan on doing much rafting or canoeing—whether for better fishing, hunting or camping, or just for the thrill of river rid-

Raft bronc-riding whitewater. (*Photo: Norman Strung*)

ing—you owe it to yourself to study this definitive work on the subject. Its discussion of river morphology is the most comprehensive one you'll find outside sophisticated scientific journals, and the detailed look at craft selection, handling and maintenance makes it a bible for whitewater enthusiasts.

Reading the Water

To most people, a river appears to be little more than a channel of moving water, not very complicated and not all that impressive. But a river rat—or a budding one—should know better.

A river or stream is in fact an intricate interweaving of many different channels and currents. Along with the obvious downstream flow, there are also places where the current moves upstream, cross stream and in circles. This diversity of currents is most pronounced in a stretch of rapids, and can plainly be seen there. Your job as a rafter or canoeist is to dodge the adverse currents, and pick the channel that will get you through the rapids with the least difficulty.

To become adept at interpreting river signs, you have to read more than this or any other book. You must practice by reading the water. Walk along a fast stretch of a small brook or stream, and look for miniature replicas of the features discussed here. Launch a twig canoe and follow its journey through the current. Notice how it is held up in some places; whirled around a rock eddy, grounded on a partly submerged obstruction, and run swiftly down the main channel. Anticipate where the twig will end up, and take note of current subtleties that alter its course. When you can predict with some accuracy the path the twig will take, you have gained some insight to the behavior of running water.

On a larger scale, the rafter or canoeist must do the same thing before entering a stretch of whitewater. He must scout ahead for obstructions, figure a way around them, and launch in a spot that will take him through with a minimum of effort. An expert can do this almost reflexively, based on many hours of practice, but the less skilled should study a rapids thoroughly before running it—getting out of the water and walking along the bank for a better view if necessary. This can't be over-emphasized. *Always scout a rapids thoroughly before running it.* And, again, experience on the water is the only way to learn successful route planning.

Here are a few obstacles you should be aware of:

Sleepers: A sleeper is an obstruction submerged enough to allow water to run over it, but not so much that a raft or canoe can clear it. In a gentle current, sleepers will do little more than give you a light bump on the bottom; but in fast water, a run-in with a sleeper can tear a raft bottom, or jar a canoe with teeth-gritting force.

To perceive a sleeper you must be alert for detail. Depending on the size of the obstruction, and its depth below water, a sleeper's wake can be seen on the surface in an upstream "V." The depth of the obstruction is relative to the distance between the obstruction and the apex of the V. However, there is no pat formula for this, and on-the-water experience is the only way to accurately gauge the obstruction's depth.

Suckholes: Suckholes are glorified sleepers that are deep enough to float over, but are hazardous in another way. The eddy beneath the sleeper is the problem. The powerful force of the whirling water floats you in tight circles, literally trapping your raft in a frothy merry-go-round.

The best medicine is prevention. Scout ahead for suckholes, which appear as a bulge in the river, and steer around them.

Rollers: Rollers are standing waves created when the circular movement of fast-flowing water is broken, causing the water to pile up on the surface like an ocean wave.

You'll see rollers formed where fast water meets slower, deeper water, or where a sharp turn in the riverbed causes the water to pile back on itself in a wave. The most notorious waves are called haystacks, and can easily flip a raft or canoe.

Judicious scouting and course choosing will steer you clear of hay-

Ropes were needed to pull this craft from the containing power of a suckhole.

stacks. Experts can flam their way through, but don't try it unless you know what you're doing. Skirt them instead.

Surface Obstructions: Your prefloat scouting should point out most of these. Be particularly watchful for fallen trees or debris piles that lodge across the current. Water flows through them, but solid objects such as your canoe or raft can't, and will be pinned between the jam and the current. If you go overboard, there's always the horrid possibility of becoming trapped underwater in the arms of the debris tangle.

Midstream rocks also pose a collision hazard. A canoe or raft can be "wrapped" around a rock, and held there by the force of the current. (Unwrapping a raft is discussed in a later section. In fast water, it's not as easy as you might think.) A protruding rock will create the appearance of an upstream-pointing V, with water piling up at the apex.

Falls: For our purposes, a falls is any section of water having nearly vertical relief of more than a few feet. Although some people tackle the smaller ones, it's not a practice to be encouraged. There's always the chance that your craft will broach at the drop and capsize, or flip stern-over-bow over the edge—not to mention the frothy water you'll end up in at the base of a falls.

Again, scouting is the ticket. Spot the falls and portage around them if no alternate channel exists.

There are a few more deductions an astute observer can gain from a river that can make the difference between planned runs and unwanted surprises.

The condition of the water is the first clue. Is the river at full pool? Or is it running at a low-water stage? One hint lies in the turbidity of the river. Chocolate brown water is a sign of significant runoff and consequent high water. Ditto for water filled with debris such as driftwood and tree branches. On the other hand, clear, or at least clean water, free from excessive sediment and flotsam, indicates the river is not at full flow. Check the banks for further indication. Bleached, water-washed rocks and exposed undercut banks are the perimeters of normal high-water flow. If you spot either, the water is not at full pool.

Once you have an idea of the speed and height of the water, you have a better handle on the potential fury of the rapids. During full pool, more water is pushed through the banks, increasing volume and flow. A dangerous rapids at low water can be impassable during high, and you'd need to do more scouting and portaging in such an instance. Conversely, during low water many rapids become more docile, hence easier to run. (Some hazards, such as sleepers, are sometimes amplified during low water.)

The next thing to watch for is an increase in gradient. The steepness of the riverbed determines, in part, the speed and ferocity of the water; the steeper the gradient, the more violent the water. Banks that rise ever-increasingly are ominous signs. So are gorges, where the diameter of the river thins and more water is forced through a tight area. Treetops can be helpful; if you notice them ahead, appearing low to the horizon, a sizable drop may soon come.

Slow water and placid pools on a spirited river are warning signs that something ahead is holding back the water—it may be a falls, narrow rapids or gorge.

Once you hear the rapids, look for telltale Vs in the water. Those that point upstream and toward you should be avoided; they indicate obstructions. Vs that point downstream, as a chute between two boulders, beckon you to a passable channel.

Look also for the frothing tops of standing waves. From back in the rapids they may appear to be little more than innocuous ripples, but as you drop to them, their true identity shows, too late to avoid if you aren't alert to their presence beforehand.

Another way to predict the severity of a river's tough spots is by consulting maps and local canoeists or rafters. Rapids are universally ranked as to the degree of difficulty they pose, and familiarity with the rating system will let you know what to expect. For example, locals may tell you that the river you want to float is mostly Class II. If you're fairly competent with your craft, you'll know the river will be a safe run.

According to the American Whitewater Association, the rating system breaks down like this:

CLASS I: Occasional small rapids with low, regular waves a foot high or less. Course is easily determined. Rescue spots all along. Water is shallow.

CLASS II: More frequent rapids. Eddies and whirlpools are not troublesome. Ledges under three feet high, with a direct, uncomplicated chute. Course easily determined. Waves up to three feet, but avoidable. Water less than three feet deep.

CLASS III: Long rapids, maneuvering required. Course not easily determined. Waves to five feet high, mostly regular, avoidable; strong crosscurrents. Good rescue spot after each rapid.

CLASS IV: Long rapids, intricate maneuvering. Course difficult to determine. Waves to five feet, irregular and avoidable; or up to three feet and unavoidable. Strong crosscurrents, eddies.

CLASS V: Long continuous rapids, tortuous. Always scout. Very complex course. Waves large, irregular, unavoidable. Large-scale eddies and crosscurrents. Few rescue spots. Require decking (for canoes).

CLASS VI: Long continuous rapids without let up. Very tortuous, always scout. Waves over five feet, irregular, unavoidable. Powerful crosscurrents. Special equipment required. Involves risk of life.

Note that changes in water level, and consequent flow velocity, alter the ratings somewhat. During a flood, a Class II might blossom into a IV. In times of low water, a Class V might quiet down to a II. Talk to locals and river-related authorities to determine the condition of the water you wish to float. And don't attempt to run anything beyond your certain ability.

General Whitewater Safety

Never was the proverbial ounce of prevention more applicable than in a discussion of running whitewater. To stifle a lot of possible troubles, burn into your mind these safety basics.

Equipment

Your safety or lack of it often rests entirely on your equipment and you can stack the odds in your favor by heeding the following rules:

Always wear a life jacket in, on and around rapids.

Modern improvements have taken much of the bulk out of life vests, allowing you more freedom of movement. Whitewater requires a jacket with a minimum 20 pounds of buoyancy. A "heads-up" jacket—one which floats you on your back with your head above water, even if you're unconscious—is a good choice.

Wear a helmet in especially tough, rocky stretches.

The best type for this purpose has a chin strap which widens near the helmet for temple protection.

Use only quality canoes and rafts.

A shocking number of people attempt to run rapids with crafts that are nothing more than toys, most commonly, the small rubber or vinyl rafts made for swimming pools. The price of good equipment is high, but proven reliability makes for money well spent.

Carry plenty of rope.

Two 100-foot coils of ½-inch manila rope, a spare coil of 200 feet, and a hand line of 20 feet attached to the bow or stern is not too much. Rope comes in handy for beaching, tracking through falls or rapids, righting after a flip, rescuing a man overboard and many other chores. All in all, rope is valuable stuff.

Wear the proper clothing.

In cold water consider donning a full-fledged wetsuit. It keeps you warm and dry even in freezing water. Lacking a wetsuit, wear a wool outfit covered with a light shell of water-resistant nylon.

Hypothermia is a constant threat when the air or water—or both—is cold. Pack along spare clothing in case you need to change into dry warm duds.

Have a first aid kit along, and accessible, at all times. And know how to use it.

Maintain a healthy repair kit and always take it on every trip.

The specifics on what to pack and how to use it are discussed later in this chapter.

Thoroughly check all equipment before a trip.

Inspect canoes for dents or gouges and repair weak spots. Rafts should be checked for leaks by running water gently over the tubes while watching for bubbles. Check brand-new rafts as well—a number of perils could befall them en route from the manufacturer to you.

Paddles should be examined for signs of wear and breakage. Replace those which appear excessively ragged. Always stow away an extra paddle in a canoe or raft. If one snaps off on a boulder or drops into the river, you won't be stuck in the center of a swirling rapids without a paddle.

Not-So-Common Sense

If there's one quality short of blissful abundance in adventure-seeking whitewater novices, it's plain old horse sense. When whitewater spray mists against the cheek, and the roar of rapids fills the ears and catalyzes the adrenaline, normally sane and sensible people do some weird things. To wit: one person perished in the froth of Georgia's Chattooga River while attempting to negotiate the Class III-V water in a craft made of Styrofoam coolers. An exception? An unofficial but knowing source tells me that over 20 people have drowned in the Chattooga since the release of *Deliverance*, a movie which revolves around a canoe trip on the Chattooga.

Then there is the large number of deaths that occur during high water all over the country. We needn't dwell on the details, but the point needs to be stressed: a wild river is not a gentle teacher if you throw caution to the wind and do something stupid.

A basic list of lifesaving precautions includes the following:

Research rivers you plan to run.

Look at maps, talk to guides, dam operators, local fishermen, anyone who might know the river and any special hazards it may pose.

Know your limitations in ability and equipment.

You can't run Class V water in an open canoe, and it would be foolhardy to try. As a less extreme example, you may not be able to run Class III water, or, for that matter, anything over Class I. Whitewater running is learned by stages; first the easy stuff, then moderate, and finally the difficult. You can't safely jump from easy to difficult, any more than you could jump from driver's education to the Indy 500.

Before you leave on a float trip, inform someone of your plans and your expected time of return.
Don't float alone.

On rough waters you should always travel in a group. One boat runs the rapids while the others watch and stay ready for rescue if necessary. Aside from the safety factor, you can also glean a great deal of whitewater savvy from observing your buddy-boats run the rapids, both from their smart moves and their mistakes. This maxim of never floating alone is vitally important. Obey it always.

Scout all rapids, particularly those that aren't clearly visible from upstream.

On easy stuff, you may not need to do anything more than observe the rapids while holding position upstream. In tough spots, don't hesitate to inspect the water from the quiet banks of shore.

Beach the boat and walk along the bank to study the water. Toss a chunk of wood in the water and watch the current toy with it. Memorize the location of suckholes, haystacks and sleepers, and plan the easiest course around them. Consider your entry carefully, for it can make the difference between a smooth ride and a frantic one.

There's an old saying among canoeists that goes something like: "No one ever drowned on a portage."

Those wise words relate the prudence of portaging around water that may be too tough for your equipment, ability or mortal limitations. No matter how good you are, there are rivers that are better. It's no contest, and only a fool attempts to make it one.

Any water you have doubts about should be circumvented; either by lining the empty boat through the rapids from the safety of shore, or by making an all-out portage, carrying craft and equipment around the whitewater. Dodging a dangerous rapids is not lack of courage, but abundance of good sense.

Don't overload your craft.

Rafts are sluggish critters to begin with, and an overpacked one is dangerously unresponsive. Canoes, on the other hand, are comparatively light and agile, and need to be for safe whitewater navigation. Overloaded, they respond lethargically to the paddle. A canoe should ride with at least six inches of freeboard all the way around, and the more the better.

Prepare for a run by securing life jackets. Fasten all gear snugly; you don't want equipment banging around the boat in the middle of a rapids. Booze and boats don't mix.

Although it may be exhilarating to run the water while light-headed, it just isn't good sense. Alcohol fogs the senses and impairs the reflexes, and both of these animal-level attributes are vital to river-running.

It might also be tempting to run wild water at nighttime. Again, the ride may be delightfully sensuous, but it could end up as a nightmare. Visibility is a crucial requisite in safely threading your way through whitewater. Nighttime is no time to be on rough water.

Canoeing

When one man takes a canoe through rapids, he kneels slightly aft of amidships and choose one side on which to paddle. Normally he doesn't change sides during a run.

When two men pair up in a canoe, the running procedure becomes a little more complicated. Both men must work to make the canoe do the same thing at the same time. To keep order, one man is appointed the captain and he gives the commands. There are two schools of thought on who should be the captain, the bowman or the sternman. One side proclaims the strongest, most skillful paddler should be at the rear of the canoe, the other favors the experienced canoeist in the bow, where he has a better view of obstructions and upcoming water. Experiment with both combinations and choose whichever works best for you.

The commands should be short, clear and thoroughly understood and agreed upon before entering whitewater. Keep them simple, such as, "back," "set right," "draw left" and so on.

Each man also chooses a side on which to paddle, and he does not change sides once in the rapids. Strokes and speed are varied to suit the water, but not to move faster than the current to gain control, as is commonly believed.

Broaching

When one end of the canoe hangs on an obstruction, and the other end swings downcurrent, turning the side of the craft upstream, the canoe is broached. A broached canoe is easily swamped by fast currents, or horseshoed around a rock. It must be straightened instantly by the canoeists.

If you are expert enough to swing the canoe about-face with draws and prys, and can do it quickly, you may be in the clear. If not, try this: as soon as the canoe broaches, swivel in your positions (both you and partner) making the bowman the sternman, and the sternman the bowman. This is regarded as sloppy form by canoeing pundits. Unless you are more interested in epicurean form than survival, use the about-face when things get rough.

Avoiding Obstacles

If you're alert and competent in your paddling, you'll avoid most obstacles, but occasionally may get a little too close for comfort. The following advice is also frowned upon by purists, but it works in a pinch.

If the culprit is a midstream rock or log, the bowman should plant his paddle blade securely against the object and push against the shaft. At the same time the sternman should complement the obstacle-fending with a stroke capable of moving the stern outward, away from the rock or log.

If the obstruction is a tree branch or other elevated hazard, the bowman should resist the impulse to grab the branch while attempting to force the canoe away. The upward pull raises the center of gravity and facilitates swamping. There is also a chance that the current will broach the boat if the bowman latches on to a stationary object. If the branch must be grabbed, it should be by the sternman, for the current will merely straighten the boat, rather than broach it.

When Obstructions Are Unavoidable

Say you suddenly find yourself broached to the current and swinging broadside into a rock. Collision is inevitable, and your first impulse is to

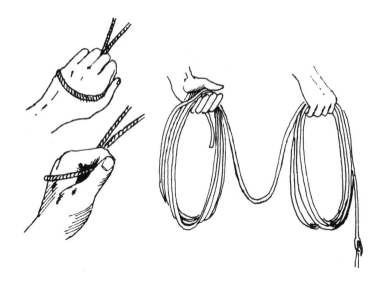

Never tie a rope to yourself if it's attached to a raft or canoe. Instead, hold it with your fist and fingers as shown at left. To release the rope, simply open your hand. The drawing at right illustrates the best way to hold a rope for throwing.

lean back and away from the rock. For your own sake, fight that impulse.

Leaning back and away from an obstacle increases the canoe's underwater surface area, increasing the current's pressure against it. A canoe that hits a rock in this fashion may be pinned against it or snapped in half. A much better reaction is leaning forward, toward the obstacle, so your submerged canoe surface is decreased and the current push lessened. Often the canoe rises high in the water and sweeps around one side of the rock without damage.

Capsizing and Swamping

If the canoe starts to swamp, jump out on the upstream side. Never get downstream of the canoe. If you fall out on the downstream side, dive or seek refuge in a rock eddy while the canoe sweeps past you. If you can catch the submerged canoe, straddle it horse-fashion and ride it through the rapids. The heavy, water-filled canoe will seek the deeper channel on its own, and make it through rough water with little difficulty in most cases.

But what if the canoe flies by? In a rocky stretch of water, float on your back, with your feet pointing downstream. If the water is fast but comparatively rock-free, swim on your belly, headfirst downstream and across.

If a rescue boat throws you a line, do not attach it to yourself. Grab it inside your fist, as shown in an accompanying illustration, but do not fasten it around your body or tie it in any way. Should ths rescue boat capsize, you won't be dragged with overpowering pressure through the rocks and rapids. By simply opening your hand, the rope will be released.

Sometimes a capsized canoe will be "wrapped" around a rock—that is, pinned against the rock by a river's mammoth push. Often a wrapped canoe can be freed by employing a combination of pull ropes and branch levers. If that fails, you'll need shore lines and possibly a winch to free it.

Emergency Repairs

On short jaunts you needn't pack a bulky repair kit; just enough to repair minor damage. If serious repairs are needed, you can hoof it back to your car and work on the canoe at home. For this you need carry little more than a compact kit, including silver-backed tape and epoxy glue. Longer trips, however, require a bit more.

> **A complete aluminum repair kit should include:**
> One roll of silver-backed duct tape
> Epoxy
> Small rubber mallet
> Hand drill and bits (that match the size of
>   the rivets and bolts)
> Rivet kit
> Two sheets of tempered aluminum alloy
> Metal file
> Pliers
> Tin snips
> Rubberized caulk
> Six 5/32-inch bolts with nuts

Dents are perhaps the most common ailment, and the easiest to fix. Sometimes a sharp smack with the side of your fist or palm is all that's necessary. Other times you'll need to bang away with the rubber mallet. The procedure is the same used for pounding out a dented car fender: tap around the edges of the dent and work in tightening concentric circles toward the middle. If the dent involves straightening a bend, hold a flat rock on the outside of the dent for rigidity, as an auto repairman uses a dolly.

Cracks and holes are next on the agenda, and they require a bit more work. First clean and file down jagged edges around the puncture. Next, cut an aluminum patch to cover the damaged area, allowing ample overlap onto the undamaged area around the hole. Fit the patch to the hull and drill bolt holes in each corner. Bolt on the patch securely, then drill rivet holes at half-inch intervals along the edge of the patch. Remove the bolts and patch, and file down rough spots around the drilled holes. Spread a liberal coating of caulking around the inside of the patch and bolt it back on. To finish the job, secure the patch with rivets, remove the bolts, and seal the bolt holes with caulking.

Silver-backed tape and epoxy can be used for minor repairs of a fiberglass canoe, but more serious damage requires specialized materials.

A fiberglass repair kit includes:
Large square of fiberglass cloth
Large square of fiberglass mat
Hardener
Polyester resin
Silver-backed tape
Epoxy
Coarse-grained sandpaper
Sharp scissors
Small putty knife
Folding cup
Small wood file
Small paint brush

To patch a fiberglass puncture, first clean and dry the inside of the damaged area. Next rough it with the file and sandpaper to aid adhesion of the patches.

On the outer side of the hole, epoxy a patch of silver-backed tape to serve as a backing for the filler. Make a putty by shredding fiberglass cloth and mixing it with resin and hardener, until you have a consistency resembling window putty (stiff, yet pliable). With your putty knife, pack the filler into the hole, smoothing it evenly.

You're now ready for the patches. Cut three squares of fiberglass cloth a couple of inches larger than the hole, and cut a piece of fiberglass mat an inch larger than the cloth. Cover the damaged area with the four patches, placing the mat on last. Use the paint brush to soak the patches thoroughly with a resin hardener mix.

If time is of little importance, go fishing or somehow kill a few hours, while the patch hardens. If you must set off downriver as soon as possible—say because of an emergency—you can use the canoe an hour or so after the patch hardens.

Rafting

Despite the opinion of the uninformed, it takes considerable skill to command a raft adeptly. Raft control is equal to water reading, as safe-running prerequisites. Oarsmanship maneuvers must be practiced in slow water to make them reflexive once you tackle a rapids. After mastering the craft, there are a few common trouble spots you should be prepared to handle.

Collision with a Rock

It's not unusual to find yourself on a crash course with a midstream boulder. What you do in the ensuing seconds between near contact and collision is vital; the difference between momentary holdup or hours of backbreaking labor.

First look at what happens if you do the wrong things. The raft broaches against the rock while the titanic force of the river slaps the raft against the rock and holds it there with immense pressure. This pleasant phenomenon is known as wrapping a raft, and pull-lines, cut air tubes and sore backs are common in the arduous task of unwrapping.

With that tucked in an accessible corner of your mind, consider the less insidious alternatives. As you approach the rock on an inevitable head-on, spin the raft so that it cartwheels off the rock and around one side. If that's impossible, try to hit it bow first. Just before contact, the people in the stern should jump to the center of the raft, allowing the current to slide under rather than against the raft. This raises the center of gravity and makes it easier for the raft to spin off and around the rock.

If the raft does broach, and you end up broadside to the rock, captain and crew should immediately jump to downstream side of the raft—that nearest the rock. The same principle of high gravity applies, and the raft will wheel around the boulder. Failure to do this will cause the upstream tube to be sucked under, flooding the raft and clasping it inextricably around the rock. It's wise to inform your passengers of this procedure well before you enter a rapids, and perhaps formulate a command just for that purpose. When the skipper yells "Downstream side!" or some such command, every crew member should react instantaneously.

If you're caught broadside against a rock, but not swamped, shift the crew to the end of the boat closest to the edge of the rock, keeping them on the downstream side of the raft. Have them push and kick off the rock while you lay back on the oars with all you've got. If that fails, work with the river by utilizing the same force that's holding you. Tie several plastic garbage bags, sweaters, blue jeans—anything that will hold and attain water weight—to a line, and fasten the rig to the end of the first boat you want to go around the rock. (This is a makeshift sea anchor, discussed in Chapter 8.) Secure the line tightly to the desired end of the raft and heave the improvised drag anchor to the side of the rock around which you want to travel. As the pull of the anchor spins the raft off the rock, man the oars and prepare to retrieve the anchor.

A final alternative to the anchor technique is preferred by some. When safe, one of the crew jumps overboard and pulls the raft around,

If you end up broadside to a rock, have all passengers jump to the downstream side of the raft, raising the upstream side to facilitate a spin-off.

If you're pinned against a rock, use the force of the current to help you by fashioning a makeshift sea anchor.

using himself as a drag. (But he never ties the rope to himself, since that would be as risky as Russian roulette. The force of the current could tighten a rope in one cutting, bone-crushing yank.)

Man Overboard

Occasionally, a raft will turn into a bucking horse and one or more of the occupants will be tossed adrift. Instruct your passengers of the potential dunking, and how to cope with it. (The same procedure applies as that for canoes; stay upstream of the craft, don't fight the current, tread water while floating on your back with your feet out in front of you. If you can re-enter a raft, do so. Otherwise wait until you drift into calm water, then swim downstream and to shore.)

A grab-line, tied tautly around the outside of the raft, is good insurance against losing a man overboard. But keep the line tight and not hanging into the water, or it may catch on a rock and cause the entire raft to dump.

If someone in your crew falls out, alert your companions immediately. Don't row until you know precisely where the person in the water is. A rap with an oar blade could gash or render unconscious the very person you are trying to help.

When you locate the person, maneuver to avoid bumping or pinning him with the raft. Other rafters should not dive in to help unless the overboard passenger is hurt or without a life jacket. More people in the water only complicate matters.

An Overturned Raft

If you can't avoid a flip, jump clear to the upstream side when possible. Hang onto the overturned raft, climbing atop it if the water conditions allow, but abandoning it if trouble lies ahead. Make for shore instead. The raft will see itself through the rapids. A later search will find it stranded a mile or so downriver.

In a comparatively quiet stretch, you may be able to grab the raft's bowline and drag the boat to shore. Grab the rope, but remember not to tie it to yourself. Once ashore, inspect the raft and equipment for damage and loss.

If you wish to right an overturned raft in calm water, tie one or several lines (the more the better) to the downstream side of the frame, stand on the upstream side, and heave back on the line with all you've got. If you're lucky, the raft will flip rightside up.

Unwrapping a Raft

One of the most unpleasant chores a rafter can undertake is trying to peel his raft from a rock when it's being held there by literally tons of pressure. Study the accompanying illustration to first get the picture, then note the following.

A hand winch or block and tackle is desirable, but in a pinch it can be replaced with whatever manpower is available. Fasten the winch line to the side of the raft closest to an edge of the rock. This line, the hauling line, should be attached to at least two points so that the pull is equally distributed. Tie the line securely to a sturdy D-ring, or cut a hole in the floor and tie the rope around tube. Another line is tied to the opposite end of the boat, functioning as a hand-line for pulling the extricated raft to shore.

Unwrapping a raft.

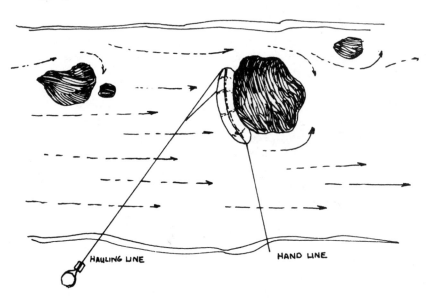

HAULING LINE   HAND LINE

Use a nonstretching rope like manila or Dacron for this chore. Nylon is too elastic; it stretches and wastes precious pulling power.

If the raft won't pull free, a bit of surgery may be in order. Cut a couple of feet off the bottom near the submerged gunwale to reduce the current's grip on the boat. If the raft still won't pull free, lengthen the cut another foot or so.

If all of this fails, you'll have to leave your raft and return during the river's low-water stage. Contact nearby property owners and relevant authorities, and inform them of your predicament, explaining that the raft is yours and you intend to return for it. You might also want to pin a note in an obvious place on shore, to deter salvagers from removing and claiming your expensive raft.

Raft Repair

A basic kit includes:
2 square yards of patching material (same as raft material)
2 pints contact cement
Bottle of hardener (if needed for adhesive)
One-inch brush
Large sheet of emery cloth
Sharp scissors
Several upholstery needles for stitching
Heavy nylon or Dacron thread, waxed
Silicone rubber seal for patching and replacing valves

Patching a raft rip is a fairly straightforward task. First the area around the patch must be cleaned and dryed, then roughed with emery cloth. The patch undergoes the same treatment.

If the rip is small—less than a couple of inches—you won't need to stitch it. Anything larger, though, must be reinforced with sewing thread. Space your stitches no more than one inch apart, knotting each stitch as you go along.

Next cut two patches, one for each side, with at least three inches of overlap allowed for the undamaged area around the rip. Spread a generous coat of cement on the outer side of the raft and the inside of the patch. When the cement becomes tacky, press on the patch evenly, rubbing it smooth with your hand to eliminate air bubbles. The same procedure is repeated on the other side of the rip.

Air-tube repairs are handled the same way, except that only the outer side of the tube can be patched. Always reinforce a tube rip with sewing thread before patching.

10

Recreational Vehicles: Using Them Safely

RVs have become an integral part of the outdoor recreationist's world. Camper units, four-wheel-drive rigs, snowmobiles, trailbikes—all have opened formerly limited access areas to a wide number of outdoorsmen. The impact on the land and resources has not always been favorable, and some of us bemoan these places that in the past entertained only a handful of people. But there are two sides to the coin. RVs have added much to the outdoor experience of people who use them sensibly and safely, and perhaps have enhanced their appreciation of the land. Regardless of either argument, RVs are here, and apparently they will remain for a long while. Our concern now is seeing that you operate the assorted machines without killing yourself or someone else.

Snowmobiles and Safety

Most of this advice has been kindly provided by the International Snowmobile Industry Association (ISIA) and the Snowmobile Safety and Certification Committee (SSCC).

Every winter, over a million people hop aboard a snowhorse and take to the woods and fields. Whenever that many individuals participate in any pastime, be it snowmobiling or basketweaving, there's bound to be accidents and injuries, and snowmobiling has its share. The machines themselves are relatively safe. Only about five percent of all recorded snowmobile accidents result from faulty technology. Manufacturers have been quick to mend mechanical deficiencies in their machines, though some of the older models have a few unsafe features such as exposed drive train, lack of clutch guards and malfunctioning brakes. The only solution for that problem is to be extra careful when handling such an ill-equipped rig, and test all operating devices (throttle, brake, steering) before zooming away. New machines are safer and are now being inspected by an independent safety team from the SSCC, which puts its label on the front of every snowmobile meeting stringent requirements. If you want to be assured of getting the safest machine possible, don't buy a snowmobile that isn't adorned with an SSCC Certification label.

As for the other 95 percent of the snowmobile accidents, only you and other snowmobilers can reduce that figure. A good place to begin achieving that goal is by following a few general precautionary practices.

> Snowmobiling takes you outdoors during the most severe times of the year, so it pays to be conscious of cold dangers and dress accordingly. Remember the wind-chill factor, and tuck away a complete survival pack as preventive medicine for a mishap.
>
> Don't go alone on extended trips or through unfamiliar areas. A machine breakdown or an accident or injury might be irritating and uncomfortable if assistance is near, but it could be fatal if you're on your own.
>
> Always leave your starting point with a full tank of fuel, and never use more than half of it before beginning a return. (A seemingly obvious practice that is often forgotten in the exhilaration of a cruise.)
>
> Before embarking on an expedition, file a travel plan with a friend. Should something happen that prevents you from returning on schedule, your contact can notify authorities.
>
> Never, never drive while under the influence.

So much for commonsense generalities. Now let's focus on the core of the safety problem—improper handling of the machine.

Speed

Snowmobiling experts say that, without question, most accidents can be laid at the door of people driving too fast. Speed is an exhilarating thing to many people, and a machine that can skim the snow at 60 to 90 miles per hour is a hard temptation to resist. For safety's sake, however, fight that temptation like the devil.

Speeding snowmobilers commonly collide with assorted obstacles— logs, rocks, trees and branches, parked cars, fences, guy ropes and barbed wire. If you seek a breathtaking ride by riding over the snow, any of a wide number of objects will provide it, literally. The answer to all of this is simple: Drive at reasonable speeds, especially in unfamiliar areas or near junctions of heavy traffic. Take into account the condition of the snow and the configuration of the terrain when calculating safe top speeds.

Jumping

The experts are in agreement on jumping: Don't do it. Jumping a snowmobile is a tricky and dangerous business, and you should never try it. The machine can flip, you can be thrown on landing impact, you could collide with another machine or obstacle, and so on down the list. Repeat: *Do not make intentional jumps.*

The time may come, however, when a hill or bump suddenly drops away from you and you find yourself in the air. If this happens, immediately stand up in a semi-crouch, with your knees bent to absorb shock and your arms stiffened to avoid crashing into the windshield. Apply a bit of throttle, and brace for a jolting landing. As you hit, ride out the bump and repercussion bounces that may follow. If you are thrown, relax your muscles and roll with the impact, both to avoid breaking bones and to get out of the way of the falling snowmobile.

Carrying Passengers

If you must carry a passenger, have him sit behind you if an adult and in front of you if a child. Instruct your passenger to lean with you on turns and to always keep his feet on the running boards. Drive slower than you would alone to compensate for the extra weight and bulk of the passenger. Warn him of upcoming bumps, or protruding twigs and branches that may whip into his face. Never carry more than one passenger at a time.

Many people enjoy towing their kids or friends in a sled. This is fine, providing the hitch is a rigid bar. A piece of rope or other supple material is unsafe because it lacks control; the snowmobile may stop, but nothing will prevent the sled from ramming into it.

Another towing rule requires that you go slowly, especially on rugged terrain.

Riding Positions

How you sit on your snowmobile affects your safety. For example, if you sit in the usual position on the seat while riding over bumpy snow, you can damage your spine. Much better is a kneeling stance, assumed by placing one foot on the running board and the opposite knee on the seat. In this position, your legs absorb the shock of bumpy riding. In place of the kneeling stance, you can assume a "posting" position, where you half-stand and half-sit with a foot on either running board. This is also good for running rugged terrain.

Regardless of the type of position, make the most of your body weight by leaning toward the inside of a turn. The machine will respond by banking to the inside, making your turn easier and safer. Never use your foot as a drag to assist in rounding a bend. It's an enormously dangerous tactic, and there's no real need for it anyway.

Crossing Roads

Always approach roads slowly and pause at the crest of the bank to wait for traffic to clear. Be careful when descending the drop to the road, and cross in a straight line. Don't run along the sides of roads, and never ride on bare pavement.

Riding on Ice

Every year a number of snowmobiles crash through the ice, and a few lives are lost. If you decide you must travel across a lake or river, be sure you have at least six inches of clear ice beneath your machine. Don't travel in an unfamiliar area without first consulting a local warden or ranger to ascertain the condition of the ice.

Ice presents another hazard by its very nature. The stuff is impossible to get a good grip on, whether with a tire or snowmobile track. Allow for more stopping distance, and go slowly around turns, or you may find yourself in a skid or spin. Be especially careful at night.

Night Driving

Night driving in unfamiliar territory can be dangerous, and the experts say you shouldn't attempt it. But on familiar trails, night riding on snow can be great fun. Before departing, check to be sure your lights are functioning properly, and wear reflective, or at least light-colored clothing. Drive slowly when it's dark, and never overdrive your headlights. Stay off ice or obstacle-littered areas.

These are the basics of snowmobiling safety, but there is more to know. A safe snowmobiler is one who knows his machine and how it operates; who has studied his service and maintenance manual, and who puts his knowledge to use by obeying the rules of proper driving. If you would like more information on the subject, plus a brief rundown on maintenance and trouble-shooting, write for the Snowmobiler's Safety Handbook, Snowmobile Safety and Certification Committee, Suite 311, 1755 South Jefferson Davis Highway, Arlington, Virginia 22202. This 38-page booklet contains a wealth of information, and is free for the asking.

Campers, 4WDs and other RVs—
Avoiding Breakdowns

A high percentage of RV breakdowns results from misuse or neglect on the part of the operator. Working parts aren't inspected for signs of wear, dashboard gauges are forgotten and various clanks, gurgles and clatterings are ignored. This neglect later leads to needless trouble and exasperation. It's a lot easier and less time-consuming to have a neighborhood mechanic replace worn out belts on your motor home than it is to be stranded in Podunk, U.S.A., where neither the parts nor skills for repairs are available.

It should become ritual to check your rig before, during and after a trip to see that it is maintained properly and functioning smoothly. At the start of a sojourn, test all belts for tightness and look for fraying and signs of wear; check the oil, battery water and transmission fluid levels; regulate the air in the tires to match the suggested poundage; squeeze all hoses, especially the water hoses stemming from the radiator and water pump, to test their pliability. Replace them if they are hard and stiff to the touch.

On the road, acquire the habit of glancing frequently at the dashboard gauges. They can often alert you to approaching trouble before it becomes too serious to handle. The temperature gauge tells how hot the engine is—an especially important factor during the summer months. The oil gauge measures the amount of pressure pushing the engine oil. When there's low pressure, the oil can't circulate and lubricate the moving parts which desperately require friction-reducing lubrication, and your expensive engine locks up from the heat.

The ammeter shows you how much electrical charge is being produced by the alternator or generator. When everything is functioning normally, the needle settles squarely in the middle of the gauge. (On those models that have needle gauges, that is. Some have red lights that flash when you have electrical problems.) If the needle rides to either side, to "discharge" or "charge," something isn't kosher in your electrical system. The problem may be as serious as a failing alternator, or as minor as a loose fan belt.

Whenever the gauges tell you trouble is brewing, stop immediately and examine the engine. Don't try to drive on with the notion of finding help in the next town, because a small problem could mushroom considerably if ignored for even a few more minutes. This is particularly true of oil troubles. When an oil light flashes, stop at once and check the oil level. If it is low, you may need only to add a quart or so from the spare cans you should always carry. Once the oil light shuts off, drive to the nearest garage and recheck the oil level to determine whether or not there is a leak.

If you stop because of an oil light and discover that you are not low, don't attempt to drive on. Get to a mechanic by hitchhiking or by phone, and have him inspect the oil system. Again, do not try to drive a rig that isn't pumping oil. You won't make a mile in most cases before the pistons heat and expand in their cylinders, eventually freezing in position and causing all sorts of expensive damage. If you do a lot of traveling in remote areas, where no mechanics are within reasonable range, you had better bone up on your auto-repair techniques and pack along spare parts, manuals and tools.

If your engine suddenly overheats, as engines commonly do, pull off the road and step on the emergency brake. Shift the transmission into neutral and run the engine at a brisk idle to allow the fan and water pumps to operate. Turn off the air conditioner, if you have one, and turn on the heat. Jack it up to full blast. It may be uncomfortable in the cab, but the heater fan cools the engine. Open your hood to allow more cooling air to pass over the engine, and wait until the heat dissipates before attempting to open the radiator cap. Once the engine is cool, or at least not steaming hot, slowly and evenly twist off the radiator cap while pressing down on it. Protect your hands from hot water or steam by placing a glove or ball of rags between them and the cap. Allow the steam to escape before removing the cap completely, or it might shoot up in your face.

If the water level is normal, you may have problems with the thermostat or water pump. Allow the engine to cool completely, then drive to the nearest town for repairs. Don't gun the motor at stops and starts, live for a while without the aid of air conditioning, and the engine will stay cool longer. If you have a long way to go, keep the heater on full blast until you get to town. It's about as comfortable as a sauna, but there is little alternative.

When the engine overheats and the radiator water is low, there are a number of causes. You may have busted a water hose (usually obvious to the eye), developed a leak in the radiator (not so obvious) or just plain forgotten to add water at an earlier stop. In any case, keep the engine running while you slowly fill the radiator with water. Never pour water into a hot, semi-empty radiator when the engine is off. Get a mechanic as soon as possible and have the cooling system examined. Incidentally, if a leaking radiator hose is the culprit, have both radiator hoses replaced, and not just the leaking one. This prevents a later repeat of the same trouble.

The best way to thwart overheating in the first place is to regularly examine all belts, pumps and regulators that affect the cooling system. It's also important to keep the system clean. Whisk away bugs, leaves and dirt that accumulate in front of the radiator core; they clog the pores

The highway distress sign: an open hood and a white cloth tied to the antenna (in this case) or door handle.

and restrict air flow. During hot weather, avoid the common habit of strapping bicycles or motorcycles to the front of your grill; they also block air passage.

Next, have the battery tested and charged or replaced if necessary. Cold weather saps battery power considerably, sometimes in half, and a weak battery won't have enough juice to start the engine. While working with the electrical system, change or clean and regap the spark plugs and points for easier starting.

Ice-caked fuel lines are a common winter malady, and in really cold weather you may want to resort to anticondensation additives for your gasoline. Moisture is less apt to form in full tanks, so it pays to keep your vehicle fueled to capacity.

If all of your precautions are seemingly in vain, and you suddenly find yourself stranded along some road in a malfunctioning vehicle, it helps to know the universal signal of motorist's distress: an open hood and a flag of white cloth tied to a door handle or radio antenna. And if you must hitchhike for help, you'll probably find that today's highways are full of suspicious, cautious people who speed up and swing into the lane opposite your outstretched thumb. However, there is a remedy for this paranoia: carry a small gas can along—even if you don't need gas—and hold it in your hand in an obvious way. Your odds of being picked up increase markedly. Once most people realize you're in distress, and not interested in robbing or molesting them, they're willing to give you a lift to the nearest gas station.

Tire troubles sometimes afflict RV owners, and the best remedy is to buy high-quality tires from the start, and keep them adequately filled. Always check tire pressure before a trip. Look also at the amount of tread wear and the condition of the sidewalls. Tires that have abrasions and cuts, or tread worn below 1/16-depth in more than a couple of consecutive grooves should be replaced.

A flat spare is next to worthless, so be sure you are carrying a ready-to-use tire and rim at all times. On especially rough roads, such as the Alcan Highway or many Baja backroads, two spares are added insurance that you will make it safely to your destination.

If you notice unusual swaying or tugging to one side while driving, you probably have a low tire or the beginnings of a flat. Pull over at once and check it out. If it is a flat, chances are the tire is reparable if you haven't been riding on it too long.

Cold weather poses different problems. The saying, "prevention is the best cure" may be trite, but it applies to wintertime driving.

The first item on your winter checklist is to test your antifreeze protection. If you're protected to 40 below, you are safe in most areas of the country. Use a Glycol-based antifreeze; it has a low freezing point and a high boiling point, which makes it a good all-year product. Your windshield washer reservoir needs antifreeze just as your radiator does, and a variety of nonfreezing mixes are on the market. This is important, because slush, sleet, road salt and mud can solidly cake a windshield.

On-Pavement Driving Tips

Driving pickup campers, jeeps and assorted coaches of reasonable size is not much different than driving a large car. But the moment you hook up to a trailer—whether for towing a boat, camper or travel trailer —you take on a substantial length of vehicle. There's nothing difficult about handling such a rig, but there are a few tips you should keep in mind.

Before you move an inch, your car and trailer should ride nearly level. There should be no "V" formed by the dipping rear end of your car or truck and the slanting front end of your trailer. If you can't seem to eliminate the sag, you may have to jack up your rear end suspension with air shocks or heavy-duty springs.

If you're toting a travel trailer, load your gear judiciously, keeping the heavier items on or near the floor and the light stuff up high. Anchor any loose objects solidly to prevent them from being tossed and juggled en route. Close all cupboards and cabinet doors, and latch and lock the entrance door.

Inspect the whole rig in a last minute safety check. Test the turn signals and brake lights. Clean the taillight lens if necessary to make sure your trailer will clearly flash the signals you want it to. Kick the trailer tires for tradition's sake, and while you're at it, check them for wear and air pressure.

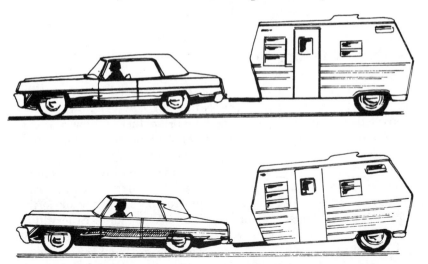

A trailer should ride level with the towing vehicle, as it does in the top draw-ing. The rig at bottom has a perceptible sag, which makes for poor handling on the road.

Once on the road, remember your new increased length and drive accordingly. Allow more room for passing, changing lanes and turning. Don't cut corners as sharply as you would with a car, or you'll find your-self jumping curbs and maybe a few pedestrians. When coming to a stop, do so smoothly and gradually. A sharp halt may cause your trailer to swing about and jackknife. If your rig has a manual brake for the trailer, ease it back before stepping on the car brake to keep your tow in line.

Laws in most states say a trailer must move slower than other traffic, and you can avoid a few citations by heeding the rules. You'll also avoid a lot of sudden stops, sharp turns and other unnerving maneuvers that accompany high speeds. But if you find yourself piling up a line of traffic behind you, the safe and courteous thing to do is pull over at the next turn out and allow the cars to pass. You are not only doing your turn for mankind, but you rid yourself of annoying tailgaters as well.

Some people are initially frustrated when they attempt to negotiate a boat ramp or tight camping corner while backing their trailers. A little practice before the trip is the answer. Find a vacant parking lot and make a few trial runs by backing your trailer between a couple of empty garbage cans or boxes. Place your hand at six o'clock on the steering wheel and move it to the right to make the trailer swing right, and to the left if you want the trailer moving portside. For best results, avoid "oversteering" by backing slowly, and turning the wheel a little less than you think you need to.

Off-Pavement Driving Tips

It's a fact of life that if you drive off the main roads often, you'll run into your share of lousy conditions. No matter how careful or dextrous you are at the wheel, you will at one time or another find yourself stuck. You can cut these unpleasant moments to a minimum by observing the rule of three "Ps"—prevention, preparation and perspiration.

Let's look first at prevention. A good working maxim for rough-road driving is: if you aren't reasonably sure you can get through safely, don't go any farther. Park the vehicle where you are and walk in if it's feasible, or admit defeat and turn back to where there's easier driving. If you think you might be able to drive through, at least stop the vehicle and walk ahead to examine the road. Test the ground for firmness, and consider the clearance between your rig's underbelly and the boulders or gullies that block your way. Walk up the road a bit to see if conditions improve or worsen. There's no sense in risking a tough section of road if you can only travel a few yards before running into impassable conditions. If you're in doubt, get the devil out.

On muddy or wet stretches, when you make up your mind to plow through, give it an all or nothing attempt. Many people get stuck because they chicken out in the middle of a bog and start to slow down. That is a fatal move, because momentum is the best thing you have going for you. Select your best course, then run it at a safe top speed. Often your forward push is enough to drag the rig through a couple of feet of mud, to a spot where the tires can find traction and take over. The same applies for plunging through patches of deep snow—go reasonably fast and you'll make it; try to crawl over, and you'll bog in a minute.

Slick roads provide another hazard: it's easy to slide out of control and into a ditch or down a slope. This usually happens because of one of two conditions—either the wheels lock during braking or turning, or the driver is going too fast to maintain solid traction. The latter trouble is usually easy to correct. Coming down a hill, run with your transmission in low gear and touch your brakes lightly when you feel yourself picking up unwanted speed. Never jam hard on your brakes on a slick road, or you'll experience the first problem—wheel lock. The brakes grab hold, the tires freeze in position, and you swerve and slide out of control. The same thing happens when you brake hard while turning, only the inertia of the turning car amplifies the loss of control. Instead, jab your brakes with light pumps to decelerate safely.

On the other side of the coin are traction problems resulting from overacceleration. Too much gas will cause a climbing rig to fishtail on a slick incline. If you anticipate trouble ascending a slick hill, arrange cargo weight so it rides over your drive wheels. (Usually the back wheels; place heavy objects in the trunk or rear of the vehicle and passengers in the back seat.) Try to get a running start up the slope, and decelerate as you lose momentum. Follow the clearest path you have—a dry lane on a wet road, a clean or packed track on snow, a firm spot on mud. Sometimes the untrammeled snow or dirt on the road's edge will get rough enough to provide essential traction. If you can't make headway on the main road, give the shoulder a try.

Preparation is next. We discussed briefly in Chapter 3 the basic gear that should be a part of your RV removal kit, but it's time for a closer look.

Chain is an important item. You should carry at least 20 feet of thick, sturdy links with a hook attached to one or both ends for towing and hand-winching. Also carry tire chains, either the full-size type or the smaller (and less effective) emergency variety.

I've mentioned that you should carry a shovel (a folding one if you'd like), ax, 50 feet of sturdy rope and a heavy-duty jack. The standard jacks that come with most new vehicles are wholly inadequate for rough-and-tumble driving. Buy one that is capable of solidly lifting and supporting a heavy load. Since much of your jack work will be in mud, snow or soft ground, bring along a wide plank about a foot or so long to prevent the jack bottom from pushing itself down rather than the vehicle up. If you have lots of room, pack a couple of three-foot, one-by-six-inch planks for giving traction to half-buried wheels. Throw in a couple of short two-by-fours to block the wheels while the vehicle is on the jack, and you have a pretty good removal kit. If you are traveling roads that might have numerous deadfalls blocking the way, bring along a light chain saw or, lacking that, a buck saw.

Beachcombers should include a square of thin-meshed wire screen for supporting a jack on sand.

The last ingredient for getting over rough country is the most time-consuming one: perspiration. Once you are stuck, you'll lose a lot of it getting out.

The first, and easiest, method of extrication is one you've doubtless tried yourself a time or two. One or both drive wheels are spinning deeper and deeper into a rut of sand, snow or mud. You step on the gas and the car rocks forward slightly. At the peak of the forward rock, you let off the gas or step on the clutch and allow the vehicle to roll backward. At the height of the backward movement, you engage the clutch or step on the gas and swing a little farther forward than you did the time before. The rock and roll is repeated with ever increasing motion until the stuck tires pick up enough momentum on a forward swing to lift out of the rut. If it doesn't work at first, you chuck handfuls of traction-giving sticks, pebbles, cinder, etc., in to aid the progress. On sand you deflate your tires to roughly eight or ten pounds of pressure before attempting

Anyone who frequents the backroads is wise to invest in a good winch.

to drive out—the increased surface area of the deflated tires provides more traction.

If that fails, whip out your shovel and dig a path for your tires to follow, lining it with those planks you brought along, or twigs and pebbles if that's all you have.

But you discover you're really buried deep—to the axles or higher. You can't wait for the snow to melt or the mud to dry, so you face the fact that you have a bit of dirty work ahead. Out comes the jack. You mount it on the foot-long plank carried for that purpose and jack each wheel clear of the hole. Next you fill the holes with whatever is on hand that is solid, and cover them with the three-foot planks. If chains will help out, you attach them to the tires while the vehicle is up on the jack. If you're religious, you pray. If not, you pray anyway. If everything goes smoothly, you get out of your predicament. Or you move a few feet and become mired again, and then the whole process begins again.

A serious outdoorsman, who spends a lot of time driving over backroads—and perhaps in places that don't even qualify as any kind of road —should forget the tedium and inefficiency of jacking and shoveling, and employ the cool effectiveness of a power winch. The kind I'm thinking of is one of those light, 12-volt electrical dreams that mount on the front frame or bumper of your vehicle and is capable of pulling up to four tons. One will set you back anywhere from $375 to $500, depending on the model and amount of cable you buy. Once you have it, you'll never need to worry about common rough road conditions again.

Rigging a winchline so that it performs at peak efficiency is an art in itself.

The most common situation, perhaps, consists of a vehicle bogged in some sort of mire. The winch cable is stretched out ahead of the vehicle and attached to a sturdy object capable of holding the weight of the ve-

Rig using a deadman to winch its way up a snowy road.

hicle. This could be a tree, large boulder, other vehicle—either heavier outright or anchored via rope or chain to another object—or a "deadman." A deadman consists of one or two objects, usually iron bars such as old car axles, pounded or buried into the soil. Once the cable is secured to the bracing object, the winch is switched on. Slowly but surely the vehicle is pulled from the bog and onto firmer ground.

The bracing object is an important part of the setup. It must be sturdy and able to take more strain than the vehicle, or the winch will pull the brace in, rather than the vehicle out. This is especially important to remember when using one vehicle to pull another.

Should a situation arise where you have nothing available for an anchor—say no trees or large boulders are present and you haven't a deadman—scrounge around for a log, fencepost or signpost and fasten your winch cable to it. Bury the makeshift deadman in the ground as deep as possible; the weight and resistance of the soil may hold the rig in place until your vehicle is winched from its trap.

When winching a vehicle up a steep incline, follow to the side as it progresses uphill, and place logs, rocks or woodblocks behind the rear tires. Should the brace suddenly give way, or the cable snap (though it rarely happens), your rig won't roll downhill.

It takes an awesome amount of pull to break a cable, but a sudden snap can pop a wire line surprisingly fast. For this reason, when pulling another rig, don't try to aid your winch by backing up. A slip of the tires or a change in traction could jerk the cable with enough force to pop it like sewing thread, sending the bottom vehicle downhill like a recoiling rubber band.

A winch can do a lot more than pull you out of mire and up steep slopes. Rather than break your back hanging an elk carcass at camp,

Burying a makeshift deadman.

pull it up with a winch. Use the winch to lift logs and large rocks out of a road; to right an overturned car or truck; to pull your family car out of a snowbank or ditch; or, slung over a tree, use it as a hoist for the front end of your vehicle while you make backcountry repairs.

The winch cable is run under the vehicle and fastened to a sturdy object to pull it backwards.

A winch can be used as an emergency hoist for making back country repairs.

11

Lost!

When I was a lad of 11 or 12, my family took a short vacation to Michigan's gorgeous, and at that time very wild, Upper Peninsula. While my parents and sister lounged in the cabin or went sightseeing, I cast pike lures relentlessly into the copper-tinted waters of the nearby lake, and explored local blackberry thickets for signs of deer and bear.

One day I left the trail that wound from the cabin door through a wall of birch and spruce, to step into the realm of woodsmen. My plan was to bushwhack into the forest, spot a bear or two, and work my way back to the trail.

I'd gone maybe 100 yards when my woodsman's confidence began oozing perceptibly. The conditioned security of the trail was gone. And there were bears in the woods! I faked the cool, calculated appearance of a man making a vital decision, and reckoned it was better not to go any farther. I mean, I didn't want my mother to worry if I didn't get back before nightfall.

I turned back the way I came and headed out—a little faster, perhaps, than a cool, calculated woodsman would.

I walked 200 yards without hitting the trail. I moved off in a different direction and walked for ten minutes before stopping. Still no trail. At this point, all attempts at confidence went to hell. I stumbled along frantically, occasionally sobbing and occasionally swearing—and feeling guilty for both. I must have walked for 45 minutes before I crashed through the brush and tripped onto a dirt road. Even though I was terrified and panting heavily, I recognized the sinuous road as the access to our cabin. I had clawed a large half-circle through the woods from the original trail to the road. Now, with the comfort and security of a known path under my feet, I quickly regained composure and strode down the lane to the cabin, thinking I was one hell of a woodsman at that. But deep inside I knew then, as I know now, that it was mindless luck that I blundered onto the cabin road.

The experience was stamped firmly in my mind. Getting lost was no fun. In fact, it was downright disconcerting. Through the years I've learned another fact about becoming lost: in most cases there's no excuse for it.

It doesn't take much time or skill to become proficient enough with map and compass to keep your bearings. Anyone who ventures outdoors should make the effort to learn basic navigation and savvy. Once the basics are learned, and applied, it becomes difficult to seriously lose your way. Sure, even experts become confused now and then, and occasionally they get lost, but the odds are against it.

Maps

I once took a college course in map reading and was simply amazed at the information maps contain. A good geographer can discern from a map the type of terrain; kinds of wildlife and their habits; interesting land features; and even the geological history of an area. When you combine this potential knowledge with low cost and easy availability, maps become one of the best bargains around.

The type of map you use for outdoor work is important. Regular road or county maps can be of some help in very civilized areas, but are of little use in more remote lands. Without question, the best map for the average outdoorsman is a topographical survey map. These show elevation contour lines at evenly spaced intervals. The map scale varies, but generally falls somewhere between an inch equaling four-tenths of a mile to six miles. The larger the scale—that is, the smaller the area covered by an inch of map—the clearer and more accurate the detail. Topo maps tend to confuse people who see them for the first time, but actually they are among the easiest maps to read. Each has a color and symbol key for land features. Learn these well and map reading becomes easier, and more informative. The accompanying illustration will simplify map interpretation.

Topographic maps are available from a number of agencies. The best are from the U.S. Geological Survey. For maps covering areas east of the Mississippi River, write to U.S. Geological Survey, Washington D.C. 20244. For regions west of the river, contact U.S.G.S., Federal Center, Denver, Colorado 80225. Maps of Canada can be obtained by writing the Map Distribution Office, Department of Mines and Technical Service, Ottawa, Ontario. For Alaska maps, write U.S.G.S., 520 Illinois Street, Fairbanks, Alaska 99701. National Forest Service maps are available either from regional offices located throughout the country (mostly in the West) or from the central office in Washington, D.C. State fish and game departments also have maps available to sportsmen.

Generally, the best way to order from these sources is by first requesting a map index. From the index you choose the appropriate number and name of the map you require. Prices will be listed, usually running from 25¢ to $1.50.

Also useful for outdoorsmen are airphotos. Airphotos cost more than topos and are more difficult to obtain, but offer sharp detail. Viewed with stereoscopic glasses, the photos provide a three-dimensional look at the terrain. The photos cost from $1.75 to $9 each, and the glasses will set you back another $3.50. To purchase them you must locate your county office of the U.S. Department of Agriculture and look through its photo index for the maps you want. You then mail a completed order form along with your remittance. This all takes time, and you would need to do this months in advance of a trip to be assured of getting your maps before you leave.

Boaters also need maps. There are many types of navigation charts

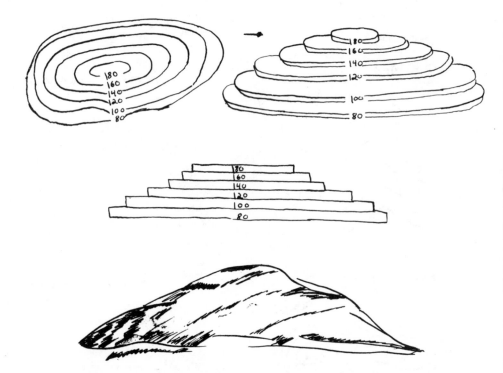

Map contour lines draw a clear picture of the actual terrain—if you can read the lines accurately. The above drawings illustrate a few of the more common map features and how they are interpreted.

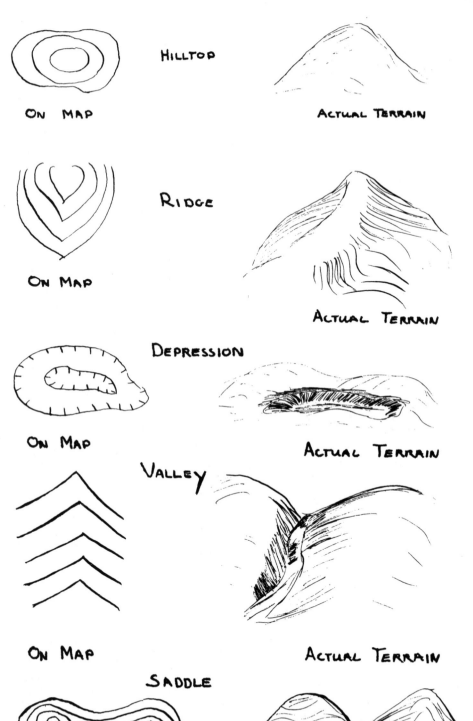

HILLTOP

ON MAP

ACTUAL TERRAIN

RIDGE

ON MAP

ACTUAL TERRAIN

DEPRESSION

ON MAP

ACTUAL TERRAIN

VALLEY

ON MAP

ACTUAL TERRAIN

SADDLE

ON MAP

ACTUAL TERRAIN

that show water depth, buoys, currents and such: pilot charts for making long-distance voyages (available from Oceanographic Office, U.S. Navy); sailing charts for plotting courses on the sea; coast charts for navigating bays and sounds along specific areas; harbor charts; small craft charts available from the Coast and Geodetic Survey that show navigation needs for heavily used boating areas; and assorted inland maps which are available from the U.S. Army Corps of Engineers and the Geodetic Survey. The Department of Commerce also offers inland and coastal water charts. For smaller areas, marinas or bait shops often sell crude, but helpful local maps, sometimes hand-drawn. Any map, as long as it is accurate, is better than none.

Drawing Your Own Map

What if you've exhausted all possibilities and still can't find a map of your destination? Or what if you don't have time to look? Then draw your own map. It may not be precise, and it won't look very professional, but it will be enough to get you back safely from your excursion. The technique is fairly simple.

As you travel, mark down any characteristic landmarks on paper. Estimate the distance between each landmark and write it on the map. If you have a compass, mark the direction of travel you take away from a landmark, or the direction you are traveling when you spot it. On your return trip, you will view everything in reverse order. If a granite outcropping stuck out on your left when you were traveling north, it will obviously be on your right when returning. This crude method keeps you oriented to your surroundings.

Compasses

Whenever compass techniques are discussed in books or articles, the result is invariably confusing to the beginner. The actual act of using a compass is simple, but reading or writing about it is difficult. To fully understand written information on basic orientation, the average beginner needs to take his compass in hand and work out the instruction in his own mind. Suddenly, everything will click.

There are many types of compasses around, and I don't intend to discuss them all, but will focus attention on three styles.

The first is the orienteering or Slyva compass. It's attached to a transparent rectangular base, which often folds in half to pocket size. The edges are ruled. A large arrow is etched or printed on the front of the compass, and is the direction-of-travel arrow. It points wherever you aim

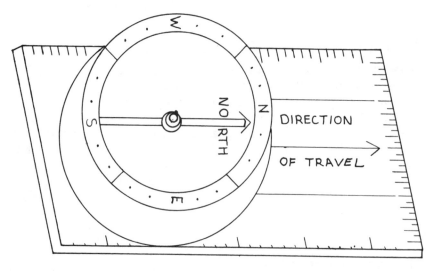

Orienteering or Slyva compass.

it and not necessarily north. The function of the direction arrow will become clear later.

The second type of compass is the lensatic or engineer's model. In the rear is a hinged metal tab equipped with a small magnifying lens that enables you to easily read degree marks when taking bearings. The front of the compass has a hooded sight for lining up and chartering landmarks. The tab and hood fold down to protect the compass face and fit easily into a pocket. The lensatic model is more sophisticated than the orienteering compass, and is a little more difficult to use.

Lensatic compass.

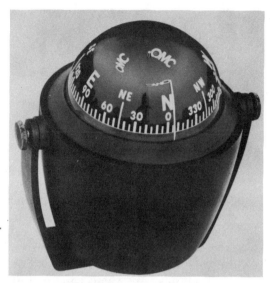

Boaters need a marine compass.
(Photo: Outboard Marine Co.)

Either model can be purchased for from $3 to $50, and with care will last a lifetime.

For boating, a hand-held compass is limited. Engine vibration jiggles the needle constantly, making it impossible to take a reading while the craft is running. If waves bob your boat, you can't even take precise readings with the engine off. To solve this problem, try a marine compass. This liquid-filled model is mounted on either side of the keel, within easy view of the helmsman. A good location is slightly forward of the wheel. The compass has a floating "lubber's line" which swings to give you a reading for whatever direction the bow is pointing. With this compass you can stay on a reasonably straight course without difficulty.

Even if you use a marine compass, carry along an orienteering or lensatic model, too. If you must beach the boat, the pocket compass will allow you to take easier land readings.

Basic Principles

All compasses, regardless of type, have a few things in common. First, they all point to a highly attractive area known as the magnetic north pole. They don't point anywhere else unless something is interfering with the magnetic field. A rifle, knife, car hood, belt buckle, or any other metal object, can provide that interference. If you're toting a firearm, set it down well away from your compass when taking a reading. If you're carrying lots of metal, you may have to set the compass on a log and back away until the needle settles on north.

All rocks are magnetized by the earth's field when they form, and some have enough power to mess up your reading. Magnetite, for example, is an iron ore that can swing your compass needle 180 degrees off north. Northern Michigan, parts of Minnesota, Ontario and other iron-rich lands are noted for the tricks they play on compasses. If you are in iron country, keep this in mind. You may want to check your compass with some natural direction finders to be sure. However, rock interference is comparatively rare. When in doubt, believe your compass and not your instincts.

Another thing all compasses do is point to magnetic north, not necessarily true north. Don't let this confuse you. The magnetic pole is not exactly in line with the geographic north pole. In most locations, your compass points a few degrees east or west of true geographic north. This is known as declination. In the United States you can get a true north reading if you are somewhere on a straight line from the southern tip of Florida, through Chicago, to the northern tip of Michigan's Upper Peninsula. Anywhere east or west of the line gives you a slightly false reading of north. You must compensate for this by adding or subtracting the declination (number of degrees off true north line) from your reading.

If you are east of center, subtract the declination from your needle reading to find true north. West of true north, add the declination. For example, near my home in Montana the declination is about 18 degrees. When I'm in the field and want to find true north, I add 18 degrees to whatever my compass shows as north. When I'm fishing or hiking in eastern Tennessee, where the declination is three degrees east of the line, I simply subtract three degrees from my compass reading to find true north. For half a buck you can buy a declination chart of the United States. Write for Isogonic Chart of the United States No. 3077, U.S. Department of Commerce, Coast and Geodetic Survey, Distribution Division C44, Washington D.C. 20235. There is also a less sophisticated chart illustrated in these pages.

Just how important is declination?

For short trips it doesn't matter much, particularly if you are only five degrees or so off true north. But if you are planning a hike of several miles in the country that is 20 degrees off north, the error margin becomes considerable.

Using Map and Compass

The first step in using a map and compass is orienting the map. To do this, simply set your compass on top of your map and move the map until its north-south lines run in exactly the same direction as your compass needle. Don't forget to adjust for declination if you deem it necessary. Many maps have the declination listed near the key, so you need

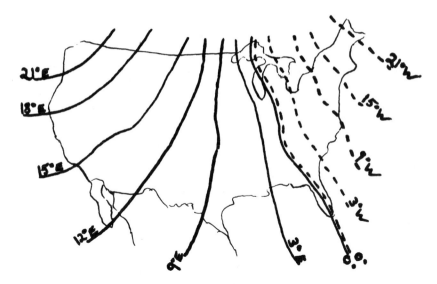

An isogonic chart of the United States shows declination from true north for various parts of the country.

only to refer to the map bottom to figure how much to add or subtract. Your map is now lined up exactly as the country faces you. To chart a path by map, follow these steps:

Locate on the map the place you want to reach and line the sighting arrow of your compass on a straight path to it. Wait for the needle to align with north again, then take a degree reading on the sighting arrow. If the reading is, say, 40 degrees northeast, that is the line you want to travel. Jot down or remember the reading. Next, standing in the same place, sight your compass in the same direction—in this case, 40 degrees east of north. Find a landmark that is directly in line and aim for it. Walk to the mark and from there sight another one. In this way, you jump from landmark to landmark until you reach your destination. The distance to the mark depends greatly on the country. In northern forests the distance may be 100 yards. In mountainous terrain it may be six miles. To return to your starting point, you simply travel in the opposite direction, using the same landmarks if possible.

This sounds easy enough, but in most country worth hiking it's hard to travel a straight course. You may have to dodge swamps, ravines, lodgepole tangles and other obstacles. To beat this, there are a couple of auxiliary techniques.

When you come to an obstacle in your path, say a patch of doghair pines that is littered with deadfalls and tangled with branches, take a 90 degree path to one side of the stand. Take even strides and count them carefully. When you are clear of the trees, walk in your previous direction until you bypass the obstacle. Then turn 90 degrees back toward your original path, again counting your steps carefully. When you

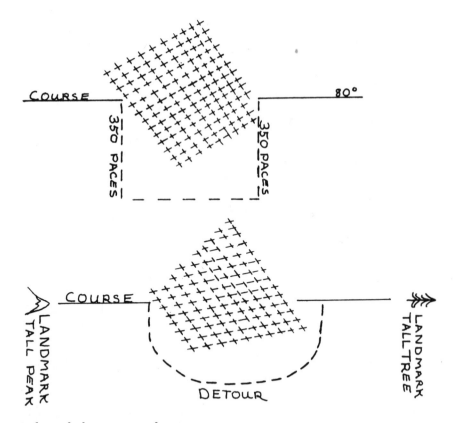

Right-angle bypass around swamp.
Lining two landmarks to stay on course.

have walked the same number of steps as you did when you first left your path, you will be very close to being on the same line of direction you began. The accompanying illustration will make this clear.

This technique will work only under certain conditions. If the obstacle is small and the terrain fairly level, the right-angle bypass is effective. If the detour is a long one, or an uneven one, things get more complicated. If the terrain is very irregular, 50 steps in one place will not equal 50 steps in another. For getting around in areas with obstructed visibility, it is still a good trick to know. But in places that allow long-distance views, there is often a better way.

If the landmark you are aiming at is a prominent one, and you can spot another obvious landmark behind you, forget about counting steps. Walk around your obstacle. Then head back in the appropriate direction until the landmarks line up again, one in front and one in back. This is a simple but effective way of staying on course, and is particularly useful in the open West. Be sure, however, that the landmarks line up evenly both before you swing off course and after you return to it.

There are a number of other tricks that help you keep your bearings.

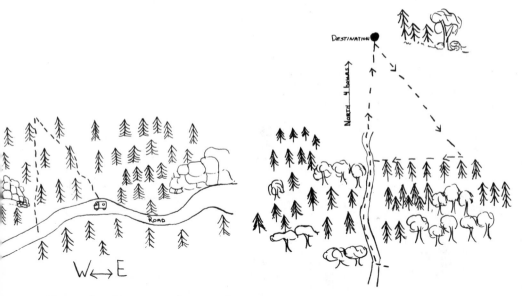

Using a baseline to avoid getting lost.

If you need to pick up a narrow trail head, record your walking time from the trail's end to your turn-around point. Aim slightly to one side of the trail as shown, and walk back, traveling for an extra half-hour or so to be sure you are parallel to the trail. Then turn and walk at right angles to the trail until it is found.

One of them is to establish a baseline of sorts as your return point. The baseline may be a road, trail, stream or railroad track that runs north-south or east-west. If you camp or park your vehicle near such a line, finding your way back is easy.

Say you want to hunt grouse in an area you have never seen before. You park your car on a road that runs roughly east and west. (Check this with your compass.) You grab your gun and emergency pack, and begin hunting north. Consult your compass occasionally to stay on a northerly course. You hunt for an hour and decide to head back. If you simply hunt straight south for another hour or so, you'll be back at the road. This is easy.

The only problem with this technique is that upon hitting the road, you may not know in which direction your car lies, and hike the wrong way for a mile or so. To overcome this, plan to deliberately overshoot your car to one side. For example, leave the car and hunt in a slight northeast direction. To get back, aim straight south. When you hit the road you will be directly east of your car.

Sound like an easy way to keep on course? It is, but there's one catch: Always check your compass when starting out in country you don't know thoroughly. If you know which way your baseline runs and the direction you started out in, you can find your way back with no trouble —even in the dark.

Landmarks can help you make a mental map of your route.

Not every camp can be pitched against a baseline. Sometimes you must bring yourself back to an exact spot by using your compass and woodsmanship. The landmark and compass technique described earlier will work nicely, even on a zigzag course, but you can augment the compass by following a few guidelines.

First, if you are plotting the course with map and compass, don't draw the walking line directly through swamps or over ridges and ravines. These barriers make it easy to become turned around and confused. Your contour map will point these out. Plan for them in advance and work out a zigzag course—which is really no more than a series of small straight-line courses. See the illustration.

Another way to know your whereabouts is to form the habit of looking behind you occasionally to see what you have just passed. Landscapes tend to appear differently when viewed from opposite angles. If you imprint on your mind the land behind you, it will be familiar on your return trip. Also, make special note of unusual or obvious landmarks. If you have a poor memory, mark these with pencil and paper. Jot down the distance between each landmark, too. In a sense, you will be drawing a rough map of your travels.

To estimate the distance between two points, simply check the traveling time from the first mark to the second. You can either note the time traveled or the distance in yards or miles. If you're on level ground, it's sufficient to only record the time. For example, if you spot a lightning-split cottonwood at noon, and your next landmark appears an hour later, you can mark on your mental or actual map that an hour's walk will get you back to the cottonwood. In hilly country, this doesn't always work. Going up takes much longer than going down. It could take an hour to reach a second landmark if the walk is all uphill; going back, you could reach the first point in 15 minutes. This is fairly obvious, but should be taken into account in appropriate areas.

Another way to judge distance is to know your walking pace. To learn yours, time yourself when walking a known distance. Don't try to beat the clock, but simply walk at your normal hunting or hiking tempo. Do this in various types of terrain; you may make excellent mileage in flat country, but poop out easily when climbing a steep trail.

The average man walks about four miles per hour when walking steadily on flat land. In the woods, where you often must break the rhythm of your gait to duck a branch or step around a deadfall, you may be cut down to two miles an hour. In rugged mountain country, puffing up a winding mountain path, you may do only one mile per hour. If you are wearing a backpack or heavy rucksack, you'll make even less mileage. At any rate, time yourself until you can judge with fair accuracy how far you have traveled. This can be invaluable knowledge if you become confused in the woods. If you don't arrive at a destination when you think you should be there, check the time and figure how far you have walked. You might discover you are only a mile or so short of camp. Many a nimrod has walked until he was only a quarter mile from camp, but, suddenly thinking he had walked too far, turned around and crashed off into the bush in the opposite direction—lost.

One other word about keeping your bearings. Although landmarks are valuable aids, don't depend on them entirely. If a fog rolls in, or a storm seals the sky, visibility will be limited. You may not be able to see your marks, no matter how prominent they were in clear weather. This is a good reason to use landmarks in addition to your compass. Should the marks become obscured, your compass savvy will get you out without problems.

If You Are Lost

But suppose, regardless of all the above know-how, you do become lost. What do you do?

The first advice is: *Don't panic*. This is extremely important, probably more important than anything else. But if you're like the average lost person, you will become initially frightened. It's normal, but don't let it get out of hand. Just remember that being lost doesn't have to be serious. If anybody knows where you are (and someone should), you can be sure they will be concerned about you if you don't show up by nightfall. Telling yourself these things brings the whole situation into focus. If you have your emergency pack or other equipment, you have very little to worry about.

When you first realize you are lost or confused, stop immediately.

Find a log or rock or grassy knoll and sit down. Consider where you could have gone wrong. If you have a map, take it out and scrutinize it. If the whole thing seems jumbled and you can't remember anything, don't panic. Fold up the map and forget about it momentarily. Look around you. Look at the trees and the sky and look for something beautiful. You must find some beauty in the outdoors or you probably wouldn't be there in the first place. Really think about nature. Don't let yourself view the woods as something strange and alien to fight or escape. Doing that only spurs hasty judgments and brings back your deadliest enemy—panic. If you can exercise the self-discipline it takes to ignore your situation and appreciate your surroundings, you can live through your emergency easily.

Okay, you're ready to face the situation realistically. Get out the map and compass and see where you went wrong. How far back did you become confused? Did you know where you were two hours ago? If so, find that place on the map; you can't be too far from it.

If you can't work out a return route to your satisfaction, or if the map still confuses you and you're still a little nervous, then build a fire. The fire will civilize the place and remind you that you have some knowledge of woods-lore. If it's late in the day, plan to spend the night. Remember, it's much better to stay put if you don't know where to go anyway. Using the information in Chapter 16, build a temporary shelter.

Make your camp as comfortable as possible. Eat only a small amount of emergency rations; save more for the next day. If you have good reason to believe a search party will be looking for you, don't plan on leaving your camp. Do your part by sitting tight and waiting it out. Utilize all the signaling potential you have. (See Chapter 17.)

In the morning, if a search party is not likely to be looking for you, or if emergency conditions force you to find your own way back, act carefully and methodically. If you know the trail is reasonably near, there are a couple of ways to search for it. Remember to take pains not to become more confused or lost.

If you have a map and compass, align the map's north with your compass north. Look for prominent landmarks in the distance and see if you can spot them on the map. If you find one, sight it carefully with your compass and take a degree reading. Next, draw a line on your map that passes at the same angle through the landmark. Now look for a second landmark. It should be easier the second time because the first mark will orient the terrain to the map. Take a compass reading on the second mark and draw a line through the map mark at the appropriate angle. Where the two lines cross is roughly your position. This is the triangulation method. Using this method, you should have no trouble comparing where you are with where you want to go. If you find, for example, that you are roughly four miles east of your trail, simply set a compass course and follow it.

You should practice triangulating in familiar country a few times to

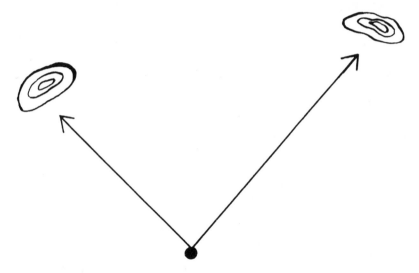

Triangulating your position.

get the hang of it. If you foul it up in a real emergency, it could get you into deeper trouble. There are times, though, when it just isn't possible to use the triangulation method. There may be no recognizable landmarks nearby that are marked on the map. Or, for some reason, you may not have a map along. Then you must search for your trail a little more crudely.

One way is by methodically covering the surrounding area until you pick up signs of your previous travel or come to country you recognize. There are all types of patterns you can follow: circles, squares, rectangles, zigzags or whatever—just be sure you are able to find your way back to your bivouac camp. Take a compass reading in a direction where you guess the trail is, and head out. Mark your path carefully by overturning rocks, making log pointers, placing red tape on tree trunks, or, in dire situations, by blazing tree trunks with a knife or stone and by breaking off branches to point the way back. Whatever means you use, be sure that you can get back easily. Walk in one direction until you have exhausted the possibility of picking up the trail. Follow your marked course back and repeat the procedure in another direction.

If none of this works, you are no longer "confused" but officially lost. Here, familiarity with the general area can help. Recall to the best of your ability any roads, railroads or major waterways that border the tract of land in which you are lost. In northern Alaska there may not be a road for 200 miles in any direction, but in most states a road of some type is reasonably near. If you know a road borders the southern boundary of the area, follow your compass south to reach it—if it is feasible. If you remember that a railroad runs along the western edge, try to get to it. If your food supply is running short, live off the land as much as possible. (See Chapter 13 for details on this.)

If you don't know the area well enough, or you simply can't remember if the road was north or south, then you must keep your eyes and ears alert for signs of civilization—the rattle of a freight train, the toot of a car horn or a factory whistle, the buzz of a chain saw or snowmobile. Any of these can lead you to help. Smoke curling in the distance could be from a fireplace, or a cut in a hillside could be a road. Check them carefully. They also may aid you in getting out. If a hill is nearby, climb it to extend your view. If you spot a road or cabin, mark it with compass bearings and aim for it.

If you can't find a sign anywhere, pick a direction you think is likely to take you out and follow it with your compass. But before you travel, pin a note in an obvious place telling who you are, what condition you are in, and what day and direction you left the bivouac camp. If you don't have paper and pencil (part of your emergency pack, remember?), make a rock arrow pointing in the direction you're traveling.

While you travel, search constantly for signs of civilization. In mountain country, begin walking downhill. If you come to an old logging road, or a dirt road of any sort, mark well the place where you first emerge. If the road is level, make an arbitrary choice of going right or left. Logging roads tend to branch off into the woods. Where the branch splits off from the main artery a "Y" is formed. If you approach the "Y" from the neck—that is, so the crotch of the "Y" points at you—you are most likely heading deeper into the woods. Think of the "Y" as an arrow of sorts. The open end is the back of the arrow, and the stem points the direction you should travel. If the arrow is pointing at you as you approach the forked roads, you are probably going farther into the woods. Turn around and walk back up the road, staying on the main lane when confronted by a fork.

Directions Without A Compass

As you can see from the above information, virtually all methods of finding your way out of the woods depend on knowing directions. Lost men invariably walk in circles when they ignore directional signs, wasting their time and energy. But what do you do if you don't have a compass along? Perhaps it was lost or damaged. Or maybe you were careless and just didn't bring one. How do you find directions then? Well, there are a number of ways, but first be warned that none of the natural direction finders are as convenient or accurate as a compass.

You can use the sun to determine east from west, but only in a general way. The sun rises slightly south of east and sets slightly north of west. If you want to travel due west or east, compensate for the north-south declination. When traveling north, the sun should hit your right shoulder in the morning. At noon it will be directly on your back, during the afternoon on your left shoulder. Remember this and you can travel a fairly straight course simply by watching the angle of the sunlight.

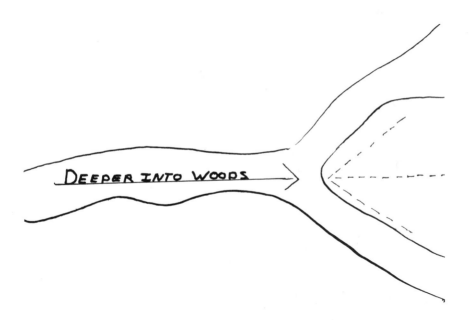

If you come to a fork in a road while lost, consider the crotch of the fork as a pointer. If you approach it from the side indicated by the solid arrow, you are most likely heading deeper into the woods. If you approach from one of the forks, as shown by the broken-line arrow, you are probably heading out of the woods.

On cloudy days, when the sun is not directly visible, determine the sun's position by rotating a signal mirror or shiny knife blade so that it reflects surrounding light. It will glint most obviously when opposite the sun.

If you have a watch handy, you can determine direction more precisely (assuming the watch is running on correct time). Point the hour hand directly toward the sun. South will be exactly half way between the hour hand and 12:00.

If no watch is available and you don't know if it's morning or afternoon, you can still utilize the sun to find direction. Find a thin, straight stick and push it into the ground. Mark the tip of its shadow with a small pebble or stick. Wait 15 to 30 minutes and mark the tip of the new shadow. The line that joins the second pebble to the first will point roughly west.

A host of other shadow techniques exists for finding directions. Most, however, take hours to do properly and involve rather complicated steps. If the sun is shining, one of the above methods should work.

When sunlight fades and the skies darken, stars become efficient compasses. The North Star, Polaris, is the most accurate natural guide available. Polaris always shines in the northern sky, and is easily spotted. First, search for the Big Dipper, a group of seven stars which are arranged to look much like an old-fashioned water dipper. The Big Dip-

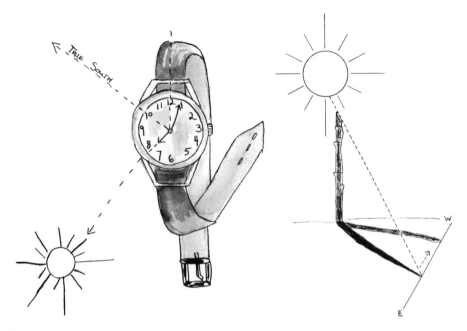

Using a watch to determine direction.
Determining the direction by shadows.

per is easy to see. Its stars are of the brightest magnitude and it appears fairly low in the sky. The two stars that form the lowest side of the dipper's cup are known as the pointer stars. Extend the line formed by the pointer stars for roughly five times their length and there will be Polaris, the North Star. Polaris twinkles brightly and stands out among adjacent stars. To be certain you have found the North Star, follow the pattern of stars that lead out from Polaris; they should form the Little Dipper. The North Star is the last star on the handle of the Little Dipper.

If the stars are partly obstructed by trees or fog, you can find the general direction by observing any star closely for movement. Push two sticks into the ground two feet apart, lining them up with a chosen star. The back stick should be shorter than the one in front. Sight along the tops of the two sticks until you are centered on a star. Watch closely for movement. If it dips, it's in the west. Stars in the north sky will glide to the left, while those in the south move to the right.

Once you've determined directions, you still must be able to travel in an approximately straight line. Often, you can use landmarks much the same way as you'd use them if you had a compass. And as described earlier, by keeping the sun on one side of you in the morning and on the other side in the afternoon, you can move in one general direction without wavering. In thick woods where landmarks and sunshine are generally inconstant, follow a line made by sighting down three objects. In most cases, you'll use trees. As you approach the nearest tree, auto-

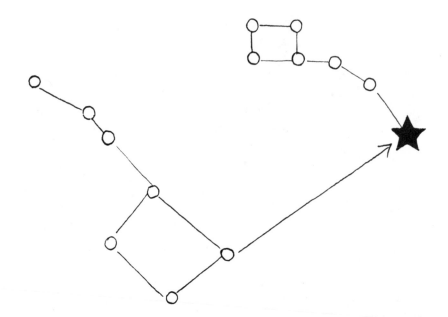

The bottom stars of the Big Dipper point to Polaris, the North Star. Polaris is the last star on the handle of the Little Dipper.

matically line up another beyond the next two. This will keep you on a straight course. However, you must line up *three* trees. Two will not suffice. In especially thick timber you can forget this rather tedious method and fashion a "lodgepole" compass. Find a long, straight pole—such as a 20- to 30-foot deadfall—and clean it of branches. Point it in the direction you want to travel and begin walking. The long pole will not be able to turn in the thick timber and will prevent you from doing the same. In especially dense copses of trees, you may have to push the pole through part way, then walk around and pull it out from the front. It is not a fast way to travel, but it will keep you from circling aimlessly in heavy timber.

In more open country, when landmarks aren't visible, the wind can sometimes aid you in moving in a straight line. Say the wind is blowing from the west. If you are moving north, the breeze will brush the left side of your face. By keeping the wind on your left cheek, you will continue walking north. However, microcurrents sometimes occur in canyons and wooded slopes. These blow in varying directions and are worthless as steering aids. Use the wind as a steering guide only when it is obviously a steady, prevailing gust.

If Lost While Boating

Every time the subject of being lost is discussed, boaters are invariably excluded. It's true that most of the information given for terrestrial

In thick woods, a "lodgepole compass" will keep you on a straight path.

navigation applies equally to water-farers, but a few tips need to be stressed.

Anyone who skippers a craft in waters that are remote or intricate enough to get lost in had better take pains to keep himself oriented. Map and compass are absolute necessities. Know where you are on the map at all times. Look back often and search for markers or natural features that will guide you when returning. Islands tend to look amazingly alike. If you pass more than a few, they lose their worth as landmarks. But there may be objects on the islands that are noteworthy.

Even so, don't rely too heavily on markers. Fogs are especially common around water, and they will cloak your vision. In low visibility you must depend on your compass to steer you home.

If you suddenly discover yourself lost—or confused if you please—stop immediately. Don't turn into channels or backwaters looking for a way out. You'll only get more confused and eat up fuel in the process. Stop and consult your compass and map. If you can spot landmarks, try the triangulation method described earlier to determine your position. If that fails, sit tight. In most waters someone will pass by reasonably soon. If you're boating in a more primitive area, such as a chain of North Country lakes, ready your signaling gear in case a bush plane passes over. In more dire times, when you must find a way back on your own, proceed systematically. Record your bearings and travel distance on paper. Probe in different directions until you spot something familiar or are able to find your place on the map. Don't burn fuel needlessly. Run your engine at steady speeds, without gunning it.

If you have an emergency radio (which you should carry on any boating trip in remote waters), use it often. If you still can't find your way out, you will have to use every signaling device possible to attract help. (Study carefully Chapter 17 on signaling.)

In Conclusion

Losing your bearings is irritating and embarrassing, but in most cases it's not as serious as it once was. Efficient, knowledgeable rescue crews are on duty in most areas, and if you stay calm and act rationally, 90 percent of the time you will soon be found. If you're carrying an emergency pack, as you always should, a few days in the woods, in all but the severest conditions, should be no great hardship. Even without the pack, a thinking man can easily stay alive for the duration of the mishap. Don't misunderstand me. Getting lost is not something to be taken lightly. But lost people do have excellent survival odds—if they can combat panic.

PART III

*Developing
Emergency Skills*

12

Predicting the Weather

With a little savvy, a little reckoning and a little luck, it isn't hard for an outdoorsman to maintain a good batting average at short-range weather forecasting. Often a weather-wise nimrod can provide a better forecast than media meteorologists, because the latter use information gathered well before the broadcast or printing, whereas the amateur weather watcher has up-to-the-minute changes and observations to work with. Also, the pros have to deal with weather on a wide scale, predicting for large, divergent areas, while the amateur concentrates on that bit of land within his immediate sight.

Weather is of vital importance in relation to emergencies, because a large number of mishaps are climate-orientated—a hunter sealed in the mountains by a sudden blizzard, a boater facing rough seas because of an unexpected squall, and so on. If you can predict the weather with some accuracy, you can thwart these types of difficulties.

Clouds

Clouds are the most obvious weather signs, but they are not indicative of the weather if viewed without reference to the wind and, sometimes, the barometer. Beginning meteorologists are often surprised to discover that cloud typing is a fairly intricate study. Just about everyone knows that fluffy, cotton-ball type puffs of cloud are called *cumulus*, but there are also variations of *cumulus* that create *altocumulus, cumulus lenticularis, cumulonimbus,* and so on. The subject is truly a complex one on a scientific level, but we needn't go that far to satisfy our

Cumulus cloud.
Stratus cloud.

purpose. In this chapter we will discuss only a few cloud varieties.

Cumulus clouds are the billowing puffs of white clouds that you often see against a backdrop of clear blue sky. Cumulus clouds are good news, because they forecast fair weather if they drift about without changing form. But if they begin to build up vertically, forming prominent "heads," they are turning into storm clouds. When the head flattens out into an anvil shape and the lower portion of the cloud darkens, you're looking at an ominous parcel of air.

Cirrus clouds are long wisps of condensed moisture that float high in the sky, looking as though they were painted there with thin, feathery brush strokes. Cirrus formations, also known as "mare's tails," are generally fair weather clouds, but keep your eye on them. If they multiply noticeably, and if the wind is steady from northeast, east or south, they spell trouble. Late-season hunters and fishermen should be especially watchful for increasing mare's tails; they portend blizzards and snowfalls.

Stratus clouds are low clouds having little or no layering in a vertical

Cirrus clouds.
Nimbus cloud.

sense, often appearing more as a gloomy gray blanket covering the sky and obscuring the sun. Stratus clouds often bring long sessions of drizzly rain or light snow flurries, but, coupled with northeast to south winds, are capable of heavy precipitation.

Nimbus clouds are low and formless, usually having large patches of

Cumulonimbus cloud.
Cirrostratus clouds.

The beginnings of a mackerel sky.

dark blue or gray. Nimbus clouds usually accompany precipitation, or are direct forerunners of it.

These basic cloud types often intermingle to form progeny like *stratocumulus*, a low, fluffy but unlayered dark cumulus cloud that warns of upcoming showers; *cumulonimbus*, a dark, building cumulus cloud that also carries showers; *nimbostratus*, a low, dark carpet of cloud that brings long showers on northeast or south winds; *cirrostratus*, high, dark wisps of ice clouds, bringing precipitation within a day if accompanied by northeast or east to south winds; and *altocumulus*, also known as a mackerel sky, since the layer of small, patchy clouds resemble mackerel scales. A mackerel sky is a warning of upcoming rain or snow, usually within 15 hours.

Wind

Wind carries the weather, and is often a good clue of what is to come. Generally speaking, north, northwest and southwest winds bring good weather, while wind from the south, east and northeast bring snow and rain.

Shifting winds also tell a story. Cloudy skies laced with winds shifting from northwest to northeast or southwest to southeast are bad-weather harbingers. Even under a clear sky, winds that yo-yo between southwest and southeast are warnings that rain is likely. On the other hand, a rainstorm spiced with northeast to south winds is breaking and clearing if the wind shifts to a westerly direction.

Be particularly wary of a south wind; it brushes your cheek with a moist, sweet breeze, but is the envoy of an upcoming storm in disguise.

On a south wind's tail is often a low-pressure front, which in turn draws thunderstorms.

An east wind is also a danger sign in most areas. East winds are moist, and their presence usually means a falling barometer (low pressure), hence an upcoming storm front. Wintertime easterlies bring thick, heavy snow.

Wind changes are also noteworthy when used in conjunction with a barometer reading. If you're afield and don't know the barometer reading, but can tell by natural signs (which we'll discuss shortly) that the barometric pressure is rising or falling, you can determine the weather with more certainty. The following chart, from the Official U.S. Coast Guard Boating Guide, is a good reference for calculating wind-barometer data. The barometric readings are given for sea level. Add .1 inch for every 92 feet of altitude at your location. (Or skip the numerical reading all together, and work—more crudely—with just the up and down fluctuations in pressure.)

Wind Direction	Barometer (Sea Level)	Weather
SW to NW	30.10 to 30.20 and steady	Fair with slight temperature changes in 1 or 2 days
SW to NW	30.10 to 30.20 and rising rapidly	Fair, followed within 2 days by rain
SW to NW	30.20 and above and stationary	Continued fair with no decided temperature change
SW to NW	30.20 and above and falling slowly	Slowly rising temperature and fair for 2 days
S to SE	30.10 to 30.20 and falling slowly	Rain within 24 hours
S to SE	30.10 to 30.20 and falling rapidly	Wind increasing, with rain in 12 hours
SE to NE	30.10 to 30.20 and falling slowly	Rain in 12 to 18 hours
SE to NE	30.10 to 30.20 and falling rapidly	Increasing wind, rain within 12 hours
E to NE	30.10 and above and falling slowly	In summer, with light winds, rain may not fall for several days; in winter, rain or snow in 24 hours
E to NE	30.10 and above and falling fast	In summer, rain probably within

		12 hours; in winter, rain, snow, increasing winds
SE to NE	30.10 or below and falling slowly	Rain will continue for 1 or 2 days
SE to NE	30.00 or below and falling rapidly	Rain with high wind, followed within 36 hours by clearing and in winter, by cold
S to SW	30.00 or below and rising slowly	Clearing in a few hours, fair for several days
S to E	29.80 or below and falling rapidly	Severe storm imminent, followed in 24 hours by clearing and in winter, by cold
E to N	29.80 or below and falling rapidly	Severe NE gale and heavy rain; in winter, heavy snow and cold wave
Going to W	29.80 or below and rising rapidly	Clearing and colder

Other Weather Clues

On a less scientific basis, but still reliable, are the many other clues that can help you decipher the weather. Let's look briefly at each of these.

The color of the sky is worth noting, particularly at sunrise and sunset. "Red sky at morning, sailor take warning; Red sky at night, sailor's delight," is an old bromide that has sound scientific backing. A red or dark orange sunrise usually brings rain or snow within a day. Similarly, a dull red orb of a rising sun peeking through gray clouds also spells precipitation.

In the evening, a red or dark orange western sky promises good weather for the next day. So does a violet-colored sky with blue traces above the clouds. A golden horizon, scratched with strokes of green at the perimeter, tells you high winds are in store for the morrow. A gray night sky usually means you'll get rained on the next day.

A rainbow can tell you much about the near-future weather. If it occurs in the morning, a squall is in the offing. A midday rainbow usually accompanies unstable weather, and a night rainbow informs you that the storm has passed. Since most storms originate from the west in the Northern Hemisphere, a rainbow in the morning appears before the storm, and, conversely, at night it appears after the storm.

Sun dogs—rainbowlike bands appearing around the sun in the morning or evening—indicate colder weather is on the way. In wintertime, sun dogs warn you of an approaching cold front, one which may bring extremely frigid weather.

Dew is a reliable short-range weather-teller. If you awake in the morning to find the grass laden with droplets of dew, you're in for a fair day, at least for the first half of the day. Conversely, early morning grass that is not wet from dew promises you a day with precipitation. "When the grass is dry at morning light, look for rain before the night," is one adage to remember. Another: "When the dew is on the grass, rain will never come to pass." During the colder months, dew takes the form of frost, and hence a good frost is indicative of good weather, while a lack of frost spells rain or snow.

Smoke is a poor man's barometer, for it drifts in relation to the barometric pressure. Smoke that curls straight up from a fire or chimney and dissipates quickly is a sign of high pressure and continuing fair weather. But smoke that rises a few feet, only to level off and drift thickly along a horizontal path, indicates low pressure and upcoming rain or snow.

An outdoorsman with alert senses can sometimes smell a storm before it arrives. This is not as fantastic as it sounds. Prior to a storm, low pressure fronts move in, releasing odors held captive by the preceding high pressure. The result is a richer, thicker profusion of odors from grass, animals, rubbage, swamps, marshes and other odoriferous objects.

Cloudy, low pressure days create a ceiling over the land that echoes sounds noticeably. Consequently, prior to a rain or snow, everyday sounds seem clearer and exaggerated. A barking dog, the hollow thudding of an ax against wood, or a buzzing chain saw—all these sounds travel farther than they normally do. You can also hear the difference in the woods. Before a rain the forest is a quiet place, hushed and muffled perceptibly.

Your sense of sight can also aid in your weather guessing. High visibility over salt water is a bad sign, since the normally salty haze is dissipated by unstable air movement. When you can see far along the sea, prepare for rain or snow.

You sometimes hear elderly folks moan about their corns and arthritis before a storm, and science tends to back up these claims. Low pressure causes injuries to ache, stiff joints to throb, and the people bearing them to become irascible. Don't dispell such aches from your prognosticating; they may be the most sensitive weather instruments you have.

At night, cirrus clouds blanketing the moon create a perceptible ring around that celestial body, which many people are fond of for weather forecasting. Actually, a ring around the moon is a limited prophecy;

roughly half the time you get rain the following day, the other half you don't. Used in conjunction with other weather indicators, a moon ring is at least worth noting, but be warned that it is not very conclusive evidence.

Another commonly accepted night weather sign is the clarity and profusion of stars. Unfortunately, clear nights don't tell much about the next day. In fact, unusually bright stars blanketing the sky may be the forerunners of a morning rain or snow storm.

A good indicator of changing winds is a tree leaf. Leaves grow in relation to the prevailing wind, and a shift in that wind turns them over, so that their tips curl back and their undersides are exposed. A tree with curly leaves is warning you to check the weather; a storm might very likely be on the way.

The Birds and the Bees

Animals of many types respond to weather changes with subtle quirks of behavior. If you're alert to these, they can back up your findings from wind, clouds and natural barometers.

Most of us know that birds perch before a storm. The low pressure prior to a storm creates air that is less dense than usual, and birds have a harder time flying through it. When you observe telephone lines, tree limbs and other perches littered with birds, it's a good bet that low pressure is moving in. When they do move, they fly low, struggling along, rather than gliding with their usual grace. Also, waterfowl tend to fly low when bad weather is in the offing and high during fair weather. Biologists explain this by claiming that low pressure has an uncomfortable effect on waterfowl ears; the effect is lessened by low flying.

Birds give other warnings, too. Sparrows and swallows, diving and circling low to the ground, are feeding on assorted flying insects that emerge because of the high humidity preceding a storm. Migratory birds such as waterfowl and woodcock fly with cold weather at their backs, and when you see large flights of geese, or notice unusual numbers of woodcock in your upland covers, a cold front isn't far behind.

Bees swarming about indicate that the next few hours will be fair. On the other hand, if no bees are buzzing around flowers or offal, wet weather may be in store. On days when bees won't leave their hives, you might want to follow suit and not leave the dry comfort of your home.

Flying insects in general act peculiar just before a storm, flying and buzzing erratically. Greenhead flies in particular are annoyed by oncoming rain, and often vent their anger by biting human flesh.

Spiders are good short-range weathermen, for on clear days they build long webs and pace around them actively. When rain is in the cards, the webs tighten and become fewer, and the spider sits lethargically near the middle. Just before a big rain, the spider will leave its web completely. If it stays on the web after the rain starts, it's likely to be a brief, light shower.

And then there are a host of other animal-lore weather guides, less usable and practical, but worth mentioning at any rate. An elk herd that bolts and runs suddenly, for no apparent reason, is a clue that a major storm is descending on the area, usually within a few hours. This is a great tip, assuming that you can spot a free-roaming elk herd (not easy in most places) and that your presence is not the reason for the stampede. A somewhat more reliable and practical elk sign occurs a day or two ahead of a storm. Then the elk leave the high country summer range and migrate to their lower winter range. En route to the wintering area, with a storm pushing them, they will move more boldly than usual, and you may spot one or two crossing a road in front of you. All elk tracks eventually lead to lower elevations or protected slopes. If you notice such a migration, deep snows are likely to fall in the high country.

It's said that coyotes yammering during midmorning are a sign of bad weather soon to come, but my own experience doesn't bear this out. It's also said that the depth of a bear's hibernation den is relative to the amount of snow which will fall that winter: the deeper the den, the less snow; the shallower the den, the deeper the snow. Personally, I'd like to see some authentication on this one. But even if you accept this as true, there's still the task of finding a bear's den.

As far as I know, it matters not a whit how early or late the groundhog emerges from its den. Whether or not it sees its shadow is entirely its own problem, for it has no bearing on the weather. Along these same lines, the thickness of an animal's fur or the amount of food it caches for the winter indicates that the previous year was a good one for food and health, but it doesn't predict the upcoming weather. A beaver can have a heavy pelt and the ensuing winter can be the mildest on record, or it can have a flimsy pelt and face a harsh winter.

Putting It All Together

An accurate weather forecaster doesn't rely on one or two signs to make a prediction. He gathers all the evidence he can, weighing each against the other while shaving the facts down to a conclusion. For example, you may notice towering, dirty cumulus clouds overhead and predict rain. But the other factors, wind and barometer, may be such that the rain will fall someplace other than where you're standing. A better method would be to observe the cumulus clouds and then make a few more observations to narrow the odds for an accurate forecast.

Say the grass at your feet is dew covered, and the wind is steady from the north. Both are good signs. A truck roars down a road some distance from where you are standing, but its noise doesn't seem especially loud, as it would in a low pressure area. A walk to some nearby wildflowers finds a number of bees buzzing around the stamens in search of nectar. The leaves on a nearby shrub are hanging point-down, rather than curled back as they would be in humid, prestorm weather. These are more good signs. All seem to indicate fair weather, and those moisture-laden cumulus clouds are not likely to dump their water burden on you.

Now look at an opposite example. The sky is gray with low floating stratus clouds, mixed with what appears to be some dark forms of cumulus. The wind is steady from the south, and the balmy air has curled the broad leaves of the maple tree in your front yard. There is no noticeable dew on the ground, and the smoke from your neighbor's chimney is drifting horizontally across the rooftop. Your hair is a bit unruly from the humidity. So far all signs are bad. A walk to the backyard scares a bunch of blackbirds which were perched on telephone wires, and that clinches it. Rain is on the way, and you decide to abort your plans for trout fishing and spend the morning tying flies or reloading shotshells instead.

If you're outdoors—camping, hunting or such—and you notice an upcoming storm, don't wait until it's too late to react. At a flash of lightning, begin counting slowly, one count per second, until you hear thunder. Every fifth count signifies one mile, hence a count of ten means the storm is two miles away, and could be upon you in minutes. Get to shelter immediately. If you must find or build a shelter, make sure the entrance faces away from the storm. Since winds in this hemisphere circle low pressure fronts counterclockwise, you can determine the direction of the storm by facing the wind. The storm will be coming from your right.

13

Finding Food

Learning to gather wild food is a two-fold endeavor. First, there is the fun you have learning how to set a primitive snare or identify an edible plant—skills that tie you to a heritage of woodsmanship and outdoor savvy. Second, the knowledge you gain could save your life. Even if you never need to stave off starvation with wild food, you experience a certain comfort and satisfaction in knowing that you could find food if you had to.

The food I'm talking about is not necessarily gourmet cuisine. In fact, some of the recommended survival food tastes awful. Remember, however, that in an emergency you seldom have the opportunity to do—or eat—what you like. Instead, you must do the best you can. I have had people tell me in positive tones that they would never eat such survival fare as insects, trash fish, and so on. I can't say for sure, but I'd bet that given several days to develop an appetite, these same people would be ready to eat just about anything. When your belly is empty, all your preconceived notions about food quickly vanish.

Don't get the impression that all wild food tastes lousy. Some of the edible plants are very palatable when eaten raw, while others become tasty when boiled or parched. Animal flesh is generally satisfying to the taste buds—or at least it's not offensive. Insects, surprisingly, are not bad at all. If you have the means to prepare these items properly, they can indeed become gourmet fare. But when dug, clubbed, trapped, or shot in the woods, with no preparation or condiments save water and fire— the foods are rarely something to relish. They will keep you alive, though, and that is your only concern in an emergency.

You need a variety of food items to keep you going for more than a few days. If you were lost in an area that had excellent fishing, eating fish would be enough to get you by if your mishap ended in a few days. But when foraging for emergency food over an extended period, strive to gather a variety of essentials; and don't burn up more energy than your food will provide. Spend part of your time catching fish, part of the time digging roots and tubers, and the remainder picking berries. This way you have a better chance of maintaining a healthy diet. The fish provides proteins and essential vitamins, the roots starch and the berries sugar.

Here are a few more basics to remember when in need of food.

Animal food is generally more nutritious than plant food, but be sure you eat the fat as well as the meat. Meat provides proteins, fat gives you carbohydrates and energy. The heart, liver and lungs of most animals can be eaten when cooked and are nutritious. But beware of eating organs that have lumps, spots, sores or parasite holes.

Plant tubers are rich in carbohydrates. Many of the more fibrous tubers are difficult to digest. Cooking, if only parching near a fire, tends to make digestion easier.

Berries provide sugar—energy—and often have other needed vitamins. Most berries are tasty as well, and make a welcome supplement to any meal.

Don't nibble food throughout the day. Gather your edibles and prepare them to be eaten at one sitting. This will give you the contentment of a full meal, and your stomach a chance to digest the food properly while you rest.

Drink plenty of water. You can live for several weeks with little or no food if you flush your body regularly with fluids. But even if you are eating sufficiently, drink liberal amounts of water.

When food is in short supply, don't waste energy. Do only what is necessary and no more. Keep warm; shivering uses up calories.

Edible Plants

Although animal flesh is generally more nutritious, it's best to concentrate most of your effort on harvesting edible plants. Plants are sta-

tionary, and you needn't chase them through the woods or immobilize them with a bullet or club. Botanists claim there are over 120,000 edible species, and at least a few of these can be found almost anywhere you go.

You'll probably be content with learning no more than a dozen or so edible species. It never hurts to know more; it may hurt to know less. Practice identifying plants while fishing or hiking, know which parts are usable and how they are prepared. Better still, find someone who has a reliable working knowledge of edible plants and ask him to point out useful species. Make a mental note of the characteristics of the plant—the type of flower, leaf, fruit, stem, etc.—*and* the habitat.

Once you learn to identify plants, harvest a few to familiarize yourself with the edible parts and to sample the taste. Thin-stemmed plants having usable roots and tubers can be murder to pull out intact. Invariably, the stem breaks and the root is left buried in the earth. A digging stick—a three-foot length of sturdy branch-wood, carved smooth at the handle and beveled near the bottom—will help you overcome this. Insert the stick on the upslope or backside of the plant, eight to ten inches from the stem. Loosen the soil by churning back and forth. Remove the stick and dig into the ground about a foot in front of the plant. When the stick is a foot or more deep in the soil, lean back and down on the handle. The entire plant, root, tuber and all, can be lifted out.

For those unfamiliar with plant anatomy, here are a few useful terms of edible plant parts:

> TUBERS are starchy, underground storage compartments for plants, that generally occur at the end of the root. Many plants have edible tubers, and though they sometimes are fibrous and bitter tasting, they often can be eaten raw—an important consideration for emergency use.
>
> ROOTS AND ROOTSTALKS are generally knotty, spindly fibers of white, starchy material that anchor the plant in the soil and filter water and nutrients. These are often edible and, like tubers, may require a digging stick to remove from the soil.
>
> LEAFSTALKS are fleshy stems that attach leaves to the plant's main stem. Leafstalks are easy to harvest and generally are not bad tasting.
>
> SHOOTS is a term broadly used to describe a young stem. It may be sticking singly out of the ground or branching from a larger main stem. Shoots of edible species are generally moist and palatable when young—more palatable when a little salt is handy.

Other consumable parts include leaves, berries and nuts. Of all plant

A selection of common edible plants that you can find just about anywhere: (p. 179) A. Burdock, B. Glacier Lily, (p. 180) C. Chicory, D. Dandelion, E. Arrowhead, F. Plaintain, G. Cattail, H. Wild Grape.

Using a digging stick to uproot frail plants.

materials, nuts are the most nourishing. They are rich in fats and oils, can be easily harvested, and are often tasty. The inner bark of some tree species—known as cambium—can also be eaten in emergencies. The cambium is harvested by scraping away outer bark with a knife or sharp rock and peeling off thin strips of the watery underlayer.

Preparation of edible parts varies with the plant, but is simple enough to be done under most circumstances. I've included many species that can be eaten raw. These should be emphasized. In a crisis, you may not have the time or facilities to boil stems and leaves.

Many plant parts can be roasted over a fire. To avoid charring tubers and rootstalks, pack them in mud if possible before placing them on the fire coals. The mud will harden and the tuber or root will cook without burning. The baked mud breaks away from the food item easily and cleanly.

The following is a list of wide-ranging and easily recognized edible plants. Not included are consumable plants which are difficult to identify or which have look-alike poisonous cousins. The plants are illustrated through line drawings, but this may not be enough to identify some species positively. If in doubt, ask someone who knows—or consult a more sophisticated identification manual.

ARROWHEAD *(Sagittaria)* grows throughout the United States and Canada in shallow water or muddy soil of ponds, swamps and rivers. The arrow-shaped leaves and three-petaled white flowers are easy to identify. The plant grows to three feet, but has roots that may reach five feet away from the main body. The entire root is edible, but the starchy tuber is best. The roots and tubers can be eaten raw or roasted.

BARREL CACTUS (*Echinocactus*) resembles its name.
These pudgy, oblong cacti stand from two to ten feet
high and are equipped with thorny needles. Yellow
to pink flowers ring the crown. The barrel cactus is
found mostly in southwestern deserts. The pulp of the
plant can be eaten raw or boiled.

BASSWOOD *(Tilia)* is a large tree common to the eastern half of the continent. The leaves are heart-shaped
and saw-toothed; the bark is dark and shiny. Early in
spring, the buds may be eaten raw or boiled. The sap
is rich in sugar and can be tapped for emergency
energy. Basswoods grow in rich bottomlands and
moist, rocky slopes.

BEECH *(Fagus grandifolia)*: Beechnuts are familiar to
anyone living in the northeastern states and southeast-
ern Canada. The mature trees have a smooth, white-
to-gray bark and bear thin-shelled triangular nuts. In
late summer and fall, the sweet nuts can be eaten raw
or roasted. In spring, young beech leaves can be
cooked and eaten as a green. The inner bark can be
stripped and eaten raw.

BIRCH (*Betula*): Although there are several species of
birch, we will divide them into two groups: white
birches and river birches. (This is taxonomically out-
rageous, but will aid in practical usage.) First, white
birches are slender trees common to northern forests.
Their loose white bark makes them easy to identify.
The main trunk is branchless for several feet, with a
crown of heart-shaped leaves overhead. The river
birches or black birches have dark, smooth bark, and
often grow in tight copses near streams and through-

out river bottomlands. Both types of birch have a watery, sweet inner bark that is nutritious and easy to collect. The cambium layer can be peeled from the tree and chewed, or the sap can be collected in a receptacle for drinking.

BLUEBERRY *(Vaccinium)*: Blueberries and closely related huckleberries are common in burnt woodlands across the country. They also frequent edges of logging roads and trails. The berries are blue-black to red, and are sweet and nourishing.

BULRUSH *(Scirpus)*: This common plant is found in marshes, swamps and wet soils throughout the United States and southern Canada. Most people are familiar with its triangular green stem and wispy, dangling leaves. The young roots of bulrush are sweet and can be eaten raw. Also edible is the lower foot or so of the stem, which is peeled and eaten raw.

BURDOCK *(Arctium)* is a ubiquitous species normally regarded as a pest. It's easy to identify: tough, straight stems, three to seven feet high; wavy, arrow-shaped leaves and hooked flower heads. The root of this plant is edible when boiled, as are the young basal leaves. The young leafstalks can be eaten raw.

Cattails *(Typha)* are common, easily recognized and provide important emergency food. They grow in wet soils across the continent. The thick stalks, slender leaves and sausagelike spikes are easy clues for identification. Almost everybody knows that cattail roots are edible, but few realize that the plant is virtually edible from root to spike. The stem base can be peeled and eaten raw, the young flower spikes can be boiled or roasted, and the pollen fluff can be kneaded with water and baked into small cakes.

Chicory *(Cichorium intybus)* is another wide-ranging plant that occupies disturbed or gravelly soils. Chicory reaches a height of several feet, but the smaller, younger plants offer more palatable food. The wagon-wheel flowers, about an inch in diameter, are lavender to deep blue. The basal leaves are large and dandelionlike. The leaves can be eaten raw or boiled and have a tart, sometimes bitter taste. The roots are edible raw, but are better roasted.

Chokecherry *(Prunus virginiana)* is found near stream banks, rich thickets and bottomlands across the country. Chokecherry varies in size from low woody shrubs to full-size trees. In late summer and fall, the red to black berries are usable. They can be eaten raw or mashed and cooked. Be sure to remove the pit stones—they contain high levels of cyanide that can be fatal if ingested. However, if the pits are cooked with the cherries, the cyanide is rendered harmless.

Clover *(Trifolium)* is a worldwide plant that should be familiar to everyone. The yellow, pink and white flowers can be eaten raw; so can the leaves and roots. Clover, like cattails, is completely edible and easily recognized.

CRANBERRY (*Vaccinium* and *Viburnum*): For our purposes, the two different cranberries will be considered together. The *Vaccinium* cranberry grows low to the ground in marshes, bogs and pine woods. The leaves are small and oblong, and cluster around each stem. The *Viburnum* or highbush cranberry has maplelike leaves which are hairy on the bottom and smooth on top. It reaches to heights of seven or more feet. Both cranberries are red to orange in appearance, and can be eaten raw. Cranberries cling to the vines throughout winter—something worth remembering if you venture outdoors in the cold season.

CURRANT *(Ribes)*: Over 70 species of currants and gooseberries are found on the continent. The important thing to remember is that all produce edible berries. Currants thrive in moist, shaded areas, such as along stream banks, gullies, north-facing mountain slopes and shady forests. Some species have prickly stems; others are smooth.

DANDELIONS *(Taraxacum)* are familiar plants that are also useful as food. The stems and leaves can be eaten in an emergency. If necessary, they can be eaten raw, but boiling improves the taste considerably.

Dock *(Rumex)* is an easily recognizable plant found over most of the continent. The stalk is hollow and hard; usually red or brown. At the top are clusters of small green to brown flowers, arranged so tightly they appear to be small berries at first glance. Large, curly leaves stem from the plant's base. The leaves are edible raw, but are more palatable when boiled. Depending on the species, dock frequents varying habitats, from sandy loams to moist weed patches.

Elderberry *(Sambucus)*: These plants vary from shrubs to small trees. The edible fruits, which appear in late summer, vary in color from blue to black. The berries are sour when eaten off the tree, but sweeten if dried in the sun. A red variety of elderberry exists, but avoid it. A few authenticated poisonings have resulted from red elderberries. Look for elderberry along streams and moist mountain slopes.

Ferns: Many species of ferns exist, but none are poisonous. The roots and fronds of many are edible, though not especially nourishing. However, they could stave off starvation in really dire times. Ferns grow on wet ground along streams and lush woodlands. The roots can be eaten raw, but are more palatable when roasted.

Fireweed *(Epilobium)* is a valuable species to remember. It grows in moist soils along streams, in open woods, prairies and on freshly burned or disturbed sites. The characteristic four-petaled flowers, pink or lilac, grow in clusters around the stem, forming a cone tapering to the top. The stems of fireweed can be peeled and eaten raw, or boiled to taste much like asparagus. The young leaves can be consumed when boiled.

GLACIER LILIES *(Erythronium)* are easy to recognize and generally grow in large patches. If you spot one, enough for a meal will be nearby. Also known as dogtooth violets, the plants are common in moist areas of the West, but also frequent moist soils in the East and North. The plant is a few inches high; one thin stem bordered by two smooth, rabbit-eared leaves. The flower hangs down from the top of the stem, and has toothlike petals that flare outward. The leaves can be plucked and eaten raw. The green seedpods taste like string beans and the small, bulbous root is sweet and nutty.

GRASSES: The seeds of all grasses are edible. To collect these, shake the spike-tops over a cloth. The cloth, which may be your shirt or jacket, will catch the seeds, and a lot of chaff as well. The seeds are nourishing, though it takes many to provide a meal. Also, the white tips of all young grass shoots can be eaten.

HAWTHORN *(Crataegus)*: These plants are found in thickets and river bottoms from the Atlantic to the Pacific. The small trees grow rounded crowns, protected by inch-long thorns. As many as 1,200 species are suspected to exist, and all produce edible fruits. The small apples, sometimes called thornapples, are green to red and have a pulpy flesh. Taste varies from good to very poor.

HAZELNUTS *(Corylus)* grow across the continent in woods and thickets. Size ranges from a shrub to a smooth-barked small tree. The nuts are sweet and are contained in bristly husks. Hazelnuts can be eaten raw or ground with rocks into a flour for easy carrying.

HICKORY *(Carya)*: These include pecans, pignuts and shagbark hickory nuts. Hickories grow throughout the East, but are especially common in the South. The nuts are nutritious and good-tasting, with the exception of some pignuts, which sometimes taste bitter. The husks of all *Carya* are smooth.

JERUSALEM ARTICHOKE *(Helianthus)*, also known as sunchoke, inhabits much of the eastern half of the country. The tall sunflower is seen often in fields and in thickets. The flower has yellow petals and a round, brown eye. It isn't uncommon to see the plants reach ten feet or more. The tubers are thick and tasty, and can be eaten raw, boiled or roasted.

JUNIPER *(Juniperus)*: The berries of all junipers are edible, though not always palatable. These evergreens are very common on dry slopes and foothills in the West, but are also found as far east as Labrador. Junipers vary in appearance according to species, but tend to be bushlike with white to gray berries. The berries are eaten raw or sun-dried.

KINNIKINIC (*Arctostaphylos uva-ursi*), also known as bearberry, is scattered throughout the United States and Canada. This shrub lies closely to the ground in mats. Its small, round, leathery leaves and bright red berries are easy to spot. The berries are edible, though mealy and tasteless. They are important emergency food, however, because they are nourishing and cling to the vine year round. Kinnikinic grows in dry woodlands and on hill slopes.

Lichens (*Umbilicaria*): Rock tripe (left); Moss (lichen) (right).

LICHEN *(Umbilicaria)*: Also known as rock tripe, this plant grows on boulders and rock walls. It appears as a wavy, tough leaf a few inches in diameter. Most lichens are edible, but should be soaked in water to remove the purgatives they contain. They can be eaten raw—after soaking—or dried and boiled.

MAPLE *(Acer)*: The inner bark of all maples is edible, and usually sweet and watery. In spring the sap can be tapped and collected in sustaining quantities. The assorted species of maple grow in numerous habitats throughout the country.

MILKWEED *(Asclepias syriaca)* is a nationwide plant, easy to identify and usable in many ways. The plant reaches a height of several feet, but is best for eating purposes when young. When cut, milkweed bleeds a sour-smelling white fluid. The seedpods are tasty when picked in midsummer and boiled. The young leaves, stalks and buds can be eaten raw or boiled.

NETTLE *(Urtica):* You have probably bumped into this mass of stinging leaves at one time or another. The green stems and saw-toothed leaves are covered with needles and should be gathered carefully. When boiled, the leaves lose their rigidity, and serve as vitamin-rich greens. Nettles are common nationwide and are found in fields and thickets.

OAKS *(Quercus)*, in varying species, are common throughout the country. Most produce acorns, which taste good to exceedingly bitter, depending on the species. Fortunately, the bitter compound, tannin, is water soluble, and can be removed by soaking in fresh water. Acorns can be found in large quantities and thus are an important emergency food. They also can be ground with stones. The resulting flour, mixed with water and baked, produces emergency bread.

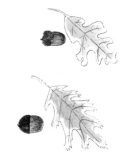

PAPAW *(Asimina triloba)* grows throughout the eastern two-thirds of the United States. You'll find this shrub in rich woods and along stream banks. In autumn, the papaw bears a banana-shaped fruit which tastes much like custard. The fruit is eaten raw, and is sweet and delicious.

Pine *(Pinus).*   Plantain *(Plantago).*

PINES (*Pinus*): All species of pine have edible inner bark and provide subsistence levels of nourishment. However, some pines taste very strong, much like turpentine. Pines that produce cones also produce nuts. Roast a pine cone in fire, then crack it open. Several small edible nuts should fall out.

PLANTAIN *(Plantago)* is found nearly everywhere and is easy to identify. The wavy, ribbed basal leaves are smooth and waxy on top. Several spiked flower heads grow out of the leaf base. The young leaves can be eaten raw, and aren't bad, but the older ones must be boiled.

POPLAR *(Populus)* is a common tree that grows along streams and rivers across the country. Depending on the species, poplar usually has heart-shaped leaves which are smooth and lightly toothed. The inner bark can be peeled and eaten raw in an emergency.

PRICKLY PEAR (*Opuntia*): In desert or very dry regions, this plant is useful for food and water. Prickly pears are green, fleshy lobes of thorny cacti which have yellow, red or orange flowers. The fruit of the plant is red to purple when ripe and can be eaten raw. Depending on locality, the fruit ripens from late summer to fall.

PURSLANE (*Portulaca*) is another common weed that is also edible. The plant grows nearly everywhere on this and other continents. The leaves and leafstalks can be eaten either raw or simmered.

RASPBERRY (*Rubus*): Includes blackberries, dewberries and thimbleberries—all of which are closely related. You'll find these low shrubs in rich woods along streams, trails and logging roads. The fruits are very sweet and provide sugar and vitamins. Young shoots and twigs can be peeled and eaten raw.

ROSE (*Rosa*): Wild rose is easily recognized by its reddish, thorny stems and gentle pink to red flowers. There are many species, and the range and habitat is wide, but roses generally grow in moist soils. The fruits—rose hips—are high in Vitamin C and can be eaten raw. The petals of the flower are also eaten raw.

SEAWEEDS: Occasionally, writers of edible plant guides declare heartily that all seaweeds are edible, and thus are great emergency food. To my knowledge, no seaweed is decidedly poisonous, but there are still a few limiting considerations. First, many seaweeds contain purgative substances that can sap your energy. Second, seaweed is often tough to digest when eaten raw and the high salt content sponges up body water—a prime consideration when fresh water is scarce. Lastly, you may find yourself mildly allergic to some forms of seaweed, which is uncomfortable at best if the plant is ingested.

With all this in mind, you still may be forced to consume seaweeds. Most are edible and contain high amounts of iodine and vitamins. Eat sea plants slowly, and only little bits at a time. If possible, wash them thoroughly in fresh water before eating. While it's true that an expert can find tasty and nutritious seaweed, the average person is better off foraging for the sea animals that coexist with the weeds.

SERVICEBERRY *(Amelanchier)* is a small shrub that bears tasty blue berries early in the year. You'll find serviceberry in open woods, near forest edges and along streams and lakes. The berries are eaten raw or sun-dried.

SOLOMON'S SEAL *(Polygonatum commutatum)*: This plant is easily recognized and is nearly worldwide in distribution. Large, wavy leaves form alternate rungs up a single stem. Red fruits cling in pairs down the main stalk. The young shoots of this plant are edible raw or cooked. The roots can be boiled or roasted.

SORREL *(Oxalis)* is another wide-ranging plant that produces edible leaves. The round leaves are attached by long leafstalks and circle the main stem. The leaves are tart and can be eaten raw or boiled. You'll find sorrel in dry fields and sandy or gravelly soils from coast to coast.

SPRING BEAUTY *(Claytonia lanceolata)*: These delicate little flowers are attached to a sizable tuber which is both edible and palatable. Spring beauties are among the first flowers to bloom in the spring; usually white or pink five-petaled flowers. They grow throughout most of the moist forests and stream banks of the continent. The tuber is attached to a frail stem, and a digging stick is generally needed to remove it completely.

SPRUCE *(Picea)*: The inner bark of spruce can be peeled and eaten raw in spring and early summer. The young branch tips and buds can also be eaten raw. Spruce are common in evergreen forests across the northern half of the continent, and in high altitudes in some southern states.

THISTLE *(Circium* or *Sonchus)* is another backyard plant that is found nearly everywhere. The leaves are large and irregular; the stems green and armored with needles. The flower head is yellow to purple, depending on the species. The young leaves of thistle can be eaten raw or boiled. The roots also are edible raw, boiled or roasted. The peeled stems, steeped in boiling water, can be eaten. Thistle is common in open field, dry soils and weed patches.

WATER LILIES *(Nymphaea)* are plants that almost everyone has seen floating in quiet lake or river waters. They appear as leathery green pads floating on the water, and have tough green stems which anchor them to the bottom. The roots and tubers are edible, and can be pulled from above or dug out with your toes while wading. Eat the tubers and roots raw if necessary; boil or roast them to remove bitterness if possible.

WILLOW *(Salix)*: The sheer abundance and diversity of this genus makes it important to remember as a source of emergency food. The inner bark, shoots and buds can be eaten raw, as can the young leaves which provide vital Vitamin C.

YUCCA *(Yucca)*: There are several species of yucca, all of them edible. The plants are found mostly in arid regions, particularly in the southern Rockies. Swordlike leaves revolve around the single stem, and yellow or green flowers cluster to form a bullet-shaped top. The flowers, buds and flower stalks can be eaten raw, boiled or roasted. Some species produce a large, pulpy fruit that tastes much like a banana. The fruit can be eaten raw or roasted.

Other Plants

As noted earlier, many more edible plants exist. Those listed are especially common and easy to recognize and use. However, be aware of local plants that are abundant. Near my Montana home, for example, arrowleaf balsamroot is a common plant that has large, starchy tubers. I haven't listed it because, to my knowledge, it is limited to the West in habitat and range. Other plants, also excluded from the list, are common and edible. Examples are various cherries and grapes that are too numerous and diversified to name individually. Also, walnuts, butternuts, chestnuts and other familiar, large nuts are available in many areas. Watch for these.

Another fact to keep in mind is, the farther north you go, the more edible species you find. In the Arctic, for example, virtually all plants are edible. The only exception is one small fungi. On the other hand, the farther south you go, the more likely you are to find poisonous plants. In tropical or subtropical areas, be certain the plants you gather are safe.

Mushrooms

Most mycologists and wild-food experts warn amateurs to avoid mushrooms unless they know them well. Many species are deadly. Others produce violent vomiting, paralysis and hallucinations. To be safe, forget about mushrooms for emergency use unless you are sure of identification. Even then, realize that they provide little nourishment anyway. Mushroom picking is a great pastime, but for emergencies, concentrate on animals and green plants for food.

In Case You're Not Certain

Say a crisis arises, and you must live off the land. All the nice book knowledge is jumbled in your mind and you can't seem to positively identify any plant. What then?

Well, there are a few guidelines for testing a plant for edibility. First, it's a general rule that plants with white, red or black sap should be avoided. However, there are exceptions. Common milkweed, which has a number of edible parts, has thick white sap. So does the edible dandelion. But if a plant is totally unfamiliar, colored sap is a warning to be careful.

Even plants with clear fluids can be toxic. To test them, follow these steps: Place a bit of the leaf, root, tuber or berry (whatever part you want to eat) on your tongue. If it burns or irritates your mouth, spit it out immediately. However, if there is no bad sensation after a few moments, chew the material lightly. Again, any adverse reaction means the plant is not edible. If the plant tastes exceedingly bad, avoid it. Remember though, that bitterness is common in raw edibles. The taste must be unusually bad.

If the flavor is tolerable, remove the material and wait a few minutes. If your mouth and tongue seem unaffected, eat a small amount of the plant. If, after a few hours, your body does not react unfavorably, the plant is probably edible. If some symptom of poisoning does occur—nausea, dizziness, cramps—induce vomiting immediately by drinking water and poking your finger down your throat.

Obviously this tasting method is not particularly desirable or effective. In a pinch it can work, but in the long run it's much better to know a few edible species positively.

Animal Food

With a little ingenuity you should be able to obtain some fresh meat to supplement your plant diet. The techniques I'm about to describe are for the most part illegal under normal circumstances.

Virtually all animal flesh is edible. This includes the whole gamut from grasshoppers to grizzly bears. For the majority of emergencies, small animals will be your mainstay. They do not require intricate trapping skills, and are easy to prepare. Don't overlook them with hopes of catching something larger and perhaps more desirable. A snake, frog or salamander may not be as pleasing a food item as a rabbit or deer, but the flesh is equally nutritious and not at all bad tasting. A slightly comforting thought to consider is no matter what animal you're about to devour—be it an ant or boiled fish head—some culture in the world probably regards it as a delicacy.

Mammals and Birds

Some of the larger furred and feathered animals likely to be encountered can be caught with bare hands, a rock or stick. One example is the porcupine. These slow, rather clumsy beasts can be chased down and killed with a club. The same applies for opossums, and in desert country, armadillos. Mice, rats and other rodents can be flushed from mulch piles and rock dens with water or fire, and clubbed as they attempt escape. Waterfowl lose their flight feathers during summer moult and can be chased and caught or clubbed. Many birds sit tightly on their nests and can be approached close enough to hit with a long stick or rock. Don't overlook the eggs or young birds that occupy the nest—all are edible and nourishing. Young fledglings (birds that have just left the nest) often are limited in their caution and flying ability. If pressed, most will offer an opportunity for a well-tossed rock or stick.

Grouse in wilderness areas are often tolerant of an approaching human. A throwing stick tossed into a group is likely to knock down at least one bird. Throw the stick with a sidearm motion, so that it spins into the flock. If you miss completely, follow the flushing birds with your eyes and mark where they land. Keep pressing them until you collect one.

Snowshoe hares, cottontail rabbits and various squirrels can sometimes be approached close enough to be stoned. All of these animals instinctively remain motionless, depending on their camouflage to hide them. If you walk slowly and stealthy toward the animal, you can often get within throwing range.

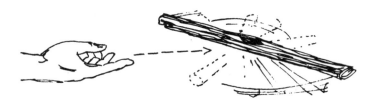

Throwing a heavy stick this way increases your odds of connecting with the target.

In winter, muskrats and beavers live in thatch houses which appear as brown mounds on lake or swamp ice, or along the banks. By stalking slowly, and quietly—I mean with absolutely no noise or vibration whatever—it is possible to pad your way to the house without alerting the occupant. A solid pointed stick, preferably barbed, is thrust through the roof and into the house. The idea is to skewer a hapless muskrat or beaver. Since muskrats tend to bunch together for warmth, it's very likely your spear will find flesh. If you connect, pin the animal down and kick apart the house. If you attempt to lift a full-size rat or beaver, it may slip off the stick and escape. This method has been used for decades by Indians and trappers, but it must be done silently or vibrations transmitted through the ice will send the animal down its underwater escape exit. Also, beavers are hefty creatures attaining the weights of 30 to 40 pounds and they can put up an awesome struggle. Have a knife or club on hand to quickly dispatch the pinned animal.

If you do have a weapon along, a firearm or bow, you obviously have more killing power and range. But don't waste precious ammo or arrows by shooting at difficult targets. A running animal is hard to hit, harder yet to kill with one shot. Avoid shooting at bears or other potentially dangerous game with small-caliber bullets. A .22 can bring down a deer, elk or moose if the animal is shot in the ear or brain, but you must be very close, and a good shot. Body shots at these large animals will only cause wounds, and waste your ammunition. Also, don't waste bullets on prey that can be killed with a club or rock. You needn't shoot the head off a grouse with a .270 if the bird is within easy stick range. Save the cartridge for something larger.

No matter if you're hunting with a Weatherby magnum or a throwing stick, your main task lies in finding a target. This is where hunting skill and savvy can save you. Even if you aren't a sporthunter, it's good emergency practice to take note of the following tips on finding and collecting animals.

The first requirement seems obvious enough: To find animals, you must first find their habitat. Many wildlife species frequent "edge" areas, places where two distinct plant communities blend together or meet sharply. A frequent example is where a forest meets a meadow. The woods offer protection, the meadow offers food. Another example of edge is a lakeshore or stream bank.

Animals are also attracted to abundant food sources. For deer, this may be a patch of nut-laden hickory or oak trees. For scavengers such as foxes, weasels or bears, the carcass of a dead animal may be a drawing card.

Once you find what seems to be a potentially good area, scout it carefully for sign. Look for runways—well-worn animal paths that wind through the woods and across meadows. Search along runways for signs of recent use. Look for fecal droppings, which will be dark and shiny when fresh. If they are dry or chalky white, they may be too old to be useful indicators that animals are still present. If you find nothing but old droppings, the animal you are chasing may be in an entirely different area. Search also for tracks. Fresh ones will be sharply outlined in dirt, mud or snow.

If you find recent sign, hunt the area slowly and carefully, pausing often to look and listen. Remember that most animals move about at dawn and dusk, and bed down in the day; plan to hunt at the most optimum times. Be very careful not to pass hidden game; don't look for entire animals, but search for irregular shapes. In forests, which are composed mostly of vertical lines, a horizontal line should be inspected carefully. It may be a bedded deer or hunched rabbit. Be alert for flicks of movement or color; a speck of black that glints may dissolve into the head of a camouflaged grouse, a branch that sways out of rhythm may be the upper tine of an elk antler. It is important that you watch much more than you walk.

When a well-used runway is discovered, you may want to hunt it in other ways. For rabbits and smaller game, you can set deadfalls or snares. For larger animals, if you have a suitable weapon, you may want to build a blind nearby and wait for the animal to pass.

In arid regions, one of the best places to wait for game is near a waterhole. Invariably, animals of all types will filter in to drink. Birds such as quail and chukar partridge water and dust in the evening, and can be likely targets for a rock or stick. Larger game—javelinas, antelope and deer—will come in for water also, and offer a chance for a rifle, bow or trap.

Snares and Deadfalls

Before launching into a discussion of trap assembly, let's take a nut-shell look at trapping basics.

Choose the kind of animal you want to catch, then set your snare or deadfall exclusively for it.

Setting up a "general" trap for any animal that wanders by is usually futile. For survival purposes, plan to catch the animal that appears to be the most abundant.

Anticipate what your quarry is going to do, then set your trap to catch it doing it.

If you spot a rabbit runway complete with fresh tracks and droppings, you can assume a bunny will pass through sometime during the day or night. Plan to catch it by setting a runway snare. If you discover a lived-in burrow, figure the occupant will eventually come out (or go in) and construct a deadfall or string snare at the entrance.

Take pains not to disturb the area near your trap. Animals view warily any changes in their familiar territory.

Do all you can to force an animal into your trap.

If you set a trail snare, form a fence on both sides of the trail that funnels into your snare. Keep the fence simple, and natural looking. For small animals, use bits of small branches as gentle guides. Larger creatures obviously require heavier fencing. The idea is to make contact with the trap inevitable.

Now to the actual construction of snares and deadfalls. There are many crafty sets, but for emergency purposes, learn to build two or three different snares and a couple of deadfalls. Keep them simple. Some sets are wired, notched, carved contraptions that resemble a Rube Goldberg invention. These are fine for showing off to friends and Boy Scout audiences, but are unnecessary in the woods.

The simplest snare is nothing more than a noose secured to a heavy object. The noose can be made from wire, fishing line, rope, shoelaces, braided vines or anything else that bears semblance to a cord and is strong enough to hold a struggling animal. The snare is placed in a likely spot—a runway, den entrance, feeding area—high enough from the ground to catch the animal's head and neck. Limp noose material needs to be propped open by small twigs or grasses. When the animal pokes through the snare, the loop tightens. On a very basic snare, the animal struggles against the line and is bogged down by the snare anchor.

A more complicated variation of this idea is attaching the snare to a bent sapling so the animal is jerked from the ground and hanged. A sen-

A simple snare.
A spring snare, tied to a green sapling, is harder to build than a simple noose snare, but is decidedly more effective.

sitive trigger holds the sapling in place until the snare is disturbed.

For squirrels, an effective trap is the leaning pole set. A long, slender pole is equipped with several nooses and propped against a tree. If a squirrel is in the area, it will inspect the pole by scampering up and down the length of it. When the squirrel becomes caught in a noose, its struggles tighten the snare more, holding it until the trapper arrives.

An effective squirrel trap is made by rigging nooses to a pole and leaning it against a live tree.
To catch perching birds, a perch snare is effective. The bird lands on the trigger to nibble the bait, the trigger falls from the weight, and the noose cinches around the bird's feet.

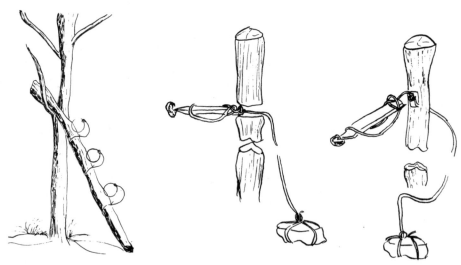

To catch birds, you can fashion a perch snare. This is nothing more than a pole rigged with a baited trigger stick. When a bird lands, the trigger falls and the snare tangles around the bird's feet. This is shown clearly in the illustration.

Another effective bird snare is a group of forked poles thrust into the ground to form an octagon. Cross poles are set across the forks and lashed down. Snares are attached to the top poles and bait is set in the center of the trap. Any bird that attempts to enter the inside of the octagon to reach the bait will become entangled in a snare. This is also illustrated.

It is possible to catch large animals in a trap, and the best rig for this purpose is a pit, foot-snare combination. A shallow pit is dug and cross-hatched with light twigs. Over the twigs spread your snare, which is attached to a heavy log or rock. The twigs and snare are covered with leaves, grass or snow for concealment. When an animal steps on the covering, it breaks through and is caught in the snare. The log or rock drag keeps the animal from moving too far or fast while you catch and kill it. The trick here is digging the pit where an animal is likely to step. This can be near a bait of some sort, or on a runway.

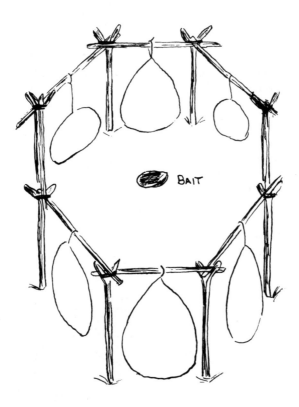

BAIT

Ground-feeding birds such as quail and pheasants can be caught with the above snare.

A pit, foot-snare trap for larger animals.

A useful supplement or alternative to snares are deadfalls. These work by crushing the animal to death with a rigged weight. Two kinds are worth knowing. The first is the classic Figure 4 set. For this, three sticks are whittled to fit together in the shape of a 4. A heavy log or

The basic Figure 4 deadfall.

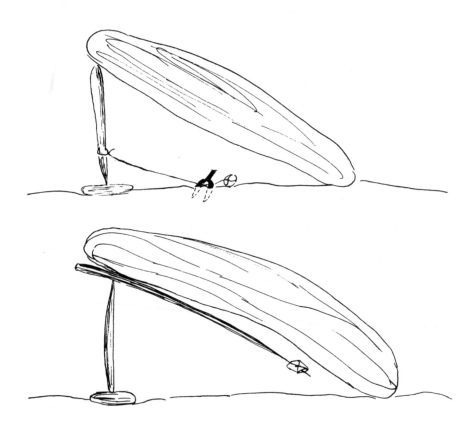

Two-stick deadfalls are less effective than the Figure 4 deadfall, but easier to build.

rock is balanced on the top stick and a bait is placed on the trigger. The slightest movement of the bait causes the log or rock to fall. The Figure 4 deadfall is handy to know, but sometimes difficult to make in the field. A simpler design uses only two sticks to prop up the deadfall. A piece of bait is tied to the supporting stick. When the bait is moved, the stick is pulled out and the weight falls. This trap is easier to build than the Figure 4, but isn't as sensitive or effective.

Fish

If you are carrying your emergency pack, you have hooks, line and maybe a lure. With this you can make an old-fashioned pole out of any long, springy green branch. Lacking commercial split shot, tie on a pebble or a small rock for a sinker. Lob your lure or bait upcurrent in streams and allow it to drift down riffles and pools and under eroded banks. In fast water, fish often lie behind stream boulders to escape the current. A lure drifted along the edge of a rock may produce a strike. In lakes, probe carefully around and through weed patches, log tangles and rock piles. In all shallow-water fishing, keep your profile low, and avoid casting a shadow on the water.

If you have no fishing gear, you must improvise. Line can be woven from bark, root fibers, thread, canvas and other materials. The technique of making line is discussed in Chapter 18. For hooks, several makeshift substitutes will do. First, search the items you are carrying for one that can be bent or twisted to form a hook. Nails will work, as will needles and safety pins. Strap attachments on backpacks can be pried apart and bent into satisfactory fishhooks. If you have nothing that will work, a gorge can be carved out of a straight, thin length of hardwood. This is nothing more than a small piece of wood or bone carved to roughly resemble the horns of a Texas longhorn. A notch is cut in the center for line attachment. The gorge is buried in the bait and swallowed by the fish. A jerk on the line swings the gorge about and lodges it in the fish's gullet.

Hooks can be made from thorny tree stems such as hawthorn and mesquite. The main branch serves as the shank, the thorn as the hook. You'll need to whittle these some to make them effective.

A forked branch of small diameter can be carved to make a workable hook. The crotch of the fork is whittled to form the hook bend. A notch is cut in the shank for line attachment.

Fishhooks can be improvised by bending a nail, carving a bone or wood gorge, utilizing a thorny branch, firmly tying a small pen-knife or carving a forked branch.

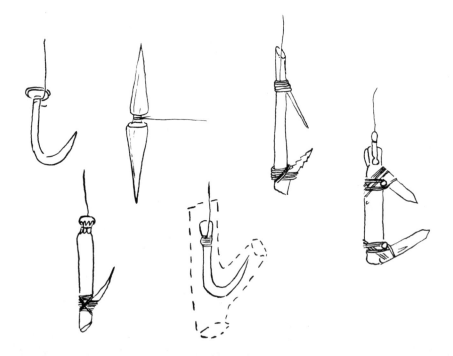

There are also a number of fishing methods that don't involve hook and line. The most primitive method is catching fish by hand. I have done this myself a number of times, and have seen it done by others. One way is to sneak up on your belly to the edge of a stream bank and peek over. If you spot a fish finning in the current, very slowly crawl your hands down the side of the bank until they near water. Let me interject what may not be obvious: you do all of this from the fish's backside. That is, you want to sneak up on it from behind. Slowly move your hands under the fish's stomach. Some advise that you rub the fish's belly lightly to calm it. Anyway, when your hand (or hands if you can reach with both) is directly under the fish's stomach, lift up steadily. When the fish nears the surface of the water, flip it quickly onto the bank. As remarkable as this sounds, it really works. Of course, your main task is locating a fish that is within reach. This method works best when fish are spawning in the spring and fall. Then they are more likely to be in shallow, clear water.

If you can't see any fish that are close enough to stalk by hand, there is an alternative hand-catching method. Walk into a shallow, clear pool. The fish in the pool will undoubtedly streak away. Reach down in the water and form a cup with both hands, keeping your body on the upstream side of your hands. (The cave formed by your hands should face downstream.) Stand storklike in this position. The idea is that when the trout reenter the pool—as they assuredly will—one will find the shade, current cushion and security of your hand-cave and nestle into it. While this is not a surefire method, and admittedly is a limited one, it does work, and may be worth a try at times.

One day on Montana's Rock Creek, I sat down on the bank to smoke a pipe and contemplate the scenery. The bank was low and my legs were in the water from the knees down. Ten minutes or so later I glanced into the water and saw a ten-inch rainbow finning lightly between my legs. Trout and other fish will fall for shade traps, and under the right conditions making one may produce some food.

Another primitive fishing method is spearing. The spear can be nothing more than a sharpened stick, or better yet, a sharpened forked stick. However, the most practical lance is the trap-spear. To construct this, first find a green branch of about an inch in diameter and five or six feet long. Split one end with a knife and rock. Insert a wedge to hold the split open, and carve pointed teeth on the inside of both halves. Remove the wedge and wind rope, bark or cord around the base of the jaws to keep it from splitting any further. The jaws are pried open and held by a thin stick. When the spear is thrust over a fish, the twig breaks and the jaws snap down on the quarry.

When ice covers the water, you can still catch fish by chipping a hole with a knife or rock and fishing through it. The best method is to attach something with glitter—a button, piece of aluminum foil or ring—to your

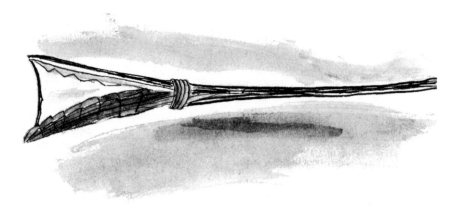

A trap-spear carved from a green branch.

hook and jig it up and down slowly. Lower your lure until it touches bottom (you'll feel the line go slack when it hits), then jig slowly and methodically, working up to the surface. When a fish hits, keep steady pressure on the line as you bring it in hand over hand.

What about baits? Well, finding terrestrial and aquatic baits is generally easy. So easy, in fact, that it may be wise sometimes to give up unproductive fishing and eat your bait!

Insects

A researcher at the University of Wisconsin, studying insects as potential food, has discovered that many bugs have higher levels of protein than beef or soybeans. Eating insects is nothing new to many primitive cultures, who owe much of their sustenance to ants, grubs and termites. However, the average "civilized" person would cringe at the thought of knocking back seconds of fried earthworm or roast grasshopper. But in times of emergency, insects can be your food windfall.

Consider the benefits. Insects are abundant, in some form or another, in all seasons and climates. Most are edible when cooked, and the taste is not at all bad. Most important, they are nutritious and will keep you alive when nothing else can be found.

Grasshoppers can be caught easily early in the morning when dampness and cool temperatures make them sluggish. You can pluck them like berries from weedstalks and grass stands. By kicking apart rotten logs you can find grubs and beetles. Other insects are found in tree bark, under rocks and logs and in thick leaf and forest litter. In winter, break open dry, standing weedstalks in search of various fly larvae. (These also make excellent emergency ice-fishing bait.)

Don't forget aquatic insects. They are easy to collect throughout the year and offer an abundant yield. Upturn underwater rocks to find these, especially in shallow, fast-moving water. In deeper water, your shirt or some other cloth tied to two poles makes a useful collecting net. Place the net downstream and on the bottom while kicking over rocks and disturbing the streambed. The dislodged insects will float into your improvised net. Incidentally, aquatic insects also make excellent baits for emergency fishing.

All insects should be cooked. Although some can be safely eaten raw, many contain parasites which are dangerous unless cooked. The method of cooking can be boiling, roasting, parching, frying or sun drying. As you can imagine, a fried grub is not an appetizing sight. But if you can force yourself to swallow it, and keep it down, it can save your life.

Other Food Sources

We have barely scratched the surface of possible foods. Frogs are common around water and can be speared, caught with a hook, clubbed or grabbed by hand. Crayfish are good to eat, as are small minnows and fish. Both can be caught by using your shirt as a net. Place the net near the edge of a weed patch and thrash the water. The small fish that dash out can be scooped up in your net.

Shellfish often are found in clean rivers and lakes. Probe the bottom thoroughly for them. The shells can be cracked with a rock and the meat boiled.

Turtles and snakes are easy to catch and kill, but be wary of both. Poisonous snakes should be pinned first with a stick and then beheaded. Beware of the amputated head—it can still bite. Bury it or cover it with a log or rock. The flesh is separated from the skin and fried or roasted near the fire. Turtles provide nutritious fatty meat and can be clubbed or caught with hook and bait. Take care to avoid the remarkably strong jaws of snappers. Turtle meat should be boiled or fried; the fat can be rendered near a fire, or even from a hot sun.

Lizards can be caught in some areas, though sometimes they are extremely fast. The best times to chase them are during cool periods when they become sluggish. Then they can be approached and clubbed. Be sure the animal is dead before you grab it. Many have painful and occasionally poisonous bites.

Another possible source of food is, unappetizingly enough, carrion. If you come upon a recently killed animal you may be able to salvage some usable meat. This could be fox-killed rabbit or leftover moose from a grizzly kill. Of course, you can't count on finding a freshly done-in animal, but you should be aware of the possibility.

Seafood

Food is plentiful in and along the sea. Many types of fish are present, and almost all are edible raw or cooked. The fish can be caught with

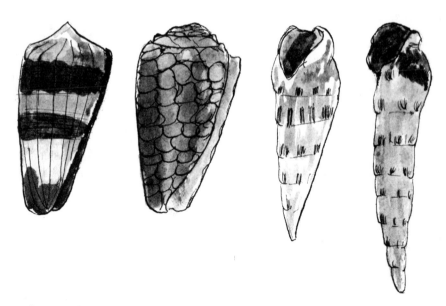

Only two types of mollusks are poisonous—cones and terebras. Fortunately, they are rare specimens, found mostly in tropical waters.

hook and line, speared during low tide or attracted by torch light at night and hooked or gaffed. During low tide, comb the beach for crabs, shellfish, lobsters, shrimp and sea cucumbers. Overturn rocks, inspect pools of water, look in crevices and burrows. Most of the animals you find are edible.

Almost all of the mollusks — clams, scallops, oysters, barnacles, conches—are edible with a couple of rare exceptions. Two types of mollusks, cones and terebras (see illustration), are poisonous. However, cones and terebras are scarce, and are found mostly in tropical waters. Black mussels in the North Pacific are sometimes dangerous and should be avoided if other food sources are available.

Most of the seashore animals can be captured by digging, grabbing or spearing. Some can be eaten raw, such as oysters and the inner muscle of sea cucumbers. Others should be cooked by boiling or roasting. Most shellfish are good boiled, as are crabs and shrimp.

Food for Traveling

If you have to travel to get out of your predicament, you will need to carry what food you have with you. If you make a large kill, such as a deer or elk, you can't pack the meat fresh. The best alternative is to dry the meat into jerky. This also works when you make a large catch of fish, or find an abundant number of small animals.

"Jerking" meat is nothing more than drying it. This is best accomplished by cutting the meat into thin strips and letting it dry in the sun. A smoky fire built underneath the meat strips will keep away flies and bugs and impart a smoke-cured taste. Before drying, cut away fat to prevent the meat from becoming rancid.

However, don't throw the fat away. Render it to liquid near a fire and mix with shreds of jerky. When the mixture is thick and heavy, in a consistency similar to ground beef, let it harden. Wrap it tightly in a bag or cloth. This is a form of pemmican, and is excellent trail food. The fat will keep you alive when lean meat won't.

Aim for Water

If you look back through this chapter, you will notice that most of the easiest-to-get food is obtained in, on or near water. This is an important point to remember. If you need food, head for the nearest lake, stream, river, swamp or sea. The largest number of edible and recognizable plants grow near water; fish, frogs, turtles and snakes frequent water, and most terrestrial animals come to drink at least once a day. In short, waterways are the supermarkets of the outdoors.

14

Finding Water

Water is essential to your survival, and you must consume sustaining amounts of it regularly. That's the nub of it, plain and simple. So without further introduction, let's discuss the purely practical aspects of water: how to carry and conserve it; how to find it; and, when necessary, how to manufacture moisture by condensing it from the air.

Carrying Enough

Regardless of where you travel, whether in water-soaked lake country or parched desert lands, you should always carry some water with you. On short jaunts of no more than a few hours, a quart canteen of water is plenty. But on longer excursions—particularly during hot weather—a quart of water just isn't enough.

A man can stay alive on a quart of water daily if the temperature is mild and his exertion is slight. But the typical day outdoors leaves the body in need of about a half-gallon of water—twice as much as most canteens hold. In extremely hot, arid regions, or with much physical exercise, it may take as much as a gallon to keep you going. If you're afoot, a gallon jug of water is a bit cumbersome to carry, so you must seek the best alternative: refill your canteen at *every* freshwater source. It's taboo to pass by a stream or clean lake without replenishing a needy water supply, and the lazy intention of filling your canteen at the next good water could get you into trouble. The next water could be ten miles away.

If you're near a vehicle, things become much simpler. Stash a five-gallon jug of water in the trunk or wherever convenient, and tap it frequently.

When you're planning a trip into arid regions, carefully check a map to pinpoint water potential. If water is scarce, plan to camp near a river, pond or stock tank at night. But remember, useful as maps are, they aren't always accurate. A stream that appears wide on the map may be little more than a trickle in actuality, or worse yet, it may be completely dry. And there's always the chance that the blue waters of the map are in reality muddy, dirty cesspools, badly contaminated and undesirable even when purified. It's good insurance, in such areas, to carry a second canteen of fresh water in your pack.

Locating Water

But what if your water runs out, and no free-flowing water is in sight? Then you must make a calculated effort to find some, utilizing all of the natural clues you can find.

Using Landforms and Geology

The terrain is your first clue to finding water. In forested, hilly country, you can locate distant streams by searching for the narrow, V-shaped drainage cuts that are carved between ridges and slopes. If you spot such a cut, there's a good chance of finding water at its base. (Water flows downhill, and is most likely to collect in the lower elevations. Your chance of finding water improves if you leave the ridges and search the bottomlands.)

If you come upon a dry streambed, follow it downhill, keeping an eye out for an emerging spring. Ephemeral streams often appear to be dry during the hot months, when in fact the water is still flowing underground. At various points the water rises to the surface, and a thirsty outdoorsman can cash in on this fact. Don't expect a gushing torrent though. The spring will most likely be no more than a trickle.

If you can't find surface water in a stream, probe beneath the surface. Sometimes the water flows through the porous gravel a few inches underground, and a little digging makes it available. But if your probing reveals thick layers of dry gravel, look elsewhere. The water has settled through the irregular bits of rock and may lie many feet below.

A word here about digging for water. Digging is work, and work means sweat. When you sweat you lose water rapidly, and in particularly hot, dry conditions, you could die of heat stroke long before you approached water. If water doesn't appear soon after you begin your excavation, give up and look elsewhere, or if you must continue dig-

Digging in a dry streambed can sometimes unearth water. X's mark the best spots to dig—at outer bends in the stream, and at the base of the steep bluff.

ging, do so when conditions aren't as severe, such as at night, or early and late in the day.

When prospecting dry washes, concentrate on the outer bends of the stream, digging into the undercut banks. Water seeps into these deeper, usually more absorbent sides. If you uncover sand in such a bend, particularly moist sand, water may be near. A scooped-out burrow in such sand could fill with water in a few hours.

Any streambed that has steep bluffs along its border is especially worth examining, since the underground water table is nearest to the surface at the base of hills. If you don't find water in the streambed, check the bluffs themselves. Look for cracks in rock walls where water trickles, or for pockets and crevices that catch and hold rain. On clay bluffs, noticeable wet spots appear where underground water is trapped in a prison of impermeable clay. Digging into such a spot may uncover a small reservoir of water.

In sandy regions, water collects and drains down the sides of steep dunes. Digging at the base of such dunes may lead to water. If the land is at sea level, like much of Florida for example, you can often dig a foot or so into the sand with your hands and strike water.

A thirsty man may be particularly frustrated to find himself along a saltwater beach, where there is plenty of water but of a type he can't use. An old water-finding trick in such places is to dig a hole into the sand, just below the high-tide line. Since fresh water is lighter than salt water, it will fill in the hole first. There's only one catch: Fresh water must be present in the sand before this can work. Nevertheless, if you

Water collects at the base of steep sand dunes and rock bluffs. In rock bluffs, look also for pockets and depressions in the rocks that may be holding water.

need water the tactic is worth a try. If rain has fallen recently, there should be enough fresh water in the sand to keep you alive.

Using Vegetation

Using vegetation, often in conjunction with landforms, is another way to locate water. Whenever you spot a clump of green growth on an otherwise sterile rock face or clay bluff, inspect it carefully. It almost assuredly means water is present. In the same vain, lush green growth that stands out from the surrounding vegetation may be a clue to an underground spring or an apex in the water table. Digging may uncover water a few inches below the surface.

Some plants are especially good indicators of abundant moisture. Ferns, for example, *when growing in isolated patches*, are veritable trail marks for tracking down water. Willows are nearly always associated with moisture, and their presence should be noted when water is needed. Cottonwoods are also water oriented, and, like willows, can be spotted from long distances. If you see a line of willows or cottonwoods in the distance, there's a good chance they border water. Cattails and bulrushes always grow in moist soils, and if water isn't present on the surface around these plants, it will be found within a foot or so underground.

Don't get the impression, though, that the mere presence of any vegetation indicates obtainable water. Plants have evolved a number of adap-

Although survival literature has overemphasized water-bearing plants, you can find sustaining amounts of liquid in some succulent vegetation, such as the barrel cactus pictured above.

tations which allow them to find and conserve water in even the harshest climates. Mesquite, for example, a thorny shrub of the arid Southwest, has roots that penetrate up to 40 or 50 feet deep. Mesquite does indicate water, but water you'd need a steam shovel to reach.

Aside from marking water-rich areas, some plants are water reservoirs in themselves. Frankly, survival literature has overemphasized water-bearing plants to the point of disillusionment. You cannot stab a cactus with your knife and take a shower in the outpouring. Nor can you always sate your thirst from a length of water-filled grapevine. You can, however, extract life-sustaining quantities of water from some types of vegetation.

Tree sap is largely water, and can be tapped at times to provide moisture, though water is probably nearby in other, more useful and obtainable forms. The celebrated grapevine can be cut and drained of juice. Make the first cut as high as you can reach, to prevent the sap from flowing upward, then cut the lower stem. You can drain the juice right into your mouth. However, grapevines are not always full of water, and even if they were, water is most likely present nearby in a more convenient form.

In desert lands, the barrel cactus is a recognized water source. Hack off the top and mash the insides with a stick or knife. A thick, gluelike liquid will collect at the bottom, and will quench your thirst. As an alternative to this approach, cut out chunks of pulp and suck out the moisture. This same technique is also used on the prickly pear cactus. The thorny skin is sliced off with a knife and the moist pulp is chewed, dehydrated and spit out.

Animal Signs

Closely observe animal movements and signs and they may lead you to water. Perhaps the most useful pointers are birds. If you see them flying in a particular direction, take note. Remember that birds fly to water in the evening and away from it in the morning. Continuous strings of doves or waterfowl passing overhead at sunset are a good clue that water can be found by heading in the same direction. Also, birds often circle a water hole before landing, and so provide another clue to watch for.

Game trails that work downhill or funnel in one direction usually point to water, especially in arid regions. Sometimes, you may see the animals themselves moving along. For example, it's common to see mule deer filter down the ridges at dusk, heading for an evening drink.

Other Water Sources

There are many other ways for a thinking man to find water. Water collects in moss-lined hollow logs and in rock cracks and depressions.

Dew collects on vegetation, and can be sopped up and used as drinking water.

It can be sponged up with cloth or a large leaf and wrung into a receptacle. Similarly, water can be soaked from moist ground or sand, or from mud, but it would need to be filtered, and probably purified.

Dew collects on grass and leaves in the early morning and again in the evening. Use a cloth to sponge up the moisture, then ring out the water into a canteen, or straight into your mouth. Dew is nothing more than cooled water vapor, and it forms wherever warm, moist air contacts a cool surface. You can capitalize on this by collecting the dew from your car hood or window, gun barrel or any other glass or metal object. Rocks also cool enough at night to cause beads of moisture to form on them in the morning. Sop up all the dew you can find; it can keep you going when no other water is present.

More obvious forms of water exist. Snow, of course, can be melted and used. So can ice. All rainwater is drinkable, and should be collected when water is a concern. Spread out your poncho, emergency tarp or even your shirt to catch the rain and channel it into a receptacle. Gather all the water possible, and when your container is filled, drink all you can. Your body is a great storage tank, and in extraordinarily dire times,

Make a rain funnel with your tarp or rain suit to gather all the rainwater you can.

you can absorb even more water through the rectal tissue—up to a pint more than you would be able to otherwise.

If you lack the means to form a rain-catching funnel, tie your shirt or any other cloth to a bush or rock and allow it to absorb rain. Periodically wring the water into your mouth or canteen.

Another way to gather rainwater without a receptacle is to dam a dry wash or drainage rill with rocks or logs. This is especially effective in desert areas, where the compacted soil holds out more water than it lets in, increasing the surface runoff. The water that collects behind your makeshift dam will be dirty with sediment, and will need to be filtered and, if possible, purified.

Making Your Own Water

Anyone who travels into dry areas should carry the essentials for making a solar still—a device that produces water by condensing it from the air. The main ingredient for the still is a six-by-six-foot square of clear plastic. The plastic is spread over a pit dug a couple of feet into the soil, and dirt or stones are placed around the edges to hold it in place and seal off outside air. A fist-size rock is dropped on the center of the plastic, weighing it down so that it forms a cone into the pit. Inside the pit, and underneath the plastic cone, is placed a receptacle of some kind—a canteen, coffee cup, hat, tin can or anything that holds liquid.

A solar still can extract moisture from the air and ground—in any terrain, in any climate.

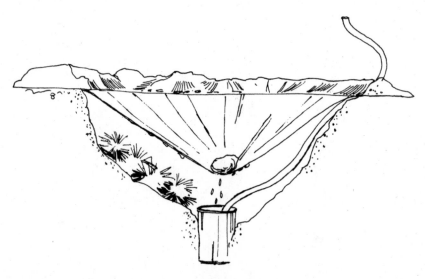

Utilizing salt water to make a solar still.

As the plastic heats from the sun, the cooler ground air condenses into water droplets on the cone, which eventually drip into the container. A five-foot length of rubber tubing is used for drinking. One end is placed in the container, and the tube is run up along the side of the pit and out of the plastic. (The tubing is optional but recommended. By using it, you don't have to disturb the still to take a drink. If you remove the plastic to drink by hand from the container, you have to wait a couple of hours for the still to begin producing water again.)

The solar still will work as is, but you can produce more water by lining the bottom of the pit with moist vegetation, such as cactus pulp. The moisture in the plant tissue evaporates water vapor into the air, which in turn condenses into water on the plastic.

Maximum condensation will occur during the day, but the still continues to produce throughout the night. It's possible to accumulate a quart or more of water every 24 hours by this method—enough to keep you alive if you conserve your water supply wisely.

The Solar Still at Sea

A variation of the basic still is useful for boaters. The basic still is made the same way, with plastic used to form a cone, but a bucket or other deep receptacle is used in place of a pit. Place about an inch of seawater into the bucket; fit a smaller container inside and drape plastic over the whole contraption. Tie the plastic tightly to seal out air, and set a rock or weight of some kind in the center to form a cone. The salt water will evaporate and condense onto the cone, and the water that drips into the container will be fresh and drinkable.

To speed up the evaporation process, place pieces of cloth or other absorbent material half into the water. The cloth absorbs the water and allows it to evaporate faster.

Purifying Water

How can you tell when water is safe to drink?

You can't really, but there are a few guidelines that help you make an educated guess.

Some extremely cautious experts advise that water should always be treated. Their argument is that it's impossible to tell when water is impure. It may look clean, may be free flowing and cold, but it can still contain deadly organisms. They say a stream may bubble up from a wilderness spring and tumble through untouched forests and still be unsafe to drink; one rotting animal carcass lodged across the headwaters could contaminate the water for hundreds of yards. I won't argue with the experts, but I'd be a liar if I said I comply with their notion of always treating water. One of the singular pleasures of wilderness travel is being able to belly up to a cold, sweet-water mountain stream and drink sloppily and lavishly; or dip a tin cup over the side of a canoe and come up with clear North Country water. I'm not suggesting you be flippant in your water treatment, but in a wilderness situation water that looks, smells and tastes clean, most likely is safe to drink. It doesn't hurt to check upstream to see if anything is contaminating the water, and if you have any doubts whatever about the quality, by all means purify it.

Any water that is near civilization should be considered unsafe to drink unless treated, as should water that looks dirty or smells foul. Water that is stagnant or heavily sedimented should be filtered and treated. In essence, any water that you are not certain is pure should be rendered safe.

There is no truth in the old saw that fast-flowing water is automatically fit to drink. Nor is there much worth in the maxim that water flowing over gravel is always pure. You can be sure that rainwater is safe to drink if collected as it falls. Fresh snow can be melted and used safely, though some prefer to boil it. Ice, on the other hand, is no safer than the water that formed it. Freezing holds germs in suspension, but doesn't kill them.

The only way to safely eliminate germs and other impurities is by chemical removal or boiling. Halazone is the most frequently cited water purifier, and can be purchased at most drugstores. The dosage varies depending on the condition of the water, but is generally one tablet per quart of water. After the tablet dissolves, shake the water thoroughly to ensure completeness of purification. Slosh a little treated water over the mouth and neck of the bottle to kill any unwanted organisms there. Let the water stand for a half hour, then sniff it. If the chlorinelike smell of the halazone isn't noticeable, add another tablet and repeat the procedure.

In a pinch, you can replace the halazone with tincture of iodine (at least three drops per quart of water) or household bleach (of the Clorox variety, two drops per quart of water). Use the same procedure of mixing and testing advised for halazone.

Contrary to some beliefs, whisky will not purify contaminated water. It may make it taste better, depending on your palate, but it in no way makes unsafe water any safer.

Boiling is the surest of all water treatments. At base elevations, water should be boiled vigorously for a minimum of five minutes. Higher altitudes require additional time. Just to be safe, boil all water for ten minutes before using.

Cloudy or dirty water may need to be filtered before it is treated. You can accomplish this in several ways. One method is to pour the liquid through a tightly woven fabric, such as your shirt or bandanna. Lacking that, use sand or grass as a filter. Remember that you can remove much of the sediment simply by letting the water sit in a cup or other container until the heavier particles fall to the bottom.

Water that is Never Safe

Seawater is never safe to drink in its natural state. It draws water and body fluids from the kidneys and intestines; makes you thirstier and, in short, can kill you rather than help you.

Recently I read a newspaper article about two men who were forced to spend 13 days on a life raft after their fishing boat sank in the Gulf of Mexico. The article said the two men "drank their own urine to stay alive." It should have said the two men stayed alive in spite of the fact that they drank their own urine! Urine has no lifesaving qualities as drinking water. Much like salt water, urine is high in body-sapping salts. Drinking it will drain what body moisture you do have, and make your water need much greater. *Never drink urine.*

The Rationing Myth

When you are thirsty, drink. That's a simple rule which should never be broken when fresh water is available. Don't try to ration your water supply, for you cannot ration water to your body any more than you can ration gasoline to a car. Look at it this way: If you need to travel 20 miles by car, you must have a certain amount of gasoline to get you there. You cannot stretch your mileage by rationing the gas to the engine a pint at a time. The engine requires one gallon of gas, and you simply can't cheat on that amount. Your water needs operate under the same logic. If you must travel on foot through a hot area, you will need, say, two quarts of liquid to retain body moisture. If you allow yourself only one quart, with intentions of rationing the remainder for the next day, you will feel the effects of dehydration. It is a useless and dangerous practice to ignore thirst while there is water in your canteen. Drink what you have. Your body can store the surplus.

I've said that you can't ration water, but that doesn't mean you can't conserve it. The two words are not synonymous. By applying a few tactics, you can stretch your water mileage, much the same way judicious driving habits increase auto gas mileage.

Keep perspiration to an absolute minimum. Wear full-length clothing if possible, and stay out of the sun. Skin that is exposed to air evaporates moisture through the pores, so cover up thoroughly. Do as little work as possible during hot hours. Build a shelter of some type (Chapter 16) and stay under it.

Don't eat any solid food. Digestion requires water, and that means further dehydration. Remember, water is much more important than food, so consider your water need first.

Don't drink alcoholic beverages. They will also promote dehydration.

Don't smoke. Smoking dries out your mouth, and increases your thirst. Breathe through your nose, keeping your mouth shut. Each time you exhale through your mouth you exude a cloud of moisture.

Don't talk. Conversation, much like breathing through the mouth, dissipates large amounts of water.

Again, drink whenever you are thirsty. If you must leave a water source, store as much water as possible in your body, and carry what you can.

15

Making Fire

It is often said that a woodsman is known by the time it takes him to build a fire. While I have always considered that rather skimpy criterion for woodsman status, there is some truth in the saying. Neophyte outdoorsmen often need half a box of matches to start a fire under ideal conditions, and gasoline and newspapers to ignite one under less favorable circumstances. A savvy woodsman, on the other hand, can begin with a match and perhaps his knife, and have tea water boiling in a few minutes—no matter if it's raining or snowing. This appears to be just a neat trick, but is actually much more significant.

Fire is used for cooking, signaling, warming shelters, purifying water and deicing clothing and bodies. Fire obviously is very important to outdoorsmen, particularly in times of emergency.

Firemaking is not a mystical skill. In fact, it is an easy one when you have matches. What separates the one-match fires from the 28-match fires is the patience and care that's exercised before a match is struck. A beginner heaps a pile of twigs and branches together and holds a match to it. The dry tinder may flare up, but the larger wood never catches. The experienced hand builds his fire with a method—arranging the materials in a way that ensures success with the first match.

Basic Firemaking

A fire is built so it burns in progressions. First you need tinder—small, dry bits of fuel that ignite with a touch of your match. Over this goes kindling, larger than tinder but still small enough to catch fire easily.

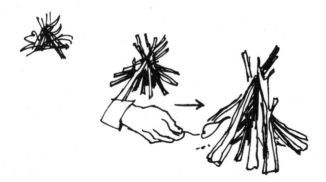

A fire is built in progressions. First the light tinder, then the larger kindling, and finally, the full-size fuel. The arrow in the above drawing indicates the direction of the wind. Note that the match is placed on the windward side of the fuel heap, so that the flames blow into the fuel.

Last is the larger fuel—full-size pieces of dry wood. In effect, to build one large fire you must first make three smaller ones. The small fire from the match lights the tinder, the larger fire from the tinder starts the kindling, which in turn has enough strength to burn the fuel. Each step

Pine pitch is one of the best tinders available. It collects in yellow, white or amber globs on conifer trunks.

is vital; mess up on one and your fire will not catch, but follow the procedure properly, and you'll need only one match.

Let's take a closer look at fire materials.

Tinder

Your ability to start a fire depends heavily on the quality of your tinder. Fortunately, no matter where you are, good tinder is present. In evergreen country, dry needles and tiny dead twigs are excellent fire-starting materials. Look for these at the base of any conifer. Also keep an eye open for pine pitch. These white to yellow globs of pine sap are among the best fire starters you can find. A chunk of pitch will burn for minutes, even in a rain.

Tree bark, in some instances, makes good tinder. The white, papery bark of birch is high in flammable oils, and rates as a top fire starter. Juniper bark peels off in dry, gray shreds and is also a fine fuel. Aspen, cottonwood and cedar are other trees that have readily burnable skin.

Small, dry wood shavings from any softwood tree will serve as tinder. Dry leaves, grasses, weed stalks and mushrooms also work. The fuzzy buds of pussy willow and the silky strands inside thistle flower heads are flammable. So are old, dry bird or mouse nests. You'll find these in woodpiles, near rocks and on the lower branches of trees.

The dry seedpods and spikes of many plants burn readily, including cattails, milkweeds, burdock, sumac, dock and goldenrod, to mention only a few. The dead woody inner trunks of sagebrush make excellent tinder. Break this fibrous wood into small, burnable sections.

If you look hard enough, you'll discover good tinder right on your person. Your hair, for example, will start a fire if nothing else is available. If you're bald, hair from your dog or a dead animal will work equally well. The cellophane and paper from your cigarette pack will serve as emergency tinder. Paper from the individual cigarettes burn, and cigar wrappings are even better. If you are carrying a camera, the film inside will light easily and fizzle and flame long enough to start a fire. Bits of thread unraveled from your coat or socks can be rolled into a ball for use as tinder. If you are really up against it, the stuffing in your car seats or the foam rubber in some boot ankle cushions can be ripped out and burned. When you're near a motor vehicle, don't ignore gasoline and oil as fire aids; they'll make flames in a hurry.

Tinder is so essential to fire building, it never hurts to carry some in your pack—particularly if you're in country where dry, burnable materials are scarce. If you need immediate fire—say you fall through the ice in subzero temperatures—the tinder is with you and ready to go. When you walk through conifer country, keep an eye open for globs of pine pitch. A chunk tossed into your pack will assure you of a quick fire when you need one.

Kindling

Kindling is the next size fuel. Often, the same materials you use for tinder can make suitable kindling, the difference being in the size of the material used. Dry underbranches from evergreens make the best kindling, and vary in size from a thin pencil to a half-inch-thick stem. Small sticks of dry wood from any tree will work, but softwoods are best. It is always better to split or break kindling before setting it on the fire. Round, bark-wrapped pieces of wood catch slowly and burn with less intensity than those which are split.

Fuel

For emergency use, don't worry about the finer points of firewood selection. It's true that hickory burns better than sycamore, but in an emergency any wood that burns is usable, and you have to take what you can get. It does pay to know that softwoods (pine, spruce, fir) start faster and burn quicker than hardwoods (oak, hickory, birch, etc.) Knowing this, you can use softwoods to start your fire and then add hardwoods to keep a long-burning, steady blaze.

Don't waste time and energy trying to cut large logs and branches into fire-size pieces. Rather, place them in the fire and burn them in two. As an alternative, you can arrange large logs in a spoke fashion around the fire, with the ends of each used as fuel. As the wood burns, a little more of the log is pushed into the flames.

Matches

The paper matches found around the house are next to useless in the woods. They sponge up moisture readily, burn for only a few seconds, and are blown out by a mere puff of breeze. Carry a book of them along to light your smokes, if you wish, but don't rely on them for starting campfires. Safety stick matches are better, but are hard to light on anything but matchbox abrasives or clean glass. For outdoor use, the best matches are the so-called "kitchen" matches, which have sulphur tips for easy lighting. You can light these on any dry, reasonably even surface: your trousers, zipper, thumbnail, ax handles, etc.

All matches must be kept dry. The waterproof safes described in Chapter 3 work nicely, or you can use plastic film containers or plastic pill bottles instead.

It never hurts to waterproof your matches in paraffin wax. Just melt the wax to liquid, swirl in the match head until it is evenly coated, and

Don't bother cutting larger wood into small pieces in a survival situation. Place the ends of the logs in the fire spoke fashion, pushing them in as they burn.

let it harden. A match thus treated can be dipped into water, yet still retain its fire-making potential.

Always have a good supply of matches with you, and carry two separate containers in case one is lost. (One in your pocket, one in your pack.) Don't use your stock of emergency matches for lighting your pipe or building everyday fires. Use other matches for those chores. The supply in your pack should be used only when necessary.

Building the Fire

Now that you have proper matches, good tinder and a healthy load of kindling and fuel, you are ready to construct a fire. If possible, select a dry, level bed on which to build. If the ground is damp with rain or snow, make a platform of dry sticks or logs for a base. Over the mound of tinder, lay thin twigs or wood shavings. Lean them against the tinder pile with enough room in between for air circulation. Over this, set slightly larger and longer twigs. Crisscross pencil-size twigs over the whole works, making sure they touch the lower sticks lightly, but also taking care not to hinder air movement by stacking them too tightly. With your larger kindling and fuel nearby and ready to use, you're ready to light the match. If a breeze is blowing, set your match on the windward side of the tinder. The wind will blow the flame into the fuel. Hold your match under or to the low side of your tinder (flames burn upward) and wait for it to catch. Keep your match in position as long as you can hold it to increase the size of the flame. When the larger twigs ignite, lean your next-size kindling onto the fire (being careful not to topple the whole works) and continue doing so until the fire is burning steadily.

The basic technique I've described will produce a "tepee" or "pyramid" fire. Some people prefer to build the entire tepee before striking the match; that is, all the progressions of wood—from tinder to larger fuel—are laid down carefully so that you need do nothing more than set a match to it and sit back while it catches. If you can construct the tepee properly the first time, it is a good method. Otherwise, start with a small fire and build it up slowly.

Depending on the weather and terrain, you'll have to alter this basic method somewhat. On windy days, build the tepee between two large logs or a row of rocks. This will prevent the wind from blowing out your match or scattering your tinder. On extremely gusty days, when the wind threatens to scatter even the larger fuel, set your fire in a pit dug ten to twelve inches deep. Two green logs placed across the entrance will hold a pan or pot for cooking. If digging a pit is impossible or difficult, place your fire on the lee side of a large windbreak—a log, rock or dirt clump. The same applies in rainy weather. You must keep your fuel dry, and if a natural shelter isn't available, rig a poncho, tarp or coat to shield the fire.

If your fuel is slightly damp, you can still get it to burn by increasing the size and intensity of the match flame. If you have packed along the candle stub recommended in Chapter 3 the task of lighting wet wood is simplified. Build your tepee around the candle, so its steady flame drys the tinder and eventually lights it. Commercial fire tablets work in the same manner. Lacking either of those, you can twist together dry grasses

On extremely gusty days, you may have to build a small pit to shelter your fire from the heat-stealing wind.

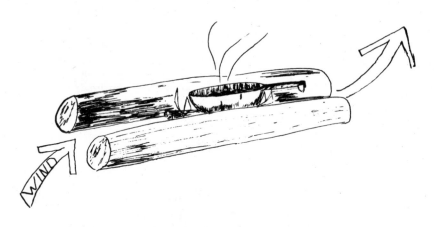

On windy days, build your fire between two logs or rocks.

or paper to make a "primer" for your fire. When lit, the primer provides a much larger flame than that supplied by a match.

Another woodsman's trick for starting fires under adverse conditions involves the use of a "fuzz stick." This is a length of thick branch—preferably softwood—which is whittled with a knife so that long, thin shavings are sliced almost, but not completely from the stick. Crisscross a couple of fuzz sticks at the base of your fire tepee and you should get a quick blaze. Incidentally, your knife must be sharp to make a fuzz stick quickly and properly, but then, your knife should always be sharp.

Once you have a fire burning steadily, don't build it too large. Big,

A fuzz stick is a bit tricky to whittle, but is an effective fire starter.

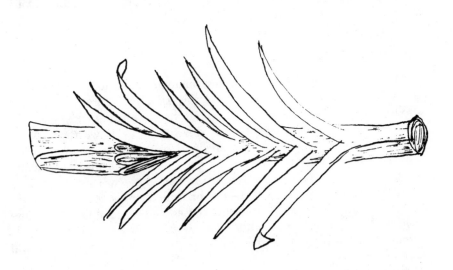

scorching blazes are voracious fuel burners, wasting wood that takes time and energy to gather. More importantly, a large fire is too hot to sidle up to for warmth without being scorched, and cooking is difficult or impossible. The best fires are small ones which will cook your food, provide warmth and save fuel.

Having declared a generality, let me immediately state an exception. If you are using a log bank or boulder for heat reflection while you sleep, a larger fire may be justified. Build a fire equal in length to your body. Sleep between the fire and the reflector. In this way, reflected heat warms the side of your body turned away from the fire.

Fires the Hard Way

If you want to fully appreciate the value of a dry match, try building a blaze without one. Making matchless fires is laborious at best, impossible at worst. Despite the oft-seen cheery prose to the contrary, you can't dash into the woods, make a few twists of the wrist with a makeshift bow and drill and produce a dancing blaze. Building a fire without matches is painstaking work, as even the experts at primitive fire building will tell you. But the redeeming point is, it can be done. In an emergency you have to make do with what you have, and what is desirable isn't always possible. If you need fire, but have no matches, primitive fire-making skills are invaluable.

All of the following methods if done properly and patiently will make fire, but be sure to try them at home, or for fun while idling away time in camp. Like any other skill, fire making with rough materials is most difficult the first time you try it, but becomes easier with practice. Don't wait until an emergency to do your practicing.

Fire by Sun

Fire by sun is probably the easiest matchless method, but has one serious limitation: the sun must be clearly shining before you can use it. When you need a fire most—in icy rain or blizzarding snow—the sun won't be visible. But on bright days, this technique is worth knowing. The idea is to intensify the sun's rays and direct them to your tinder. The best tool for this is a magnifying glass, which you may have along for studying fossils, plants or insects. If not, there are many suitable substitutes. The lens from a binocular or camera, removed from the instrument's body, will work. Eyeglass lenses will start a fire; the more powerful the correction the better. The crystal from a watch or compass, a rounded piece of broken glass, even a smooth, clear piece of ice will work.

The magnifier is held above the fuel, on an angle that catches the sun and shines a dot on the tinder. Adjust the angle and distance of the glass until you get the tiniest sun dot possible. In a few moments, smoke will curl from your tinder. At the first sign of a live spark, blow it gently enough to keep it alive, but not so much that you extinguish it. If you nurture the spark properly, it will leap into a small flame.

Using a Firearm

If you're toting a gun, another means of fire making exists. The first step in this and all other fire-making techniques is to have your tinder ready to go. Then, remove a bullet from its cartridge by tapping it lightly with a rock or knife along the crimp. Twist and pull until it comes loose. For shotgun shells, cut the plastic or paper crimp and pour out the shot pellets. (Save these. They may have later use, such as being cut and pinched on for emergency split shot, if large enough, or used as projectiles in an emergency slingshot.) With your knife or a stick, pry out the wadding. (Save this also. Shredded, it makes good tinder.) With either shell or cartridge, be careful not to spill out the remaining gun powder. Pour a bit of the powder (no more than half) into a small piece of cloth, torn from your shirt or coat if necessary. Fold the cloth in two and stuff it lightly in the muzzle of your gun. Pointing the firearm upward (to prevent spilling the powder) chamber the shell and move near your tinder pile. When the gun is fired, the cloth will fly a few feet upward and come down smoking, possibly aflame. Grab the cloth and place it on your tinder, blowing gently if necessary to keep it smoldering. As soon as a flame rises, add additional tinder and kindling.

Some authorities recommend stuffing the cloth inside the cartridge or shell rather than the muzzle, believing it more likely to flame when rigged that way. Either method works, though sometimes the cloth-laden shell or cartridge jams in the gun's action. If you're carrying a break-action gun, this is no problem. Opt then to place the cloth inside the shell or cartridge.

There's one other consideration regarding fire by gun. After extensive experimenting with the method, I'm impelled to warn that it is by no means foolproof. Quite often the cloth never catches a spark of any sort, much less a viable one. It may take three, four, maybe five or ten tries to start a fire. If ammo is in short supply, save it for bringing down game or signaling for help, and try an alternative method of fire starting.

Fire by Spark

If you have the Metal Match mentioned earlier, fires are easy to start. Scrape fragments of the metal into a small pile, then create a spark by scraping your knife sharply against the match. The spark will ignite the shavings.

Some rocks produce sparks when struck with the back of a closed pocketknife, but making fire this way is a difficult procedure. Quartz, agate, jasper and pyrites all produce sparks, at least in theory. You may discover otherwise when you try them. Sometimes it is easier to find two of the aforementioned rocks and strike them together with glancing blows; one rock being lifted upward, the other moving down. If you have the right rock, you will produce some sparks this way. Many times the sparks are too small and short-lived to even make it to the tinder pile without cooling. But, again, it is worth a try when nothing else will work.

If you aren't up on your geology, and can't tell pyrite from granite, experiment with several different rock combinations until you find one that works. Fortunately, there are many silicate rocks that produce sparks, but those already indicated get the best results.

To catch and hold a small rock-thrown spark, the tinder must be absolutely dry and highly inflammable. The spark method is a very good one if a vehicle is near. A rag lightly soaked in gasoline or oil ignites easily. A fast way to produce sparks when a motor vehicle is present is through the electrical system—assuming it still works. Cross the battery posts with a wire or metal object and sparks will jump from the metal. Or, by removing the spark plug wire from the plug and cranking the ignition, you can throw sparks a short distance, such as into a gas-soaked cloth.

Fire by Friction

Fire by friction is something everybody has heard about but few can actually obtain. In essence, two pieces of dry wood are rubbed together with enough speed and persistence to create smoldering wood powder, which is then placed in tinder and nurtured into flames. The best and easiest of the friction techniques is the bow-and-drill method.

The bow and drill operates this way. A 15-inch stick, slightly curved and an inch in diameter, is whittled to a point at one end, and bluntly round at the other to form the drill piece. A wide baseboard, preferably of the same wood as the drill, is shaved flat, and a hole is carved to receive the blunt end of the drill. A notch is cut from the hole to the side of the baseboard to allow the fine powder created by friction to be quickly dumped out on the tinder. A third piece, the socket, is carved from any hand-size piece of thick wood. This fits on the top of the drill, enabling you to apply pressure while the drill is turning. A hole is carved into the underside of the socket to receive the sharp end of the drill.

Tie a string to the bow, in the same way a bowstring fits an archery bow. You can use shoelaces for this or, better, rawhide thongs from hunting or hiking boots. A thin rope also works. Fit the string across the bow until it is tight, then knot it securely to both ends.

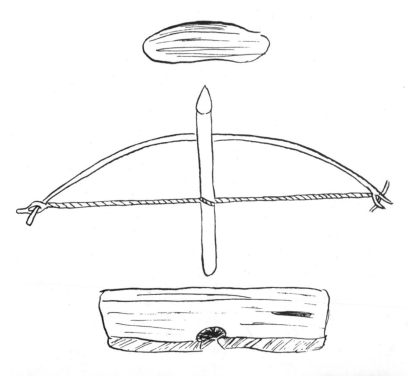

The drawing shows how a bow and drill looks in theory, the photo shows how yours will look in practice.

The baseboard is placed near your fire site, with the notch directly over or very near the tinder. The drill is placed against the bowstring, blunt side down, and twisted until the string forms a tight loop around it. The socket is fitted over the pointed end of the drill and held down firmly with your left hand (assuming you are right-handed). The blunt side of the drill is placed in the baseboard hole, and the bow is sawed evenly back and forth.

The drill will revolve quickly in a side-to-side spin. Apply firm but not overly excessive pressure on the socket to increase friction. If the drill binds, rub the pointed end along the side of your nose for the natural oil found there and try again. This helps the drill spin freely in the socket. If the drill still binds, tighten the bowstring. Hold one end of the fireboard with your foot to keep it from twisting out from under the drill.

Sweep the bow back and forth evenly. Soon you will smell the pungent aroma created by the hot wood. When smoke begins to curl out of the notch, really put your back into working that bow. Fine, brown powder should fill the notch. Watch it carefully for signs of a spark. When you see one, drop the bow and drill and turn the fireboard over onto the tinder. Do this gently so the spark isn't extinguished. If you're lucky, the spark will stay alive long enough to burn the tinder and create other sparks, which in turn are fanned into flames.

Rarely does the procedure work this smoothly. You often create a lot of smoke but no viable sparks. However, persistence pays off. Once you finally produce a healthy spark, treat it as gently as an infant. It may take a while to make another.

By using high-friction woods you can improve your odds of making fire. Poplar, cedar, basswood, yucca, cottonwood, fir, cypress, tamarack and willow are the best choices. One of these species should exist wherever there is woody vegetation.

Other friction techniques result in fire, but none is nearly as effective as the bow and drill. It is possible, though, that you would need fire and not have anything suitable for a bowstring.

The hand drill, a variation on the bow and drill, does work, but requires tireless patience and a good bit of time. A thin stick nearly three feet long is used as the drill. A fireboard is cut in the same manner described for the bow and drill. The bottom end of the drill is tapered to a dull point, and is fitted in the notch in the fireboard. Arch your hands stiffly and place them on either side of the drill, resting it against your palms. By rubbing your palms together in a rapid back-and-forth motion, not unlike a vigorous hand washing, the drill will spin from side to side. You must coordinate your back-and-forth movement with a slight downward thrust to keep pressure on the drill. This is an extremely difficult procedure and requires a lot of practice. The drill must spin steadily for several minutes before smoke will appear. Then, just when

Other friction techniques will start fires, but only with much sweat and labor. The hand drill is shown at left, the plow board in middle and the fire saw at right.

your wrists begin to throb, you must really pour it on to produce a spark. The procedure is speeded up somewhat if two people work together. The longer-armed individual places his hands high on the drill, the other person works the lower section. Once a rhythm is developed, the drill spins steadily with more pressure than one person alone could apply.

A fire saw is another painful technique that makes you a believer in the inarguable pricelessness of matches. A V-shaped notch is cut into a round length of wood. A two-foot branch is carved to match the V and is sawed back and forth in the notch. The sawing should be vigorous and constant.

A better variation on this is the "plow board." A half-log of dry wood with a V-shaped channel is carved for a foot or so along its center. The log is elevated against the tinder pile, with the mouth of the channel emptying onto it. A branch equal in width to the channel, cut blunt on one side, is "plowed" with downward strokes toward the tinder pile. Again, a rhythm is important. The branch is rubbed roughly against the channel until the smoking brown powder that's formed produces a spark, which may take considerable time.

Getting the Most from Your Fires

Once your fire is going, make the most of it. To maximize heat, fashion log or rock reflectors as described earlier. To keep the fire going while you sleep, you will need to "bank" it with thick logs. Lay two logs directly on the coals, side by side with the rounded edges barely touching. A small fire, which should last through the night, will burn between the logs.

In the morning you can rekindle the fire to cooking size simply by adding progressively larger twigs to the flames. If the fire dies completely overnight, you can still produce a blaze with little trouble. Poke under the ashes with a stick until you find either a live coal or a large spark—unless rain has soaked your ashes, one will certainly be present. Place your best tinder over the spark or coal and fan it gently until it flames. Even if you have matches in an emergency situation, this method is worth using. Any matches you save become valuable security for a later fire.

If you are without matches, and fire building is a major chore, you can take this trick a step farther. Carry your fire with you. This is not as painful as it sounds. A live coal will glower and smolder all day if given a tiny amount of oxygen. If you have a container of any sort—a tin can, frying pan, cooking pot, etc.—use it to carry the coals. If not, a piece of leather or sturdy, fire-resistant material will work. Place an inch or so of ash into your receptacle, set in your live coals (several are better than one, in case a couple die out) and cover with more ash. Sand, dry, clean dirt or gravel will work in place of ash. Cover your container tightly enough to prevent excessive oxygen from eating up the coals, but loosely enough to avoid smothering them. (You must guess on this; there is no set formula.) When you reach your next campsite, prepare the necessary fire materials and dump the coals onto your tinder. Fan the coals until they flame.

Cooking over Fire

An age-old method of campfire cookery involves a "dingle" stick. This is a slender green branch stuck into the ground at one end and leaned over the fire at a 45 degree angle. A pot of water or stew suspended from a notch in the dingle will sit directly over the flames. Meat, such as a split fish or rabbit, can be skewered and roasted right on the stick. If the ground is frozen or impenetrable for some other reason, anchor the dingle stick with two rocks or logs, placing one at the outside base for a stop, and the other on the inside for support. A more adjustable rig can be made by substituting the inner rock with a forked stick. The stick can be moved up and down the dingle to adjust the distance from meat to flame.

You can support pans and pots in other ways as well. Two stout logs, preferably green, can be laid parallel to each other for a base. Set these close enough to hold up both sides of the cooking utensil. Rocks can be used in place of logs, but less effectively. Beware of using flat rocks found in streambeds or on lakeshores. Heat from a fire can create steam build-up within the rock, causing it to explode like a bombshell. The bits of rock shrapnel could easily put out an eye or create a serious gouge. Incidentally, the practice of lining the perimeter of fire with rocks is often

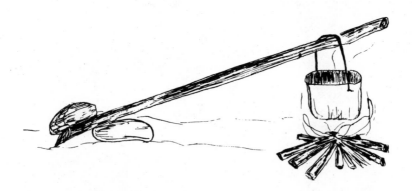

Variations of the dingle stick.

unnecessary. Unless the rocks are used as pot and pan supports or to fill some other needs, don't waste the time and energy to round up heavy stones.

Some food, such as shellfish, tiny fish and insects, can be prepared nicely in a steam pit. If you have no cooking utensils, this method is worth knowing for food that can't be skewered or roasted on a dingle stick. You needn't become carried away with the pit construction; the less energy you expend the better. Look for a natural depression that can be easily turned into a pit, and with a stick, dig until the pit is a foot or more deep. Line the bottom with rocks heated in your fire or with large coals if rocks aren't available. (You can build a fire right in the pit to fill it with coals.) Place shellfish directly on the rocks or coals and heap on wet seaweed, pondweed or other moist vegetation. The shells will open when done. Small fish and insects must be set on a base of wet vegetation, before being placed on the coals.

Remember Safety

It will do you no good to set your camp or surroundings ablaze. Even when under the pressure of an emergency, keep safety in mind. Failure to do so could result in a much more serious and dangerous predicament.

As precautionary steps, scrape away dry needles, leaves and other forest litter from the perimeter of your fire. Watch to be sure your flames don't spread. If a large, live spark is blown into flammable material outside your fire area, stamp it out. It could lie smoldering for half the night before suddenly bursting into flames.

When you leave your camp, extinguish the fire as best you can. If water is scarce, by all means do not waste it extinguishing the fire. Kick apart the ashes and stamp out live coals. Smother the whole fire-scar with sand, dirt or snow. If necessary, urinate on the coals to put them out. Do whatever is feasible to stay on the safe side.

16

Building Shelters

Shelter rates high on the list of survival essentials. If you spend much time outdoors it's a sure bet that you will be wind-blasted, sun-baked, rained on and subjected to various degrees of deep freezing. Any of these natural onslaughts can be dangerous in prolonged doses. Intense sun can cause heatstroke, sunburn or dehydration; wind and rain carry away body heat; and extreme cold can inflict frostbite or hypothermia. A properly constructed shelter fends adverse weather conditions while you wait for them to pass.

There may also come a time when you must spend an unexpected night in the woods. Perhaps you are lost or unable to travel because of injury. Maybe you are caught by darkness miles from your camp. Whatever the situation, it pays in comfort and good health to be able to throw together some kind of shelter.

The type of shelter you build depends largely on the predicament you are in and the materials you have available. However, a few basics should be kept in mind. The first of these is to squelch the impulse to build a fortress. The simpler the structure, the easier and faster it is to build. In a truly dire emergency, where shelter is the deciding factor between life and death, speed and ease of construction are vital concerns. Exertion should be kept to a minimum and you should be able to build your shelter without becoming overheated, or, in cold weather, without being drenched from chilling perspiration.

Next, make the most of your efforts by placing your shelter in a key location in relation to the wind and terrain. Look for natural windbreaks, such as thick brush, evergreen stands, rock piles or sand dunes, and build there. If heat and intense sunlight are your enemies, keep the entrance of your shelter into the wind or slightly cross-wind to capitalize on the cooling breeze. When it's cold, but not snowing, angle the opening away from the wind as far as possible. Face your shelter across the wind rather than straight away when snow is falling to prevent drifts from bottling up your entrance.

Use the same precautions discussed in Chapter 7 when choosing a campsite. Building under precarious deadfalls or snow ledges or nestling in dry stream washes and gullies can be dangerous. In your haste to find shelter, don't forget safety.

Nature's Premade Shelters

If you're alert you can sometimes find snug premade shelters that require little or no augmenting on your part. Perhaps the most obvious example is a cave. In the limestone country of the Southeast and throughout the Rocky Mountains, it is not uncommon to discover hollows and caverns in side slopes, hill bottoms and ravines. These are rarely the vast chambered tunnels pictured on Kentucky postcards. Rather, they're small, water-washed burrows or short, rock-lined halls. However, if you do come upon a cave that winds out of sight of the entrance, take care not to become lost. (An amazingly easy thing to do in a multi-channeled, coal-black tunnel.) Camp within sight of the entrance; you not only eliminate the chance of getting lost, you also are able to hear potential rescuers.

Caves and upended rocks can be found in many areas, and they simplify the task of shelter building.

In spruce country, the young saplings can be lashed together at top to form a wind-resistant shelter.

Rock outcroppings and slabs that form overhangs often make suitable shelters. Sometimes these must be supplemented with a tarp or foliage covering to keep out wind and moisture. A word of caution: Before crawling into a cave or rock crevice, search carefully for snakes or other animals that may call your potential shelter home.

In conifer country, a blustery weather shelter can sometimes be made by lashing together the tops of young, six- to eight-foot spruce trees. The bushy sides form triangular, sloping walls around your small bedding area. If snow blankets the trees, the insulating effect is vastly improved.

In wintertime, look for snow-bare hollows, formed under heavily branched evergreens. By crawling under the branches, you can spend the night in a dry, wind-protected shelter.

Another good natural shelter is a lightning-struck or wind-blown downed tree still carrying its foliage. By breaking small branches, you form a small bedding area within the mass of leaves or boughs.

Tarp Lean-Tos

If you have a tarp or large space blanket, shelter should be no problem. In almost any terrain, you can find something that will support a wind-shielding, heat-reflecting tarp.

To make one of the simplest shelters, lash a ten-foot pole four feet high on a standing tree, pitch the tarp over the slanting pole and peg down the sides in pup-tent fashion. Rigged this way, an eight- or ten-

Look for snow-bare hollows formed under thick conifers.

Fallen or broken trees are especially suitable for shelter, but a shelter can be fashioned in a standing tree as well.

Simple tarp shelter—pole, tree and tarp.

foot piece of canvas or plastic makes a quick and cozy shelter for one person.

Another type of one-man lean-to is made by lashing a single pole be-

Tarp lean-to with bough bed.

Log and tarp crawl-in shelter.

tween two trees at about head height. A tarp is tied to this crosspole and angled back and pegged or weighed down to form a sloping shelter. This lean-to works well in a light rain or in mild weather, but is too breezy to be effective in bitterly cold and windy conditions.

If you find a large log or downed tree trunk two or more feet high, you can quickly make another mild-weather shelter. Peg or anchor with weights one end of your tarp over the log. Stretch the rest of the tarp back, so it slopes to the ground in a tight triangle. Secure the low end, with a weight or pegs, and you have a crawl-in shelter.

Broken tree and tarp.

Canoe turned on side with tarp.   Shear poles and tarp.

A broken tree, slanting to the ground, also makes a framework for your tarp. Spread the tarp over the trunk and fasten down the sides with pegs, logs or rocks, forming a deep, triangular shelter.

Other structures will provide frames for your tarp. A canoe, turned on its side and propped up with oars or sticks, will support a tarp, as will an airplane wing or fishing boat.

You can also make a snug cold-weather shelter with nothing more than poles and a tarp. Two poles are lashed together near their tops and twisted to form an X. These are called shear poles. A single ridgepole is leaned into the high crotch of the X to complete the frame. The tarp is spread over the poles and weighed down at the sides. The resulting

Lashings.

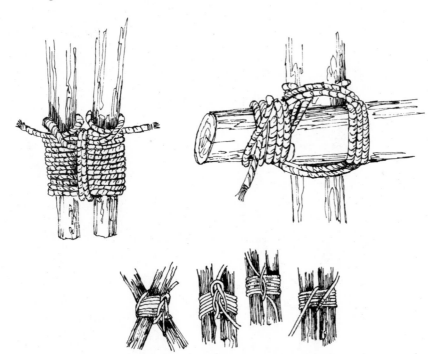

Another shelter effective in treeless areas. Use your walking staff to support the middle of the tarp, then fasten each corner to a rock weight.

shelter looks like the letter A, and is, in fact, sometimes called an A-shelter.

If your tarp doesn't have corner grommets, use a commercial Visklamp to aid in lashing. Lacking that, use a pebble as shown.

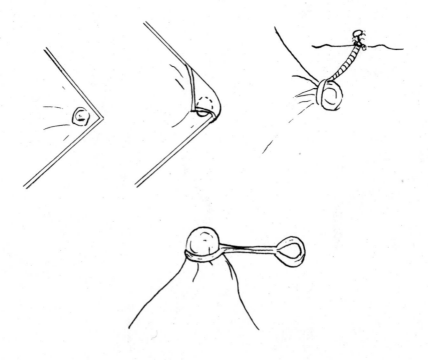

If you want to build a lean-to, but can't find a suitable ridgepole, use a length of rope instead. Fasten it tightly between two trees, drape the tarp over the line and peg down the sides in the shape of a pup-tent. In treeless terrain, you can make a shelter by leaning the tarp against shrubs or brush. Lacking that, fashion a small shelter by making rock supports. Pile a column of rocks at each corner of your tarp, making the front piles higher than those in back. Lay the tarp on the high rock stacks and weigh it down with two top rocks. Stretch the canvas back and anchor it with rocks. The resulting shelter offers protection from sun and rain.

Using Natural Materials

All outdoorsmen should spend an afternoon building a natural lean-to with no implements except a sheath knife. It's almost a sure bet that most would think twice before leaving their tarp behind on an outing. A shelter that takes five minutes to build with a tarp will take at least 30 minutes to make with branches and boughs, and the net product of the longer effort will most likely be a less effective shelter.

Making a bark-shingled lean-to looks easy in an illustration, but try cutting away slabs of the hard, corky, sometimes brittle bark which protects most trees. Birch and aspen bark peels off nicely, but you still must lay these on your branch frame solidly enough to keep them from sliding off at the first murmur of a breeze. You can make a bark and branch lean-to—if you work at it—but your task is much simpler with a tarp.

There are, however, some practical ways to build a lean-to with the materials at hand, and no guide on emergencies would be complete without them. But remember, the "I can always throw together a natural shelter" attitude can be false assurance.

Where evergreens are plentiful, a bough shelter is your best bet. One of the simplest methods is to lean several long poles or branches against a large fallen log and thatch the frame with evergreen boughs. Lay the boughs with the butts upward, overlapping them as a roofer overlaps shingles. Start at the bottom of the frame and work upward in rows. This makes a low-profile shelter that you must crawl into.

The true lean-to is a bit more difficult to build. To make the frame, lash a ridgepole between two trees, and lay a tight row of long poles against it, forming a slope to the ground. The back of the lean-to is thatched with evergreen boughs by the same shingle method described earlier. For a more effective cold-weather shelter, add sides by leaning or lashing sticks against the roof. Weave boughs between the sticks until a thick sidewall is produced. The result is a triangular structure that can be quite snug when warmed by a long fire built a bit outside the entrance.

Shelters can be made without a ridgepole by using rope (top) or by piling rocks into sturdy columns. The latter shelter is particularly useful to remember in desert situations.

Thatching a pole framework with evergreen boughs makes an effective shelter. This same method is used with other pole frames described in the text.

By using the same three-pole system described for a tarp A-shelter, you can make the frame for a bough edifice. Two shear poles are lashed together and twisted to form an X, and a ridgepole leaned into them completes the frame. Boughs are placed against the ridgepole in progressive heights, to form the sidewalls. If you can't find boughs of sufficient size to reach from the ground to the ridgepole, you can either lower the entire structure, or make a branch latticework on each side. The boughs can be woven or shingled to fill the frame.

A tentlike shelter can be made in much the same way. Lash a pole a few feet above the ground between two trees. Lean large boughs against the pole from both sides, so they form a point at the ridgepole. The butts of the boughs can be sharpened and stuck into the ground for steadiness. The end product is a small crawl-in shelter.

You can make a windproof wigwam by leaning a dozen or more poles into the crotch of a tree so they form a frame resembling three-quarters of a tepee. Weave the pole skeleton with boughs. This is especially effective when made against a tree heavy with foliage. The natural windbreaking qualities of the tree supplement your shelter.

Another forested-country shelter requires no lashings. By leaning many thin, forked branches together in tepee fashion, so they form a conelike framework (point up, of course), you have the skeleton of a small wick-iup. Boughs, leaves or grasses are layered and woven through the frame to complete the structure. Leave one small opening for an entrance. Wickiups are good shelters, being closed in on all sides, but require more work than a simple bough-and-frame lean-to.

So far, I've mentioned only evergreen boughs for making shelters from natural materials. In hardwood country, the green, leaf-bearing young branches of broadleaf trees can be used in place of the boughs, though not as effectively. Vines with thick, leathery leaves can be woven through the framework to provide a waterproof roof. In arid areas, sage-brush clumps can be made into a shelter by breaking off the light, fra-grant wood and heaping it together to form walls. Northern prairie regions provide cattails, rushes and grasses which can be woven and lashed together to form rain- and windbreaks. Use a log, rock or woody stem to provide the basic support of the structure.

Snow Shelters

In very cold weather, a small snow shelter is excellent insulation from the elements. Generally, temperatures of zero and below are required to prevent your body heat from melting the walls and ceiling. But if tem-peratures are brisk, a snow shelter can be surprisingly cozy.

You can find ready-made caves by digging into deep snow drifts that form at the base of evergreens. A hole dug in the side of the drift is an entrance that leads under the tree, where it is dry and wind-protected. Line the bottom with evergreen boughs to minimize heat loss through the snow or cold ground. You can build a small fire near the entrance, but be sure you have adequate ventilation. Heat from a steadily burning fire can cause the ceiling snow to melt to the point of a cave-in if not watched carefully.

The most basic snow shelter is nothing more than a hole or trench dug into the snow in sled-dog fashion. Using a frying pan, snowshoe, forked stick or any other digging tool you can make or find, dig a nar-row trench (wide enough for your body) a few feet deep. Line the bottom of the trench with boughs, and cover the top with a tarp or branch-and-bough overlay.

To make a true snow cave, dig deeply into the lee side of a loosely packed snowdrift. First excavate a burrow, barely wide enough to crawl through, angled on a gentle slope upward. At the end of your burrow hollow out a cave large enough to be comfortable but small enough to retain body heat. The cave is lined with boughs for added insulation. Be sure not to attempt this on a steep slope or heavy, sagging drift that might slide and bury you. Look for firm mounds of snow, or drifts on

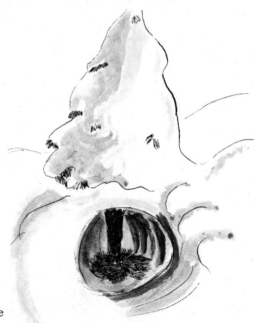

You can find a ready-made snow cave
at the base of a thick conifer.

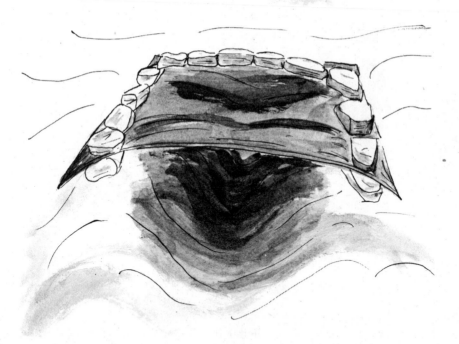

Basic snow shelter is a simple trench, covered with a tarp.

gentle slopes. Remember, when constructing any snow shelter, the smaller the shelter, the more heat-retaining ability it will have. But also realize that you cannot build a fire in a small snow cave. The gaseous release would asphyxiate you quickly without sufficient ventilation. You must depend on your body heat to keep the shelter warm.

Making a true snow cave into a deep drift or bank is more work, but under the right conditions it can be the warmest shelter you can make.

Snow blocks can be leaned together pup-tent fashion to serve as a windbreak.

Igloos are a type of snow shelter, but unless you have a snow saw and practical igloo-building experience, don't waste your time trying to build one. As an alternative, when snow is hard and crusty, you can make a shelter by leaning blocks of snow together in a row, forming what resembles a pup tent. If you lack blocks of sufficient size to make this shelter, stack smaller snow bricks atop one another to form a wind-breaking wall. In bitterly cold weather, a little water from melted snow or your canteen will freeze into an air-tight mortar for the bricks.

Other Shelters

In rocky, barren country, you can make a U- or V-shaped windbreak out of piled rocks. A fire built at the open end will provide heat. It is usually fruitless to attempt to build a closed-in rock structure. Not only is the work required considerably arduous, but the result of your efforts most likely will be a wind-raddled, shaky structure which topples easily, possibly while you're inside.

You can get protection from the sun in desert country by draping a coat or shirt lean-to style over a shrub or cactus. The effect is not spectacular, but is better than nothing. Any shade you find or make will be helpful.

Vehicles—cars, cruiser-type boats, planes, etc.—have limited use as shelters. Metal compartments have a way of magnifying heat or cold to the point of extremes. Anyone who has sat in a car on a hot day knows that it often is hotter inside the vehicle than out. In other words, you'll be more comfortable, in times of extreme heat or cold, if you leave the vehicle and construct one of the shelters described above.

About Bedding

No matter what sort of shelter you're building, some sort of bedding will improve it. In cold weather, you lose heat through conduction with cold surfaces. The ground under your shelter draws heat from you the way a sponge sucks up water. A layer of boughs, leaves or cloth—even dirt, sand or gravel—makes a space between you and the cold and significantly reduces heat loss. When it's hot, the process is reversed. You attract unwanted heat from the ground. In this case, a space between you and the earth blocks the heat flow significantly. The effect is doubled if you can get air space between the ground and yourself by forming a platform of sorts a few inches high. On the other hand, burrowing into the ground to lay your bedding also keeps you cooler. Soil, particularly sand, heats at the surface but remains cool inches below. Dig a foot below the surface and you can sometimes find temperatures 20 degrees cooler than that on top.

In cold weather, one of the best natural materials for making beds is the ever-useful evergreen bough. Lay these boughs upside down, butts pointing to the foot of the bed, in interlocking rows for the length and width of the bed. Make the bed as thick as feasible. A foot or more isn't too much. This aromatic mattress is a good insulator from cold ground, and is comfortable as well. However, although stripping conifer branches is justifiable in an emergency, it's a lousy conservation practice in general—esthetically and biologically. Do it only when necessary.

To make your bough bed, or any bed, more comfortable during cold nights, fashion an all-night ground heater. First, scratch away snow or forest litter to bare ground in a rectangle the size of your bed. Build a large, long fire along the length of the rectangle, and let it burn down to coals. Scrape away the larger, cherry red coals, but leave the finer gray ash. Cover the charred area with dirt or sand, being certain that no coals are left in the bed. The ground should feel warm to the hand when covered, but should not be excessively hot. (If it is, add more dirt or check for buried coals.) Build your bough or leaf bed over the warm ground. If the soil is frozen and you cannot find loose dirt to cover the ashes, scrape away all of the fire litter. Build your bed on the clean, but heated, ground.

Shelters and Fire

As indicated earlier, some shelters cannot be used with fires because of insufficient ventilation. Another consideration is flammability. If you fall asleep, an untended fire could catch a dried branch from your lean-to and ignite the entire shelter.

All of the open-end shelters—lean-tos, windbreakers and A-shelters—can be warmed by fire. To get the best results, the flame should be backed by a log or rock reflector which throws the heat back at you. If a rock or large log isn't available, make a reflector with two sticks thrust in the ground for support, and logs stacked against them to build a small log wall.

These are the basics of building emergency shelters, but are by no means the last word on the topic. Assuredly, there are countless variations of the rudiments. Some of them have yet to be discovered. Finding shelter from the weather, like all other survival skills, depends primarily on ingenuity. The best way to save your body is to use your head.

17

Signaling for Help

SIGNALING FOR HELP

Signaling is a necessary and vital tool for all outdoorsmen. Virtually every part of the continental United States is near enough to civilization for someone to see and respond to an emergency signal. Whether or not this is something to rejoice over is another question; but the fact remains that even the more remote sections of the country aren't that far removed from man's reach. Designated wilderness areas are carefully watched—both by tower scanners and planes—for signs of fire. Coast Guard crews chug up and down seacoast and inland waters with eyes constantly on the lookout for trouble. Add to that local wardens and rangers, state water and land patrols, bush planes and air rescue operations, private organization personnel, and you pretty much place the entire country under professional scrutiny.

People generally tend to think of signaling as something only a lost man needs. Not true. A lost man certainly does need to make himself more obvious by utilizing every signal he can, but it doesn't end there. A boater, in country perfectly familiar to him, could run his boat aground on a sand shoal and need signal devices to hail help. Similarly, a fisherman could break his leg near a stream he knows intimately and still need to signal for aid. In fact, signaling is needed most often by people who know perfectly well where they are. I stress this because signaling is, admittedly, a rather uninteresting topic. Learning signal techniques is not as absorbing as learning to build emergency shelters or set intricate deadfalls. But for the average outdoorsman, signaling know-how is probably more important than either of these other skills. Effective signaling procedures could end your troubles before they have a chance to blossom into something you may not be able to handle.

The Basics

To be effective, all signals, whether sound or sight, must be obviously different from the surrounding environment. For example, on a hazy, foggy day, it would do you little good to use a signal of white smoke. The smoke would be enveloped into the fog and your efforts would be wasted. In the same vein, shooting a gun to signal for help is pretty much a vain practice if the woods around you are dotted with other hunters. Your shots wouldn't stand out as anything out of the ordinary, even if fired in the three-shot intervals indicative of distress. Most likely a distant hunter hearing your frantic shots would smile to himself and mumble, "Some guy's really having at 'em." But if you were to beat a stick loudly against a car hood, or blow SOS blasts on a thunder whistle, another hunter might wonder at the peculiarity of the sound and follow it to investigate.

This idea of making your signals stand out drastically from everything else is of crucial importance. I mention it now because it is *the* basic consideration when signaling. This concept will be brought up frequently throughout this chapter.

Another rudiment is that three repetitions of a signal indicate trouble. It may be the three gunshots or whistle blasts, or it may be in the form of three columns of smoke, three signal fires or three letters stamped in the snow—all these declare a need for help. This is important to remember. A pilot flying over may assume you are simply a hunter boiling a pot of noon tea if he sees one fire or curl of smoke. He may very well pass over you without giving it much thought. But three fires tell him immediately that you are in trouble.

The most universal distress signal is SOS. Sometimes this can be stamped out in the snow, written out with ground letters or drawn with a snow dye. Most often it is related in Morse Code.

You may or may not want to learn the entire Morse Code. You will certainly benefit from it, but memorizing the numerous and varying combinations of dots and dashes is not simple (though it is not extraordinarily difficult either). No matter what you decide about the code, memorize the pattern for SOS. It's simple. Three dots, three dashes, three dots. This can be related with a flashlight, flag, torch, whistle, mirror and many other devices. To express a dot, make the signal brief and sharp. A dash is made by holding a dot for twice its count. So, three short, rapidly spaced blasts on a whistle, followed by three slightly longer blasts, and ending with three short notes signals SOS. Regardless of where you are in the world, a passing ship, aircraft or, very often, an individual will respond to an SOS plea.

In order for that potential rescue party to zero in on your message, you must have your signals at hand when needed. Always have your signaling means ready to go at a moment's notice. This may mean keeping your flare gun loaded and ready, or stuffing a signal mirror in your hip pocket so you can grab it in an instant. If you lack enough fuel to keep signal fires going constantly, build a fire tepee that is ready to burn with the touch of a match. Whatever the circumstances, keep your signals ready!

International Morse Code

LETTERS	INTERVALS
A	dot-dash
B	dash-dot-dot-dot
C	dash-dot-dash-dot
D	dash-dot-dot
E	dot
F	dot-dot-dash-dot
G	dash-dash-dot
H	dot-dot-dot-dot
I	dot-dot
J	dot-dash-dash-dash
K	dash-dot-dash
L	dot-dash-dot-dot
M	dash-dash
N	dash-dot
O	dash-dash-dash
P	dot-dash-dash-dot
Q	dash-dash-dot-dash
R	dot-dash-dot
S	dot-dot-dot
T	dash
U	dot-dot-dash
V	dot-dot-dot-dash
W	dot-dash-dash
X	dash-dot-dot-dash
Y	dash-dot-dash-dash
Z	dash-dash-dot-dot

The Signal Mirror

In Chapter 2 on emergency preparation, I suggested fitting a signaling mirror into your pack. Signal mirrors are inexpensive, effective, easy to use and take up little space. On a good day a mirror signal can be spotted over ten miles away. On a hazy day a mirror flash can reach a plane that you can hear but not see.

A signal mirror is not the same as a common parlor glass. Both sides of a signal mirror have shiny metallic finishes with a hole drilled at center. These features make it possible to direct your signals to an exact point, such as a rescue plane or passing ship.

Sight your target through the center hole, holding the mirror a few inches from your face. If the sun and the target are both in your zone of view, a spot of sunlight will fall on your face. You will see this in the reflection from the mirror's backside. Cant the mirror slowly in different directions until the dot on your face lines up exactly with the hole in the mirror. You will know this has happened when the dot disappears from view in the mirror. Your signal flashes are now visible to your target.

If the sun and the target are not in the same zone of vision—say, the sun is slightly behind you and to your left, and the plane is directly in front of you—the above method won't work. Because of the wide angle between the sun and target, the dot of sunlight will not fall on your face. To cope with this, hold the mirror in front of your face slightly to the sun's side. Sight your target through the center hole as before. Raise your hand (the one farthest from the sun) so that it is roughly parallel with the mirror. By gently canting the mirror, you will eventually cause a sunspot to appear on your hand. Using the back of the mirror, line the dot of sunlight up with the hole in the mirror. This directs the signals to your target.

If you hear a rescue plane but can't see it, aim in the general direction of the noise, slightly ahead of it. Anybody who has sat on a hill and watched, with the aid of a spotting scope, a partner stalk and shoot an animal knows that the sound is delayed. The hunter will squeeze the trigger, flinch with recoil, the animal will fall, and a few moments later the boom of the gun will echo to your ears. Similarly, the plane is moving ahead of its sound. How substantial the delay will depend on how far away you are from the plane. Aiming slightly ahead of a plane's noise generally puts you on target.

If you neither see nor hear a rescue plane or boat, it still does not

Using a signal mirror.

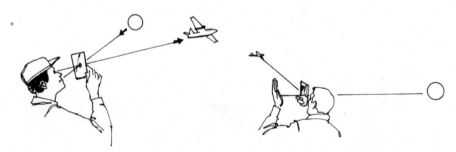

hurt to flash the mirror. In this case, make several flashes across the horizon by gently sweeping the mirror back and forth. This signaling technique isn't exhausting or difficult, so it doesn't hurt to keep at it even if the effort seems useless. There is always the chance someone will see your signals and investigate.

In a pinch, a regular mirror will work in place of a signal mirror, though it is more difficult to direct your signals to a specific target. If no mirror of any type is available, search for any highly polished or chrome-finished object. The standard advice offered in emergency texts is to use the lid of a tin can. This will work, but polish the lid, with your shirt if necessary, to make it as shiny as possible. If you lack a tin can, there are other materials that can be used. A shiny knife will work. So will a piece of aluminum foil, or a chrome-plated watch or compass bottom. If you are near a vehicle, you can use the rearview mirror, pieces of chrome ornaments or even the backside of some license plates. None of these work as well as the signal mirror, and since signal mirrors are easily obtained at most Army or Navy surplus stores, and at many camping outfitters, why take the chance of being caught without one?

Other Visual Signals

Store-Bought Signals

If you pack along sophisticated gear, you make the task of signaling somewhat easier. One of the more effective devices is a flare gun. This usually comes in a small package—a tiny gun and three or four flares. The flares are shot pistol-fashion straight into the air. They streak a hundred or so feet and explode. Day or night, it's hard for a passing aircraft or boat to miss the signal. However, be sure to use these only when help is in sight. There's little sense in wasting the precious flares if nobody is around to see them.

The same holds true for ground flares, which are stuck into the ground and lit. They fizzle and flash intensely bright light and are especially valuable in the dark. But they burn rapidly. Again, use them only when potential help is spotted.

Smoke candles or cherry-size bombs fit nicely into a pack and are worthy signaling devices. These emit thick clouds of colored smoke that are easily spotted on windless, clear days. The smoke lasts, depending on the device, from 30 seconds to two or three minutes.

If you're hiking or skiing in snow, you may want to experiment with snow dyes. These brightly colored liquids can be poured over snow to signal passing aircraft. There are a number of disadvantages to these, mainly in the limited potential they have. The dyes are also toxic and should be kept clear of food or water.

Fire Signals

Commercial signals are great if you have them on hand, but it never hurts to know how to signal by more primitive means. One of the best signals is fire. On a clear day—ideally one with no wind—smoke plumes sent up from three fires are effective distress signs. A fire-tower watchman, a pilot or even a fellow outdoorsman on an adjacent hill or ridge is likely to spot the smoke.

On an overcast day, the best signal smoke is black. If you're near a vehicle, black smoke is easy to make. Oil-soaked rags heaped on a fire create coal-black billows of smoke. So will pieces of rubber—such as matting or a spare tire (deflated, of course).

If rubber or oil isn't available, or on light days, thick white smoke will make an effective signal. This is easier to manage than a black plume. Pile any moist, green plant material on a fire and smoke will pour out. Be careful not to completely smother the flames. Another way to send up puffs of white smoke is to sprinkle water on a blazing flame, being careful not to completely douse it.

If fuel is plentiful, keep the fires going constantly. When fuel is limited, have the fires ready to go, but don't light them until you hear or see help.

At night, keep your fires going constantly, but burn them clean and hot and not smoky. You can accomplish this best by using dry wood. If built in a clearing, the fires can be spotted from the air or by tower scanners. Space the fires at least 20 feet apart if possible so the distinct sight of three fires appears, alerting an observer that something is wrong.

Sometimes a single tree, preferably a dead one, can be set afire to provide a rather glaring signal. Be certain the tree is well isolated from other vegetation; the idea is not to start a wildfire. Since setting an entire tree ablaze is a rather horrid conservation practice, do it only when absolutely necessary. Build a bonfire at the base of the tree; the dead needles will soon ignite. This works only with dead trees or evergreens, so don't attempt it on a healthy broadleaf specimen, you'll only waste your time and scar the tree.

Where you start your fire is as important as how. In mountainous country, signal fires are most effective on open meadows and clean ridges. In flat forest land build your fires in clearings, rock patches or sand and gravel bars. Your blaze or smoke must be seen. Keep that constantly in mind.

Ground Messages

Another effective way of signaling may be the letters SOS stamped out in snow or formed by piles of twigs or rocks. In order for ground letters to work well, they must stand out visibly from their background. For example, the word LOST stamped out in snow, even if done on a scale of ten feet per letter, will not stand out noticeably if the white of the letters blends with the snow in the background. However, if you fill the letters in with black twigs, dirt or rocks, it literally shouts to a passing aircraft.

In lake country, a ground signal made from branches and twigs can be built on an open sand or gravel bar. In winter, when the lakes are frozen, a dark ground letter made on the ice is easily spotted by search pilots. The important idea, again, is to make your signal stand out from everything else.

If materials aren't handy, and you need to provide some type of contrast for your ground signal, use shadows to help you. In snow, make the letters as deep as possible. Form snow mounds on the perimeter of each letter, slanting the mound slightly away from the letter so that the outside lines are not concealed. In this way you create a shadow across the indentations of your signal, making them darker and more visible. The same technique works with sand or gravel.

In densely vegetated country, you must take the opposite approach. Rather than build a ground letter, you must clear the brush to form one. In very heavy, thick growth this may not be feasible. But in high grass or weeds you could conceivably clear away enough vegetation to make an eye-catching signal. You may have to do this by cutting with your knife, uprooting plants with your hands or even burning. If it appears to be impossible to form a ground message, you may have to search for a more likely spot or, barring that possibility, use a different method of signaling.

The ground letters should be made as large as possible. An SOS that is 30 feet tall and 100 feet wide is not too big. However, if your signaling area is only a 20-foot square, you have to do what you can. There are no set rules for size, but, obviously, the larger the signal the better the chances of it being seen.

Besides the standard SOS, or HELP, there are official symbols that describe your needs more specifically and concisely. A chart of these appears on page 265. Their use is admittedly limited, but it just may happen that you will someday need something more specific than SOS. For example, if a search plane has found you, but can't land because of rugged terrain, a signal "F" tells that you need food and water. The plane can drop these staples to you while waiting for the ground crew to locate your camp. Or if someone in your party is badly hurt, the symbol "I" indicates that you need a doctor quickly. It doesn't hurt to remember these symbols just in case. If your memory is like mine, you may want to write these down on a small piece of paper and place it in your emergency pack. Wrap the paper in a couple of folds of waxed paper to make it waterproof. In this same package you might also want

Ground letters are effective emergency signals, but they need to be large, and they must contrast their background.

to include a copy of the Morse Code, plus the flag and body signals discussed next.

Body Signals

The International Ground-Air Body Signal Code can be useful if you need to signal a plane. Like the Morse Code, you needn't remember all of the signals but a few are worth memorizing.

If you need to be picked up by a plane, don't wave your arms wildly. In reasonably settled country, a pilot who isn't aware that you are in trouble may take your desperate arm waving as an inspired salutation. Instead, hold both arms directly over your head, as high as you can reach. This indicates you have abandoned your means of travel and need to be taken aboard.

If someone needs urgent medical help, lie down on your back and stretch your arms behind your head. These and a few other body signals are shown in an illustration.

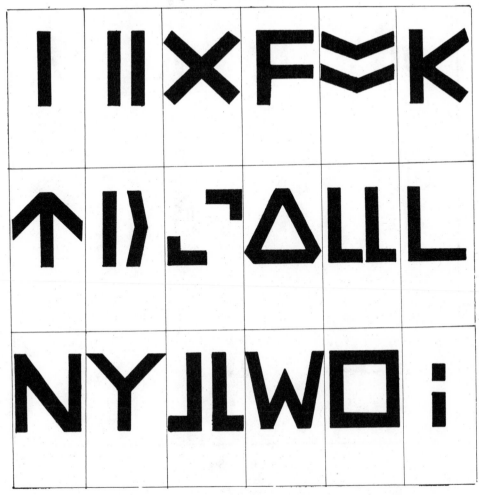

Official Ground Signals

Serious injuries —need doctor	Need medical supplies	Unable to proceed	Need food and water	Need gun and ammunition	Indicate direction to proceed
Am proceeding in this direction	Will attempt to take off	Aircraft badly damaged	Probably safe to land here	All is well	Need fuel and oil
No	Yes	Not understood	Need engineer	Need compass and map	Need signal lamp

Body Signals

Pick us up	Don't attempt to land here	All is well, don't wait	Yes
No	Need mechanical help or parts— long delay	Have working radio receiver	Use drop message
Need medical assistance urgently	Can proceed shortly, wait if possible		Land here (point direction of landing)

Flag Signals

Flag signals can be used in a couple of ways. The flag may be a specially designed signal flag or it may be a piece of your shirt tied to a stick. Most likely it will be the latter. To signal in Morse Code, swing

Morse code is easy to transmit with an emergency flag. You needn't memorize the entire code, but do remember the easy steps for signalling an SOS.

the flag in a large figure 8 on your right side to express a dot, and a figure 8 to your left for a dash. The flag is held upright and to the center of your body to indicate the conclusion of a letter. To end a word, lower the flag momentarily and then return to upright. Waving the flag back and forth in front of you signifies the end of the message. It never hurts to signal a few SOSs, just to make sure you aren't misinterpreted.

A more complicated flag system—one that may not be worth the trouble of learning—is using two flags to form letters. I include it only for information's sake. It is conceivable that somebody would find it particularly useful, and it certainly won't hurt to learn the semaphore letters, but the average outdoorsman is better off learning how to flag out a simple SOS. See the semaphore letter chart shown if you're interested in sophisticated signaling.

Audible Signals

These signals utilize noise to bring in help. The most frequently mentioned tactic is shooting a gun in three-shot intervals. This is fine except for a couple of reasons. First, although hunters generally have guns with them in an emergency, fishermen, hikers, campers and boaters generally

Letter	No.	Letter	No.	Letter	Letter	
A	1	H	8	O	V	
B	2	I	9	P	W	
C	3	J		Q	X	
D	4	K	0	R	Y	
E	5	L		S	Z	
F	6	M		T	NUMERALS TO FOLLOW	
G	7	N		U	LETTERS TO FOLLOW	(J)

Serious signallers may want to learn semaphore letters, transmitted with two flags.

do not. In other words, the average outdoorsman isn't toting a firearm. But assuming the lost person is a hunter with rifle or shotgun, the three-shot method still has some serious limitations. Most likely, when one hunter is in the woods, so are others. Shots often echo up and down the woods and it is entirely possible, and likely, that three distress shots will go totally unnoticed. In this instance, you would be better off saving your ammo. However, if you are packing an emergency whistle, an SOS blast on it will stand out from other woods sounds and is apt to bring in help. If you don't have a whistle, an empty bullet cartridge will work nicely. Suck in your lower lip and place the cartridge mouth against it. Blow sharply across the roof of your mouth and into the cartridge. The whistle tone varies with the size of the cartridge, but will be shrill and long-traveling.

If it is near dusk, or if your party is the only bunch of hunters in the woods (such as in wilderness areas or fly-in trips), the three-shot technique can work. In these circumstances, this pattern of fire will likely be noticed. Fire the first shot, wait ten seconds, fire another and then discharge the last. The first shot supposedly alerts searchers, the second two orient them as to your whereabouts.

If you don't have a gun, the signal whistle should work well. If you are near a vehicle, you can make echoing noises by banging a stick against the car hood or even by blowing your horn. As before, signal in intervals of three.

Unless help is very close by, don't shout or scream. Yelling tires you out quickly, strains your vocal chords and, worst of all, can induce panic.

Trail Signals

So far, we have discussed signals that are direct from you to a target. Now we come to indirect signaling. Say you are lost and have bivouacked for the night. In the morning you strike out to find your way back. In case someone is searching for you, you should leave trail signs to show where you have been and where you are going.

The most common sign is the pointer arrow. These show your direction of travel. You can construct pointers by making an arrow of rocks on your trail; laying a stick across a log, with the elevated end pointing in the direction of travel; blazing the side of a tree (only when necessary, please) and a number of variations and combinations. Whatever method you choose, remember to keep your directional pointer simple.

To indicate a turn, place a straight stick in line with your previous path and then fashion an arrow that indicates the direction of your turn. On a tree blaze, a smaller blaze to either side of the main blaze indicates a turn in that direction. A chain of rocks, arranged to follow a turn in the trail is an obvious and effective signal. Whatever design you think up, take pains to make it easy to follow. You may know that your

Trail signs should be clear and simple, and the directional arrow is one of the clearest and simplest.

A single blaze indicates that you are traveling a straight path. A smaller blaze placed to the right of the large blaze means you are turning right; a small blaze on the left indicates a left turn.

snapped branch means a left turn, but searchers may not. Make it glaringly obvious so that no mistake can be made.

One final word on signals: Don't abuse them. Flagging down a ship or airplane just to see if the technique works is a very foolish move.

Years ago, a canoer or boater who waved a paddle at a bush plane was signaling for help. In remote backcountry, this was taken very seriously. A pilot would often land as soon as he could, to help out. After wilderness traveling became popular as a recreation, the backcountry began to see more people, many of them inexperienced in the laws of the woods. One Ontario bush pilot told me he used to investigate whenever he saw a paddle waved. After being flagged down repeatedly for no good reason he became wary.

"Some of them just didn't know better," he said gruffly, "and said they were waving in fun. But now I'm very careful about wasting my time and fuel entertaining cheechakos."

Signaling is serious. Use it when you need it, and only then. There is still that natural law about crying wolf.

Here are two more directional pointers; the variations are endless.

18

Making Emergency Equipment

Sometimes the severity of a mishap rests heavily on your ability to manufacture essential gear. Sometimes snowshoes are needed; other times you may need to weave a fishing line, fashion a birch-bark cup, make a crude needle for stitching clothing, construct a makeshift canoe paddle and so on down an endless list. In this chapter we'll look at how to make an assortment of items, using for the most part materials found in the woods.

The following is a mind catalyst, not a "complete" text. It's impossible to anticipate all emergency gear needs, and it's equally impossible to predict all situations. For example, you may know how to make a birch-bark kettle, but that knowledge does you little good if you're in need of a water holder in the Mojave Desert, where the nearest birch tree is perhaps hundreds of miles away. The purpose of describing the following items is to start you thinking in the right direction. In most cases, you'll need to use your own imagination and ingenuity to solve your particular problem; but then, that is ultimately what survival of all types depends on: ingenuity. That one attribute is often the stark difference between life and death.

Making Rope

Rope plays a vital role in outdoor living and survival. Knowing how to make it is an essential skill.

A number of materials can be used for rope making, including sinew tendons found along the legs and backs of animals; the stalk fibers of plants such as nettle, dogbane, milkweed and thistle; strips of bark from willow, snowberry, hawthorn and sagebrush; and if necessary, from lengths of cloth cut from your clothing. In fact, any long, thin, pliable material—certain grasses, sewing thread, strips of animal hide— can be braided to form a cord varying in size from a thin fishing line to an inch-thick braided rope. Here's the basic procedure.

Take two unequal lengths of weaveable material and hold them between the thumb and forefinger of your left hand (reverse for southpaws). With your right hand, twist clockwise the strand farthest from your body, then lay it counterclockwise over the other strand, so that it now becomes the fiber closest to your body. The other strand is similarly twisted clockwise, and then laid counterclockwise over the first strand, making it once again the strand nearest your body. The same process is repeated until you near the end of one strand. Then, you must splice in another strand to continue the braiding. To do this, lay a couple of inches of the new strand over the end of the other, and twist them together. When they are connected firmly, wind the remaining strand over tightly as you did before, and the splice is complete. Continue this procedure of twisting and splicing until the appropriate length of cord is produced. Admittedly, this appears confusing on paper, but in reality it is a fairly straightforward task. Consult the illustrations to aid in grasping the principle of rope making, and then try it yourself with a couple of pieces of yarn or string to get the procedure clear in your mind.

If you have an animal hide on hand, an entirely different sort of "rope" can be made.

First, soak the hide in water to loosen the hair, then scrape away the hair with your knife. Keep the skin moist to prevent hardening, then begin cutting a quarter-inch strip from one edge of the hide. Rather than severing the strip from the hide, keep cutting round and round toward the center, producing a circular strip of rawhide. Cutting in this manner, you produce the longest unbroken length of cord possible from the hide.

Ideally, the cord should be the same diameter throughout, but it's hard to satisfy ideals in a field situation. Do the best you can to keep the cord even, and work slowly and methodically so an accidental knife slip doesn't sever the cord from the remaining piece of hide.

The best way to do this, when possible, is to sink your knife into a log, and, standing behind the knife, work the hide against the blade rather than the blade against the hide. If two knives are on hand, plant them both into the log; one to serve as a cutting blade, the other as a guide to keep the cut the same diameter.

The resulting rawhide rope can be used as is, if necessary, but can be improved if it is softened in warm water and rolled between your arched palms to obtain a nearly round shape.

This sturdy cord is known to some by its Indian name, babiche, and makes excellent lashings.

The steps in making rope: 1) (left) shows you the proper way to hold the two strands; 2) The strand closest to you is twisted counter-clockwise; 3) then it is wrapped over the other strand. This procedure is repeated until one strand ends; then 4) another strand is spliced on; 5) by twisting both tightly together. The procedure is repeated until the cord is of desired length.

Babiche is wetted before it is used, then cinched in place tightly. As the rawhide dries, it shrinks appreciably, tightening the lashed objects as solidly as if they were spiked.

Wilderness Adhesives

Sometimes the most difficult part of fashioning an emergency item is finding a way to hold loose ends and joints together without the aid of nails, glue or tape. However, with some know-how and a little luck, you can cash in on a number of natural adhesives.

Wood is understandably an abundant commodity in a forest, and there are a couple of ways it can be used to hold things together. In places where nails were rare treasures, old-time backwoodsmen whittled sturdy wooden pegs to function as substitutes. A hard, resistant wood such as hickory or birch was cut in the shape of a stubby nail, and turned evenly over a fire for hardening. For holding soft items such as bark and paper, the peg was simply driven through with a rock. For

Cutting babiche from a piece of hide is best accomplished by using two knives —one for cutting, the other as a guide to keep the cut even.

tougher items, a starter hole was bored with a knife or fishhook, and the peg was pounded into it to minimize the chance of breaking.

Pieces of green branch can be used in the manner of a clothespin. Take a springy length of branch, and split it along the center for three-fourths of its length. Use it to hold together pieces of thin bark—as for making a birch-bark cup—or for clasping together cloth or other thin materials.

Perhaps one of the finest backwoods adhesives is pine pitch. Pitch grows in white, yellow or amber globs on the trunks of many conifers, and can be melted down and spread like glue. Pitch makes an air-and-watertight sealer, and can also be used for gluing two light items together.

The thick sap of many trees, when thinned over a surface and allowed to dry, makes a tolerable adhesive. Sap accumulates near wounds and gouges in the trunk, and you can capitalize on this fact by chipping away the bark around a wound and collecting the gummy resin. Look also for small blisters on a tree trunk. Hacked open with an ax or knife, they often bleed a steady flow of heavy sap.

In treeless areas, the thick sap of many herbaceous plants can be used as a glue or sealer. One of the better species for this purpose is milkweed, which has a heavy white sap. A word of warning: Don't use the sap of an unfamiliar plant to line a vessel or container in which you intend to store food or water. If you accidentally use the sap of a poisonous species, it could contaminate your food or water.

Plants aren't your only source of glue, as many North Country natives can tell you. A fine adhesive can be made by boiling the heads and tails of fish down to a thick, mucilaginous gel. This strongly scented gunk is excellent for sealing bark kettles, and for gluing in general. A less odorous alternative is to mix any part of animal fat with tree sap in a one-to-three ratio; one part animal fat to three parts tree resin. The fat lends pliability to an otherwise brittle resin glue.

Needle and Thread

For making and repairing clothing and footwear, needle and thread are absolute necessities.

First make a needle. If you have a fishhook with you, your problem is quickly solved. Simply straighten out the hook, fasten your thread through the eye, and commence stitching. Lacking a fishhook, start searching for anything you may have that is small, thin and sharp—a safety pin, paper clip, small nail, tin-can opening key, a wire-core pipe cleaner. None of these work really well, but they do work, and that's the best you can hope for.

If you have no suitable man-made items, consider a natural substitute. Primitive people used thin slices of animal bone for their needles, and you may have to do the same. Best for this are the flat, cardlike shoulder blades of many animals. These are split into slivers and sharpened at one end with your knife.

Thread is simpler to make. Any long, thin, pliable length of fiber will work, and you can find such a fiber in the stems, roots and rootstalks of many plants. Better yet is sinew thread, made from the bands of tendon found along the backs of animals. The band of tendon is removed from the back meat and soaked in water until it becomes pliable. Then a thin thread of tendon is cut and peeled off the main strip. That's all there is to it. Keep the sinew moist while making your stitches. When it dries it will shrink and add extra strength and tightness to each stitch.

Footgear

An accompanying illustration shows how to use a triangle of cloth and a piece of cardboard or birch bark to make emergency cold-weather footwear. Study it carefully; should a time arise when you're without

Emergency cold-weather footgear made from cloth and bark or cardboard.

adequate commercial footgear, such a makeshift "boot" can be a toe saver.

If you are in need of boots and have an animal skin handy, don't overlook the possibility of making crude moccasins. Cut a large oval of hide at least twice the size of your feet. Turn the skin fur side up, and step in the center of it. Wrap the loose ends over your foot, lashing it tightly around the ankle and instep.

Makeshift socks can be formed by wrapping cloth or animal hide around your feet and ankles, leaving at least an inch of material ahead of your toes. Tie the front end off with cord to close the sock and seal out cold air.

Snowshoes

Just about any wide, flat, light object can be fashioned into an emergency snowshoe. Here are a few ideas.

Perhaps the quickest makeshift snowshoe is nothing more than one or two thick evergreen boughs, laid one atop the other, trimmed for easy walking and lashed to your boots. In slightly crusted snow, the boughs will keep you from breaking through.

Any flat board or tree slab can serve as a snowshoe. Shape the board

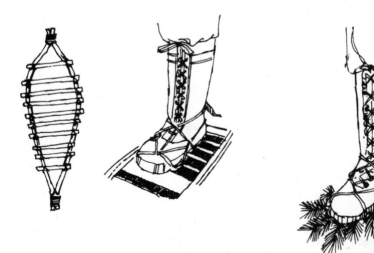

Emergency snowshoes can be made by lashing springy willow branches to the shape shown at left, or by strapping a thick layer of evergreen boughs to your boots.

to roughly resemble a traditional snowshoe, if possible, and cut out a hole for your boot toe. (This is essential for easy walking.) Bore two more holes; one on either side of the board. A rope, cord, fishing line or length of rawhide is threaded through the holes and around the board for a binding.

Another sort of snowshoe can be made by bending and lashing two springy willow branches together, and cross-fitting them with shorter lengths of willow. A length of cord is wrapped around one of the middle cross-pieces to serve as a binding. The snowshoe can be used as is, but is more effective if a piece of cloth or an evergreen bough is lashed to the bottom.

Repairing a Strap

An aggravating thing, a busted strap—whether on a snowshoe, backpack or rifle sling—can slow down your rate of travel and sometimes stop it altogether. If you lack rivets or tacks to make a civilized repair, try this.

Cut a hole three-quarters of an inch from each broken end, and pass each piece through the hole in the opposite end. When the strap is cinched tight, the pieces will bind and hold together. But if the strap is

A quick way to repair a broken strap.

not under constant stress, the broken ends may slip apart. In that case, tie a tight overhand knot with the loose ends to safeguard against slippage.

Backpacks

If you need to travel, you need a pack to carry your food and gear. If you don't have your emergency rucksack, or if it isn't capable of holding all your gear, you'll have to make a larger one.

A surprisingly workable pack frame can be made in a matter of minutes by cutting a forked, sturdy branch measuring roughly two feet long or slightly less. The straight butt section below the fork should measure roughly seven inches long. A length of rope is tied across the wide part of the fork to serve as a cross strap, and two more pieces of rope are tied from each end of the cross strap to the straight butt section, forming the shoulder straps. (See illustration.) Leave enough slack in the shoulder straps to allow them to fit comfortably over your arms. Your gear is rolled into a tarp or piece of clothing, and tied firmly to the pack frame.

If for some reason you have an extra pair of trousers on hand, you can make a small backpack easily. Stuff your gear into the hip-and-buttocks area of the pants, and tie the top shut by running a cord through the belt loops and pulling it taut. The pant legs are run under your arms and back, where they are lashed tightly to the top of the "pack."

Rafts

Survival authors are apparently fond of describing in detail the steps in building a raft, but few bother to explain the difficulties and limitations involved.

A quick, yet workable packframe can be made from a forked section of sturdy branch.

First of all, it takes considerable work and energy to construct a one-man raft, even if you have an ax, hammer and spikes (which you most likely won't have in an emergency). If you need to build a two-man raft, the task becomes much more difficult, and a raft for three or more people becomes downright impractical. Even if you do manage to throw together a floatable mess of wood, there's still the fact of traveling to confront. Log rafts are not easy to control, and you certainly can't run rapids with them. This alone rules out raft building for a large percentage of the time. Most streams and many rivers are just too fast for a rough-hewn raft. But, conceivably, there may come a time when a raft is just the ticket out of your predicament.

Figure that you'll need at least three 12-foot logs, eight inches in diameter, to support one man. The number of logs increases arithmetically with the number of passengers. How you manage to procure three sturdy, floatable 12-foot logs is a tacky question. If you have an ax, the answer is obvious; you simply go out and cut them. But since I'll venture that the high percentage of people who need a raft will not have an ax on hand, the problem may end your raft-building before it has started. (I'm not trying to be overly pessimistic about raft-building, but it's important to know what to expect.)

But assuming that you manage to find three freshly toppled deadfalls of roughly eight-inch diameter and 12-foot length, let's continue with the procedure.

Drag each log right up to the water's edge, and set them side by side. Find two thinner poles to serve as cross pieces, and lay them across the top of the raft, one at either end. Weave a long length of rope over the cross piece and around each log. Do this on both ends of the raft. Cinch the rope as tightly as possible, then tie it off at the ends with a few sturdy half hitches. For added rigidity, place another pole diagonally across the raft, and lash it tightly to both ends. The raft is now ready to see water.

Paddles

To steer and propel your raft, you'll need a combination pole-and-paddle. For this, find a long, thin but sturdy deadfall, and clean it of branches. On one end lash very tightly a bundle of broad sticks to serve as the paddle. The other end is left straight and is used to pole the

The finished raft.

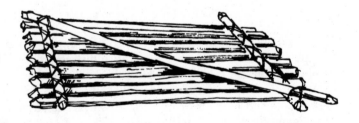

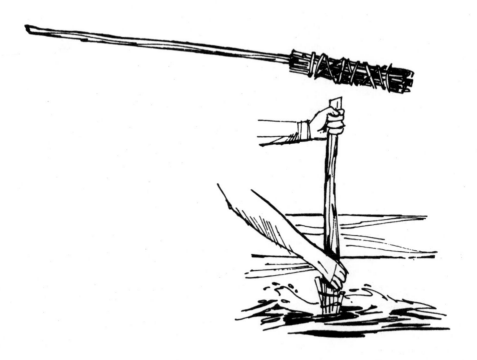

Emergency paddle.

raft through shallows and still waters. By simply flipping the pole over, you can change from pole to paddle in seconds.

If you're canoeing or boating and in need of an emergency paddle, the same procedure applies. Cut a sturdy pole so that when stood on end it reaches no lower than your chin and no higher than your nose. Tie a bundle of broad, short sticks to one end to serve as the paddle "blade."

Water Containers

The classic wilderness water holder is the birch-bark kettle or cup. A couple of examples are shown in self-explanatory illustrations. But one trick to remember if you're working with birch bark: if possible, warm the bark by rolling it over a fire for a minute. This loosens the fibers and makes the bark supple and easier to work with. However, don't let it get too close to the flame. Birch is high in flammable oils, and ignites easily.

You can also carry water by holding it in a sack made from any impermeable material—leather, plastic, canvas, etc. (See illustration.)

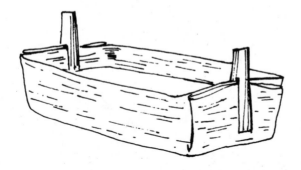

Birchbark water containers.

Light Makers

If you don't have a flashlight and need to find your way in the dark, try one of the following light makers.

Torches cast a fair length of light, and are easily made under some conditions. If you are lucky enough to be in birch country, a long strip of bark rolled tightly and lit at the top will burn fiercely for a short while. A variant of this method is to fold a strip of birch bark into a notched stick. Light one end of the bark to start your torch.

In cattail country you can make an adequate torch if you have access

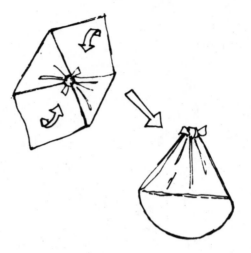

A water sack can be made from a square piece of any impermeable material, such as plastic or canvas.

Torches can be made from a roll of birchbark; a folded square of birchbark lodged in a notched stick, or from a cattail head immersed in gasoline or oil.

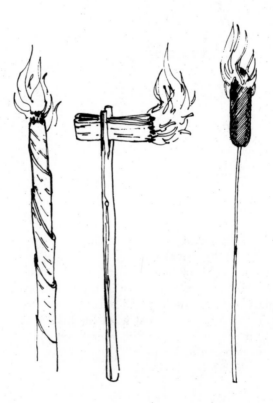

A lantern can be fashioned by
placing a candle in the narrow
opening of a glass bottle.

to gasoline or kerosene (say you're near a vehicle or have a can of white
gas in camp). Dip the sausagelike cattail head into the gas, and after
it is thoroughly soaked, remove and light it.

A makeshift lantern can be made by placing a candle (such as the
kind you carry in your emergency pack for fire starting) in a glass bottle or other transparent, fireproof object. The bottle is held upside down,
and the candle is inserted through the narrow opening. The thick bottom plate of glass must be broken out to allow oxygen to circulate and
feed the candle flame.

Sunglasses

If the bright sun catches you without sunglasses, and eye fatigue or
snowblindness threatens, make yourself a crude pair of sunglasses.

If ever-useful birch is available, strip off a rectangle of bark wide
enough to cover your eyes and long enough to reach from temple to
temple. With a knife, round the corners for a more comfortable fit, then
make thin horizontal slits for your eyes. A cord tied around the back of
your head holds the glare-cutting "glasses" in place while you travel.

If bark isn't on hand, the same effect can be achieved by using a strip
of cardboard, rawhide or paper.

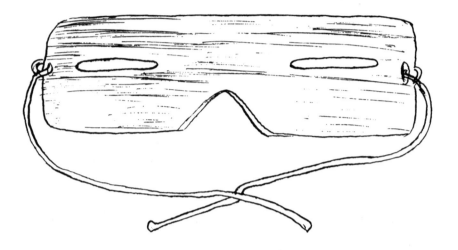

Bark mask.

Fish Lures

Once in Ontario, a partner and I experimented by fishing only with lures made on the spot. The results weren't spectacular, but we easily caught enough fish to keep us both from starving. Here are a few of our more successful creations.

A metal can opener is pounded flat with a rock. Using a short piece of monofilament line, tie a single hook to one end. Attach the main line to the other end. Again using a rock, pound the opener in the center to create a concave appearance and to add to its flutter in the water.

A metal spoon from a mess kit also produces a few fish. Work the handle up and down to weaken the metal, then twist it off. The remaining piece looks much like a commercial fishing spoon. Punch a hole through both ends of the spoon, using a leather punch from an old Boy Scout knife, and a rock as a hammer. Loop a hook on one end with monofilament, and attach the fishing line to the other end.

Trim a tin can lid with a sharp knife to resemble a pudgy heart. Crease the heart slightly in the center, and bend the rounded flaps downward. Punch hook and line holes in the front and back of the lure.

Sacrifice a pipe and make the stem into a thin surface plug. Run the fishing line through the large opening of the stem and out the narrow

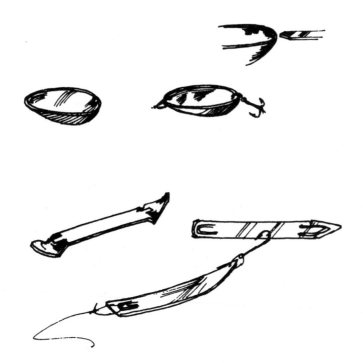

Fishing lures from spoon and can opener.

Tin-can fluttering lure.

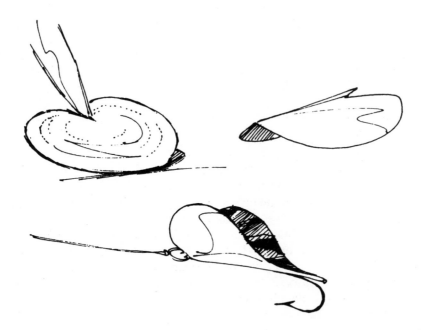

Pipestem surface plug.

Strip of fishbelly.

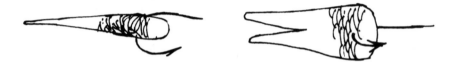

end, and attach a single hook. Seal both ends of the stem tightly with wooden plugs. The resulting lure can be twitched around lily pads and logs. Ours was chewed to pieces by energetic pike.

Unravel a foot or so of thread from a pipeless fisherman's sweater, and use it for tying a crude artificial fly. Cut a piece of orange cloth from the same fisherman's wool sock tops, to serve as the fly's tail. Wrap a thin strip of yellow shirt tail on and tie it firmly for the body. A lock of sun-bleached hair serves as the "wing," to finish off the fly.

One of the pike was killed, and a three-inch long chunk of its belly was sliced off. A sharp knife trimmed the piece of flesh so that it was a quarter-inch thick at one end, and noodle-thin at the other. A fork was cut in the thin end to give additional flutter. A hook was imbedded through the tip of the thick end, placed through both the meat and the skin, which was left on to prevent the hook from breaking through the tender belly meat. Allowed to sink to the bottom, at the conjunction of a weedline and dropoff, the lure produced the biggest pike of the trip. It served double duty as a surface lure, skittered through weeds and lily pads.

19

Learning First Aid

First aid is one of those absolutely vital subjects that most of us plan to learn someday, but never really get around to. It shouldn't need to be said that such procrastinating can be dangerous; can, in fact, cost you your life or the life of a friend. Study this chapter carefully, and practice making an emergency splint or stretcher; practice bandaging a broken nose or sprained ankle; and memorize the steps for treating snakebite, heart attack, gun wounds and all the other tragedies that occasionally plague outdoorsmen. And then let's all hope you never need to put your practice to work.

The Basics

A discussion with a medical friend made clear the first maxim of emergency first aid. "Stress one fact to your readers," the doctor said emphatically. "The absolute cardinal rule of all first aid is *'Do no harm.'* Everything else ranks second to that piece of wisdom."

Paraphrased, "Do no harm" means that your first job as a first aider is to avoid aggravating existing injuries. Do all you can to assist the victim; help him in every way possible, but don't do anything you aren't sure is correct and don't try to do more than you realistically can. After this very important step come the following.

Examine the victim thoroughly for injuries.

Certain injuries take priority over others. Serious bleeding is the most dangerous and should be attended to first. Next comes stoppage of breath. After serious bleeding is controlled, reestablish breathing. Third on the danger list is poisoning, and then comes shock. Shock accompanies many types of injuries and is something a first aider should always watch for and treat immediately.

Get help as soon as possible. Contact emergency professionals such as police, rescue squads, park service personnel, etc.

Make the victim as comfortable as possible. Act calm in front of him and don't let him see the injury if it is a serious one. (The sight of the gaping wound may induce shock.)

Don't move an injured person unless you have no alternative. Use suggested methods only, and always handle a wounded person with extreme care.

With that brief rundown on preliminaries, let's take a look at the accepted treatments for an assortment of common injuries.

Bleeding

External Bleeding

If a main artery is punctured, the victim could die of blood loss in less than five minutes, hence it is imperative that you move quickly to stop bleeding. The best way is by applying direct pressure to the wound, using a sterile compress if possible, or a clean handkerchief or your bare hand if nothing else is available. If blood soaks through the compress, don't remove it. Rather, add additional layers of cloth and continue applying pressure.

If there are no broken bones, elevate the bleeding limb to a level above the victim's heart. This utilizes gravity to reduce blood pressure near the wound, which consequently reduces the amount of blood loss. Continue to apply pressure on the wound, even while it is elevated.

If bleeding continues, you may be able to reduce the flow by applying pressure on the supplying artery. For arm wounds the pressure point is between the elbow and the armpit, in the groove created by the joining of the biceps and triceps. Grasp the victim's arm at this point with a firm clamp of your hand, pushing your thumb against one side and bracing the opposite side of the arm with the flat surface of your fingers. This pushes the artery tight against the bone, closing it partially and restricting blood flow. Bleeding from leg wounds can be slowed by applying pressure to a point located on the front of the thigh, just below the crease of the groin. With the flat of your hand, apply pressure to the artery, jamming it against the underlying pelvic bone. Care should be taken when using pressure points to stop blood flow, for direct pressure to the artery cuts off all circulation to the limb. Use pressure points only when necessary, and only until the bleeding has stopped.

Internal Bleeding

Internal bleeding is harder to diagnose, and is very serious. Bleeding within the body sometimes occurs after a fall or sharp blow, and after such an accident the victim should be examined for symptoms. Sometimes the inner bleeding may be revealed by blood flowing from the nose, mouth or ears. Other symptoms include paleness, weakness, nausea, restlessness and a weak, rapid pulse.

Keep the victim flat on his back unless he is having difficulty breathing; then prop up his head and shoulders with a pillow or backpack. If the victim vomits, turn his head to the side, but keep him still.

Do not give stimulants such as tea, coffee or alcohol; they increase blood flow and, consequently, accelerate blood loss.

If the victim loses consciousness, gently turn him on his side, keeping his head and chest lower than his hips. Get professional medical help as soon as possible.

Nosebleeds

Nosebleeds sometimes result from a blow on the nose, but other times they occur for no apparent reason. Usually they aren't serious, but a thick, ceaseless flow can result in a dangerous loss of blood. Don't ignore a minor nosebleed. Treat it at once.

Sit down and lay back your head, as if you were looking straight up and a little bit back. Pinch your nostrils together, applying light pressure for five to ten minutes. If that fails, pack gauze or a clean strip of handkerchief lightly into the nostrils and continue the pinching pressure.

Tourniquets

A tourniquet is a wide band of cloth placed above a wound and tightened to restrict all blood flow. Tourniquets are rarely needed, and should be used only when other methods won't stop bleeding. The danger lies in the effectiveness of a tourniquet as a blood dam. All circulation is stopped below the tourniquet, and living tissue is deprived of oxygen-giving blood. If blood is absent for a long period, the tissue dies, gangrene results and the limb must be amputated. To quote the Red Cross: "The decision to apply a tourniquet is in reality a decision to risk sacrifice of a limb in order to save a life."

If a tourniquet is justified, use a wide piece of cloth—never a thin strip of material such as rope or wire. Wrap the cloth above the wound (making certain that the cloth does not touch the wound) and tie a common overhand knot. Place a stick over the knot and fasten it with

Applying a tourniquet.

yet another overhand knot. Twist the stick to tighten the tourniquet. When the bleeding stops, the tourniquet is tight enough. Loosen the tourniquet for a few seconds every 15 minutes. If a physician is near, the tourniquet should not be loosened unless advised by the physician.

Artificial Respiration

If breathing stops, the human body normally expires in less than six minutes. Thus, artificial respiration should be given without hesitation. Even if the victim has not stopped breathing completely, if his breath is slow and shallow, and if his lips, tongue and fingernails turn blue, he should be given resuscitation. The following is a reprint of the mouth-to-mouth and mouth-to-nose methods of resuscitation, provided by the Red Cross. The written instructions are keyed to the accompanying illustrations.

Mouth-to-Mouth Method

If foreign matter is visible in the mouth, wipe it out quickly with your fingers, wrapped in cloth, if possible. (1)

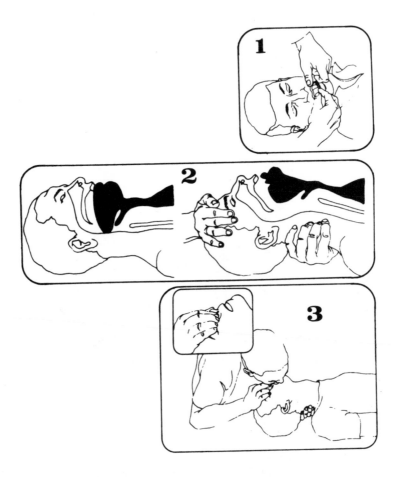

Tilt the victim's head backward so that his chin is pointing upward. This is accomplished by placing one hand under the victim's neck and lifting, while the other hand is placed on his forehead, pressing. This procedure should provide an open airway by moving the tongue away from the back of the throat. (2)

Maintain the backward head-tilt position and, to prevent leakage of air, pinch the victim's nostrils with the fingers of the hand that is pressing on the forehead. (3)

Open your mouth wide; take a deep breath; and seal your mouth tightly around the victim's mouth with a wide-open circle and blow into his mouth. If the airway is clear, only moderate resistance to the blowing effort is felt.

If you are not getting air exchange, check to see if there is a foreign body in the back of the mouth obstructing the air passages. Reposition the head and resume the blowing effort.

Watch the victim's chest and when you see it rise, stop inflation, raise your mouth, turn your head to the side, and listen for exhalation. Watch the chest to see that it falls. (4)

When his exhalation is finished, repeat the blowing cycle. Volume is

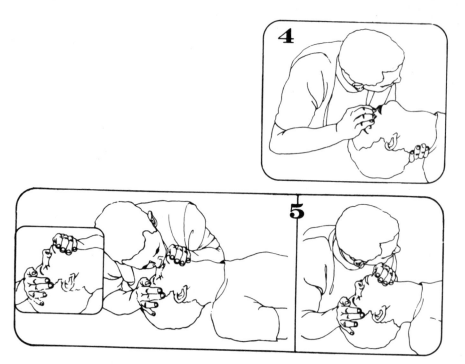

important. You should start at a high rate and then provide at least one breath every five seconds for adults (or 12 per minute).

When mouth-to-mouth and/or mouth-to-nose resuscitation is administered to small children or infants, the backward head-tilt should not be as extensive as that for adults or large children.

The mouth and nose of the infant or small child should be sealed by your mouth. Blow into the mouth and/or nose every three seconds (or 20 breaths per minute) with less pressure and volume than for adults, the amount determined by the size of the child.

If vomiting occurs, quickly turn the victim on his side, wipe out the mouth, and then reposition him.

Mouth-to-Nose Method

For the mouth-to-nose method, maintain the backward head-tilt position by placing the heel of the hand on the forehead. Use the other hand to close the mouth. Blow into the victim's nose. On the exhalation phase, open the victim's mouth to allow air to escape. (5)

Related Information

If a foreign body is prohibiting ventilation, as a last resort turn the victim on his side and administer sharp blows between the shoulder blades to jar the material free. (6)

A child may be suspended momentarily by the angles or turned up-

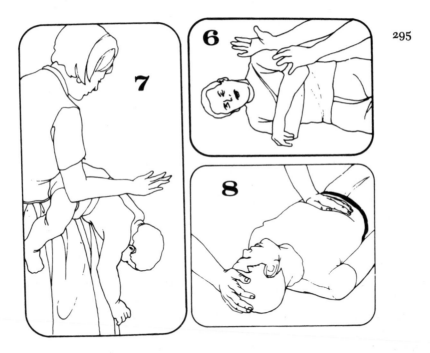

side down over one arm and given two or three sharp pats between the shoulder blades. Clear the mouth again, reposition, and repeat the blowing effort. (7)

Air may be blown into the victim's stomach, particularly when the air passage is obstructed or the inflation pressure is excessive. Although inflation of the stomach is not dangerous, it may make lung ventilation more difficult and increase the likelihood of vomiting. When the victim's stomach is bulging, always turn the victim's head to one side and be prepared to clear his mouth before pressing your hand briefly over the stomach. This will force air out of the stomach but may cause vomiting. (8)

When a victim is revived, keep him as quiet as possible until he is breathing regularly. Keep him from becoming chilled and otherwise treat him for shock. Continue artificial respiration until the victim begins to breathe for himself or a physician pronounces him dead or he appears to be dead beyond doubt.

Because respiratory and other disturbances may develop as an aftermath, a doctor's care is necessary during the recovery period.

Heart Stoppage

If you are giving artificial respiration to a person who is not responding check to see that his heart is still beating. Check the pulse at his wrist and hold your ear to his chest while listening for a heartbeat. If the heart has stopped, quickly lay the victim on his back with his legs raised to drain blood toward the heart. Support his shoulders so that his neck is arched backward, and his mouth is raised high.

Place your hand palm down at the base of the breastbone and position the other hand on top of the first one. Press down forceably, using the weight of your upper torso. After the downward thrust, lift both hands from the victim's chest. Repeat the push-and-lift every couple of seconds.

Stop every half-minute and use mouth-to-mouth resuscitation for three or four breaths to stimulate breathing. If someone is available to help, have him perform the mouth-to-mouth treatment once for every five heart-massage presses.

Shock

Shock is a condition created by blood loss, a reduced blood flow or by an insufficient oxygen supply. Shock normally accompanies severe injuries, but sometimes results from minor injuries as well. Hence it is something to always watch for.

The first signs of shock include a pale or bluish skin which is cold and sometimes clammy, weakness, a rapid pulse and increased rate of breathing. The victim may breathe with either shallow or deep and irregular breaths.

As shock advances, the victim may become apathetic because of the lack of oxygen. His eyes will appear sunken, and his pupils may dilate. His skin may appear mottled in places.

For treatment, first eliminate the cause of the shock, such as bleeding or stoppage of breath. Keep the victim lying down, and cover him only enough to prevent loss of body heat. If there are severe wounds on the lower face, place the victim on his side. If the person is experiencing respiratory problems, elevate his head and shoulders slightly. A person with head injuries may be laid flat or slightly propped up, but should never have his head lower than the rest of his body. If none of the above difficulties are present, elevate the victim's feet eight to twelve inches; this improves blood flow from the lower extremities. If there's any question about the best position for an injured person, you should keep him lying flat.

If medical help is more than an hour away, give the victim some water, preferably water that is mixed with salt and baking soda (1 teaspoon of salt and ½ teaspoon baking soda to each quart of water). The water should be neither cold nor hot, and should be given to adults in four-ounce doses every 15 minutes; children under 12 should be given two ounces. Do not give water in any of the following cases:

> If nausea or vomiting occurs.
> If professional help is less than an hour away.

If the victim is unconscious (never give fluids to an unconscious person).
If the victim is having convulsions.
If the victim has abdominal injury.

Poisoning

There are all sorts of ways a person can be poisoned. He can ingest a toxic substance, be stung by a wasp, bitten by a snake or irritated by a plant. Obviously, each type of poison varies in severity, so we'll look at the assorted poisons individually—covering those which are particularly noisome to outdoorsmen.

Ingested Poisons

Ingested poisons run a gamut from sour food to poisonous plants; from kitchen cleansers to rat poisons. If the swallowed poison is identified, administer an antidote immediately. Antidotes are printed on the containers of most dangerous materials. If a victim has ingested poison, but does not know what it was, the odor of his breath or the coloration of his mouth may provide a clue. If you have no idea of either the poison or the proper antidote, follow these steps:

Dilute the poison by having the victim drink at least four glasses of water or milk. (Only if the victim is conscious.)

Induce vomiting by sticking your finger into the victim's throat, or by giving him a drink consisting of warm water and two tablespoons of salt. However, do not induce vomiting if the victim is unconscious, has a burning sensation in his mouth, has swallowed some sort of petroleum (gas, kerosene, stove fuel, etc.) or any acid or alkali (ammonia, drain cleaner, lye, detergent).

When the person vomits, lower his face so that it is below the level of the hips (as leaning over the side of a bed) to keep the vomit from aspirating into his lungs.

If the poison is unknown, save some of the vomitus for examination by a doctor.

Contact Poisons

Most notable here are poison oak, ivy and sumac. Allergic reactions to these plants produce rash, burning and itching. In extreme cases, victims develop high fever and acute illness which lasts for several days.

Treatments:

Remove contaminated clothing, and immediately wash with water.
Continue washing contaminated skin with soap and water for at least

five minutes. Rub said area with rubbing alcohol.
For mild rash, spread on calamine lotion.
If the rash is severe, seek medical help.

Poisonous Sea Animals

Jellyfish and Portuguese man-of-war are capable of injecting a venom through tiny stinging cells. The effects of the venom vary with conditions, and produce burning pain, skin rashes, and sometimes shock, muscular cramping, nausea, vomiting and respiratory difficulty. If the tentacles stick to the skin, remove them with a towel. Then wash the affected area with diluted ammonia or rubbing alcohol. A pain reliever, such as aspirin or Tylenol, should be given.

Stinging coral also inject venom through stinging cells, and produce a multitude of small, sharp cuts which are contaminated by bits of calcium-rich material. The cuts should be cleaned thoroughly and, if possible, inspected by a doctor.

Sea urchins have numerous spines capable of injecting a potent and painful nerve poison. If you step on an urchin, tie a constricting band (like a tourniquet, only not as tight—you should be able to slip a finger easily between the cloth and your skin) above the wound. Soak the affected area in hot water for 30 minutes, or, lacking that, apply hot compresses. Get medical aid as soon as possible for removal of spine fragments.

Stingrays also inflict painful, poisonous wounds. Shock, vomiting, diarrhea and paralysis may result from stingray venom. Treat a stingray wound by soaking in hot water. Apply a bandage and seek medical help.

Poisonous Insects and Arachnids

Chapter 4 covered the list of potentially dangerous animals, and included such venomous insects and arachnids as scorpions, bees, wasps, hornets, black widow spiders and brown recluse spiders. Check that chapter for details on each individual species. Here we will divide them into general groups, placing those which require similar treatments in one group.

For insect stings, the first step is to remove the stinger, being careful not to squeeze the venom sack and release further poison into the body. If possible, make a paste from baking soda and cold cream, and spread it liberally over the sting. Apply cold cloths or packs to ease the pain, and use a calamine or similar lotion to reduce itching. If the victim has a history of bad reactions to insect bites, or is sensitized in any way, anaphylactic shock may result. Use a constricting band above the wound, apply ice packs to the sting and get to a doctor as quickly as possible.

Spider bites and scorpion stings can be more serious. Symptoms include swelling, redness and possibly spreading pain, heavy sweating, nausea and difficulty in breathing. Keep the victim warm and calm. Apply a constricting band above the bite (loosen it every 15 minutes), and apply cold compresses to the affected area. Get professional help if possible.

Snakebite

Finding the best treatment for snakebite is akin to seeking the best recipe for homemade chili. Each authority seems to have a different technique, and each one claims his is the best. What I have done here is present the two most widely accepted methods of snakebite treatment. The first way, the "new" way, is touted to be the best method, but as you will see, it has some definite limitations.

As soon as possible after the victim is bitten, apply fresh water to the bite. Ideally, the bitten area should be immersed in ice water, and should be kept in the water until the victim reaches the hospital. If no ice is available, a canned coolant or other substitute will work until ice can be obtained. (Cold streams and lakes are another possibility.) Aside from the bite area, which is to be kept cold, the rest of the victim should be covered to avoid overall heat loss. Give the patient plenty of fluids, but do not give any stimulants such as coffee, tea or whisky. Keep the victim comfortable and immobile, and assure him that everything is under control. (Panic in the victim increases heartbeat and consequently accelerates the distribution of the venom. It's important that he remain as calm as possible.) Get professional medical help as soon as possible.

The obvious limitation of this method is that a cold compress or liquid must be available for treatment. Many times, such as on a dry, rocky ridge, a snakebite may occur where there is no water of any kind, much less extremely cold water. In such a case, follow the older (and some say less effective) technique of cutting the wound and sucking out the venom. Proceed as follows:

Immobilize the victim's bitten extremity and lower it so that it lies below heart level.

If the bite is on an arm or leg, apply a constricting band a couple of inches above the wound (between the wound and the heart). Tighten the band so that it is snug, but not so tight that you can't slip your index finger easily between the cloth and the victim's skin.

If you have a snakebite kit, use the blade to make incisions through the skin at each fang mark. If you lack a kit, sterilize a knife or razor by placing it in a match flame. Make the incisions **through the skin only** and parallel with the long axis of the limb. Do not make cross-cut incisions, and do not make incisions of more than one-half inch long.

Suck the venom from the wound with a suction cup if you have a snakebite kit, and with your mouth if you don't. The venom is not a stomach poison, but you shouldn't swallow it anyway. Rinse your mouth with water after completion of the sucking, which should be continued up to 30 minutes.

Wash the wound with soap and water and blot it dry. Cover with sterile dressing.

Watch for signs of shock, and treat victim if necessary.

If the victim must walk out, he should move slowly. Medical attention should be sought immediately.

No mention has been made of antivenin injections yet, and again, each doctor seems to offer different advice on the subject. If you are carrying antivenin, an injection can be lifesaving, and since a doctor prescribed it to you (it's the only way to obtain it), it should produce no unfavorable reactions. However, there is a danger in giving antivenin to a person who has not been tested for sensitivity to serum. If in doubt, don't administer antivenin.

Burns

Thermal Burns

Thermal burns are classified according to the degree of severity. First-degree burns are the least serious, causing minor pain and reddening the skin. Second-degree burns develop blisters. Third-degree burns result in deep tissue destruction, and are very serious.

For minor first- and second-degree burns, treat as follows:

If the skin is not broken, you can reduce pain and recovery time by immersing the burned area in cold water.

Apply a wet pad which has been soaked in a solution made by mixing two tablespoons of baking soda in one quart of warm water. Hold the pad on the wound with a loose bandage.

For more serious second- and third-degree burns, observe the following:

Get to a doctor or call an ambulance if possible.

If deep in the backwoods, remove all clothing from the burn area, cutting it away with a knife or scissor. If some clothing sticks to the wound, do not try to remove it.

Cover the burn with a sterile dry dressing. Don't apply ointments, antiseptics or similar substances to a severe burn. Add additional layers of dressing, and bandage in place snugly.

Watch for shock, and treat if necessary.

Once a dressing has been placed on the wound, do not try to change it. Leave that task to a doctor.

Sunburn

Peeling, redness and possibly swelling and blistering will accompany a bad sunburn. Most sunburns can be treated by applying calamine lotion, cold cream, salad oil or any of the commercial sunburn treatments. However, don't put butter or margarine on any burn—sun or thermal. If the sunburn is severe, treat in the same manner suggested for thermal burns.

Broken Bones

Sometimes a broken bone is obvious, as in the case of a compound fracture where the jagged bone juts through the skin. Other times it may be difficult to tell if a limb is merely badly bruised or if the supporting bone is fractured. When in doubt, treat for a broken limb.

"Treatment" for fractures consists of little more than avoiding further injury. You should never try to reset a bone yourself. Handle the victim gently to avoid aggravating the wound and causing more damage. Treat for shock if necessary.

Each type of broken bone requires slightly different procedures.

Leg or Arm

If professional help is near, don't move the victim or the broken limb. Stop bleeding by using direct pressure on the wound, and bandage a dressing over the bleeding area.

If the person must be moved, splint the broken limb by fastening it to two sturdy objects—boards, poles, sturdy branches, etc. The splint must be long enough to extend well past the joints below and above the fracture. Pad the inside of the splints with soft material, and tie the

Splinting a fractured arm.

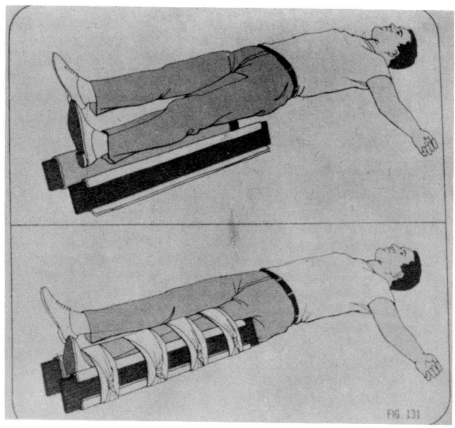

Splinting a fractured leg.

splint to the limb in at least three places. If the limb swells, the splint may need to be loosened periodically.

If possible, apply cold packs to the broken area.

Collarbone

A person with a broken collarbone will usually slouch forward, elbow flexed and forearm held across his chest while being held with the opposite hand. The collarbone area may swell and appear to be deformed.

The best treatment while awaiting professional help is to place the arm on the broken side in a sling. Make the sling wide enough to cover from the wrist to the elbow, and adjust it so that the victim's hand is elevated slightly above his elbow. Another bandage is tied so that it encircles the injured-side arm and the chest, holding the arm firmly against the body.

Fractured collarbone.

Elbow

Usually a broken elbow results in swelling right above the joint. If a break is suspected, do not attempt to work the arm to test the joint. If the arm is being held straight, splint it with two sturdy objects. If it is bent, hold it in a sling. Do all you can to avoid movement of the joint.

Forearm and Wrist

You can break a wrist bone and not realize any more pain than you'd expect from a severe sprain. Finger movement is still possible with a wrist break, though it will be accompanied by pain. If you suspect a break, place the arm in a padded splint extending from palm to elbow, and then put the injured arm into a sling, adjusting it so that the victim's fingers are four inches higher than his elbow.

If the fingers on the injured side swell or discolor, loosen the splint and/or sling to aid circulation.

Finger

Splint the finger to avoid further injury. Place the hand in a sling and consult a doctor. Lack of proper treatment can result in a permanent deformity.

Rib

A broken rib causes pain in the rib area and shallow breathing. If the rib has punctured a lung, the victim may cough up frothy bright-red blood, flecked with spots of white. If the rib has moved the other way, and has punctured the skin, an airtight dressing must be applied to prevent infection.

Keep the victim immobile and lying down. If the skin is not punctured, wrap one or more wide bandages around the chest to restrict rib movement. However, if the bandages cause pain, remove them. Also, if the broken rib appears to be depressed—pushed into the chest cavity— refrain from bandaging.

Transport the victim in a prone position only.

Skull

Symptoms of skull fracture include mental confusion, bleeding from the mouth, ears or nose, variation in eye pupil diameter or unconsciousness.

For treatment, keep the victim lying down. If his face is flushed or of normal color, prop up his head and shoulders slightly. If his complexion is pallid, lower the head slightly below the body. Apply a sterile dressing if there's a scalp wound, and hold it in place with a bandage. To move the victim, keep him in the prone position.

If the patient begins to gag or choke on blood, turn his head to one side to allow the blood to drain from his throat and mouth.

Neck and Back

A person with a broken neck will have trouble opening or closing his fingers, and he won't be able to grip anything firmly. One suffering from a broken back can manipulate his fingers, but will lack coordination and muscle control in the toes. In either case, treat as follows:

Keep the victim's neck and head absolutely still.

Cover him with blankets.

Watch the victim carefully for complications, such as respiratory difficulty or failure. Give mouth-to-mouth resuscitation if necessary, but be careful not to move the head as you do so.

Don't move the victim if at all possible, but if transporting him is necessary, move with conscious caution, for any movement of the neck could be fatal. Pad both sides of the head and neck to prevent movement, and tie the head, neck, chest and hands tightly to the stretcher (which must be rigid).

Knee

Proper treatment for a knee injury is important. Flexing of the knee can pull apart the broken kneecap and complicate the existing damage.

First, gently straighten the leg. Then place a solid splint on the underside of the leg. It should reach from the buttocks to the heel. Tie the splint firmly in place, but do not fasten it over the kneecap itself. Transport the victim carefully, keeping him prone all the while.

Foot or Toe

Remove footwear quickly; rapid swelling may make the task increasingly difficult with each passing minute. The foot should be wrapped in something soft, such as cotton or a folded piece of cloth. Refrain from movement of the foot, ankle or toes. Get to a doctor quickly.

Pelvis

A pelvic fracture is serious, since the bone protects many vital organs. Handle a broken-pelvis victim gently as follows: Keep the victim lying down, either with his legs flat on the ground or with the knees flexed up and supported by underlying padding. (Depending on whichever is most comfortable for the patient.) Bandage his knees and ankles together to prevent aggravating movements. If transporting is necessary, do so carefully, splinting the lower extremities if moving them causes the victim pain. Transport the patient on a rigid stretcher.

Nose

A broken nose is usually obviously bruised, accompanied by swelling,

Fractured pelvis.

Broken nose.

bleeding and discoloration. Sometimes the shape of the nose is perceptibly altered. Permanent deformity and breathing difficulties may result if the wound isn't attended to properly.

Stop bleeding by lightly pinching the lower end of the nose between thumb and forefinger, pressing the nostrils against the middle ridge of cartilage for at least five minutes. Apply cold cloths to the nose, while the victim holds his head back. Dress any wounds with a sterile bandage, and hold in place with cloth tied around the head. Get to a doctor as soon as possible.

Jaw

A broken jaw usually is accompanied by mild bleeding of the gums, and considerable pain when jaw movement is attempted. The upper and

Broken jaw.

lower teeth may not line up properly, and speaking and swallowing are difficult.

Gently lift the lower jaw so that the lower and upper teeth mesh. Wrap a wide band of cloth under the chin and tie the ends together where they meet the top of the head, to support the lower jaw. Should the victim begin to vomit, remove the bandage immediately and hold the jaw with your hand. When vomiting ceases, replace the bandage.

Dislocated Bones

A dislocated bone is one which is displaced from its normal position in a joint. Shoulders, fingers and hips seem to fall subject to this malady more frequently than other areas.

The patient will know if he's dislocated a bone, because the wrenching of the bone destroys surrounding ligaments and tissues, causing severe pain, loss of movement and swelling.

Dislocated bones should be relocated by a doctor, and as a first-aider, your job is simply to prevent further injury. Keep the dislocated part immobile and apply cold compresses. If the injured part is an elbow or shoulder, suspend it in a loose sling. A dislocated hip requires that the patient be moved on a solid stretcher, preferably with padding between the stretcher and the injured limb.

If you're deep in the woods, a dislocated finger may be set back into place by gently pulling it straight. However, if the bone does not cooperate, give up and seek medical attention. Incidentally, this should not be attempted with a dislocated thumb; the joint is more complicated than the other digits, and pulling may aggravate the injury.

Sprains

When the tissues, ligaments, tendons and blood vessels surrounding a joint are stretched or damaged, the area is sprained. Common sprains include ankles, fingers, wrists and knees.

A sprain is not always easy to tell from a fracture; both have similar symptoms—pain, swelling, tenderness to pressure, and sometimes discoloration of the injured area. When in doubt, always treat for a fracture. If you're sure it's a sprain, treat as follows:

Elevate the injured area, propping it up with soft objects or, for wrists and elbow sprains, suspending it with a sling. A sprained ankle should be raised a foot higher than the torso.

Apply an ice pack or other cold compress to reduce pain and swelling. Maintain the cold pack for at least 30 minutes.

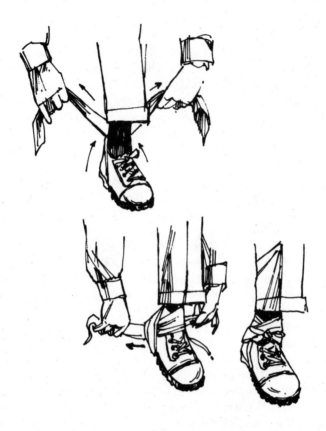

Wrapping a sprained ankle.

Have the sprain X-rayed at the nearest opportunity, for there may be a chipped bone or fracture.

If you sprain an ankle while out in the woods, and must walk on the sore joint to make your way out, try this: First, untie the shoelaces to allow for swelling, but don't remove the shoe. Next, using a long bandage or folded handkerchief, wrap the ankle as shown in the illustration. This lends added support to the ankle, making the walk out a little less excruciating.

Miscellaneous Injuries

Fishhook Removal

A deeply imbedded fishhook should be removed by the traditional

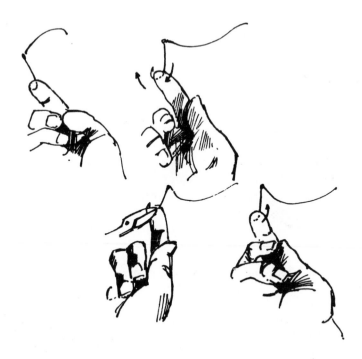

The traditional way of removing a deeply embedded hook. This is still useful if the hook is buried in a fingertip, earlobe or other thin piece of flesh.

method of clipping off the barbed end of the hook, then sliding the hook back out of the entrance hole. Use this method only when the point of the hook is protruding from the skin, as, for example, it would be if it were stuck deeply into the end of a finger. If the point is near the surface of the skin, you'll have to push it through to expose the point and the barb.

However, in most cases, there is a simpler, less painful, hook-removal technique.

First, if the hook is attached to a lure with treble or multihook attachments, remove the hook from the lure.

Next, take about two feet of fishing line, testing around 30 pounds, and tie a knot in the loose ends of the line. (If you lack such a heavy line, combine two or more strands of lighter line to form an equivalent poundage, such as two strands of 15-pound-test, or three strands of ten-pound line.)

Place the loop around the back of your hand and hold the end between your thumb and forefinger, creating a small loop of line in front

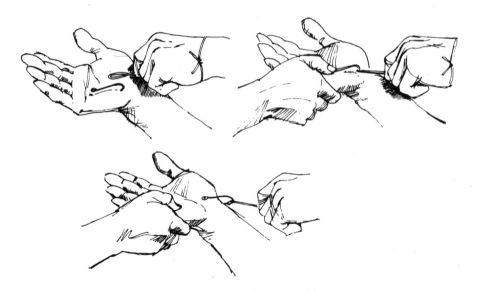

An easy way to remove most embedded fishhooks.

of your hand. Place the loop over the eye of the hook and center it firmly in the middle of the hook's bend.

With the thumb of your other hand, push down and back on the eye of the hook, and at the same time give a sharp jerk on the line. The hook will pop out of the same hole it entered, causing no additional pain or damage.

After hook removal by either method, cleanse the wound with soap, dab on an antiseptic, and bandage. If your tetanus protection is weak, see a doctor immediately.

Blisters

The best protection against blister infection is the unbroken skin around it. But if the blister is likely to break, wash it and the surrounding area with soap and water. Spread two percent iodine solution or a similar antiseptic around the edge of the blister. Sterilize a needle by holding it in a match flame, and puncture the blister near an edge. Press the blister gently to drain the fluid, then cover with a sterile dressing.

If the blister has already broken, cleanse the area lightly with soap and water, then apply a sterile dressing.

Object in Eye

Never rub an eye that contains a foreign object, or you may cause serious damage. First try closing both eyes for a few minutes to allow tears to wash out the particle. If that doesn't work, pinch the lashes of the upper lid and move the lid out and down over the lower lid to dislodge the object. If an eyedropper or eyecup is on hand, rinse the eye with plain water. If the particle still won't come out, peel back the upper lid and try to locate the foreign matter. If it is on the lid, moisten one end of a handkerchief or bandage and twist it into a dull point. Gently try to remove the object, being careful not to poke the eyeball. If the object is on the eye itself, turn your head to one side and, keeping the eye open, pour a steady stream of water across the eye (using a canteen or cup). If all of these procedures fail, cover the eye lightly with a sterile bandage and get to a doctor. *Do not rub the eye.*

Toothache

The ache can be relieved temporarily by cleaning the cavity with a swab of cotton on a toothpick, then packing the cavity with a piece of sterile cotton dipped in oil of cloves. However, keep the oil off your gums or tongue; it burns.

If the ache is in the gums or jaws rather than a tooth, hold a hot-water bottle or ice pack to the face on the side that hurts. (In sandy areas, "fry" a pan full of sand over a fire, and wrap the hot sand in cloth to serve as a long-lasting hot compress.) Aspirin, Tylenol or other pain relievers may help.

Frostbite

Prior to actual frostbite, the skin may be flushed, but as the tissue freezes, it turns white or gray-yellow. Sometimes there is pain, sometimes not.

Cover the frozen area with clothing, blankets, even a warm hand. Do not rub the area, do not soak it in kerosene, do not pack it with snow or try any other foolish remedies.

Get the victim indoors as soon as possible and immerse the frostbitten area in warm—not hot—water. Use warm treatments; never hot, for excessive heat can damage the tissue further. Give warm, nonalcoholic drinks, and once the victim is warm, have him exercise the affected parts to stimulate circulation.

Snowblindness

The glare of the sun reflecting off snow may cause your eyes to burn. It may feel as though sand particles are scratching your eyes; you may feel throbbing pain around the eyeballs and forehead. A flash of light will make you wince with pain. All of these symptoms spell snowblindness.

Get indoors as quickly as possible, and cover your eyes to seal out all light. Apply cold compresses. Wash eyes occasionally with a boric acid solution, or a commercial eyewash.

Minor Cuts and Abrasions

Wash the area around the wound. Wash away from the wound rather than toward it. Clean out all dirt and debris, using tweezers if necessary. Apply an antiseptic and cover with a sterile dressing. If the area around the wound reddens after several days, or if swelling or fever result, the wound may have become infected. See a doctor if possible. If medical help is far away, immerse the infected part in a hot solution of salt water (two teaspoons of salt to each quart of water). If immersion is not possible, soak clean compresses in the solution and apply them to the infected area for one-hour periods. Repeat treatments until a doctor can be reached.

Animal Bites

Wash the wound immediately under running water if possible. Then cleanse with soap and water. After thorough rinsing, cover with a dressing. Get to a doctor immediately. If you have caught or killed the animal, bring it along for rabies testing. Anti-rabies injections may be necessary, so be sure to consult a physician.

Heart Attacks

Heart attacks are common occurrences in the outdoors, particularly during hunting season. Symptoms of heart trouble include shortness of breath, pain in the chest or arms, pallid or flushed facial color, bluish color around the lips and fingernails, vertigo, and possible panic in the victim.

If the victim has specific ailments and medications, apply them. Otherwise, act as follows:

> Place the patient in whatever position is most comfortable, preferably lying down. If he has difficulty breathing, elevate his head and shoulders.
> Keep the victim warm, but allow adequate ventilation around him.
> Give him coffee or tea if he can drink it.
> If the victim collapses, give alternating heart massages and mouth-to-mouth resuscitation. (See other sections of this chapter.)
> Do not mention the words "heart attack" to the victim. They have a panic-inducing effect. Instead, be calm and encouraging.
> Don't transport the victim unless absolutely necessary. Wait for medical help.

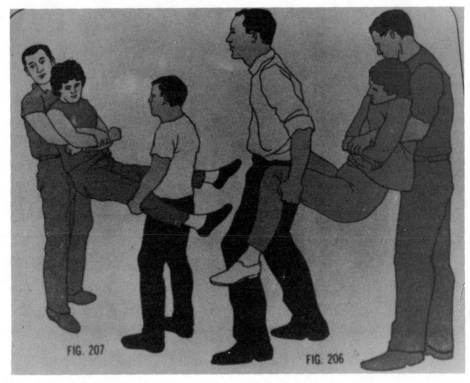

Fore-and-aft carry. (*Photo: American National Red Cross*)

Transporting the Injured

Perhaps the first thing a first-aider should realize is that more harm than good can be done while transferring an injured person. Unless it's absolutely necessary, don't move someone who is badly hurt. Send for help if possible, or if you're alone and in the outback, utilize all the signaling potential you have. But if there is no alternative to transporting, keep in mind the following recommended procedures.

Except in absolute emergencies, where the victim must be moved without delay to prevent further injury (as in a fire), take all the initial first aid steps to treat shock, reestablish breathing, stop bleeding, splint wounds, etc., before making plans to transport the patient.

If the victim is unconscious or unable to move for reasons other than trunk injuries or fractures, the fore-and-aft carry can be used. Two people are needed, one for holding the victim's legs, the other for grasping the chest. See the illustration (Figures 206 and 207).

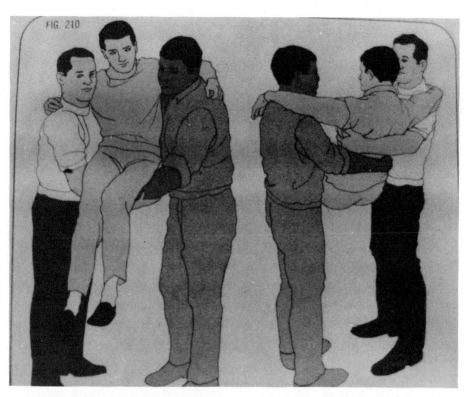

Two-hand seat carry. (*Photo: American National Red Cross*)

If the injured person is not hurt seriously and is able to cooperate with the carriers, a two-hand seat carry is a good one to use if two people are present. See the illustration (Figures 210 and 211) for details.

The best way to carry an injured person is via stretcher. You can fashion an emergency stretcher from a blanket, tarp or coat by attaching the stretcher material to two sturdy poles. Figure 234 shows how this is done.

It's best to have at least three people load the victim onto the stretcher. The loaders should position themselves facing the patient's uninjured side, one loader near the head, one near the feet, and the other at midsection. Each loader kneels on the knee nearest the patient's feet. The person at the head cradles the head and shoulders with one arm, and supports the lower back with the other. The loader at midsection supports the back and the buttocks; the third loader supports the thighs and calves.

At a command by the head loader, all three lift the victim onto their knees. One loader pulls the stretcher under the victim, and on command all three lower him gently onto the stretcher.

Unfortunately, an accident in the backwoods doesn't always find three people available for transporting. A single person can load an injured man on a stretcher by working methodically, moving the victim onto the

Makeshift stretcher. (*Photo: American National Red Cross*)

stretcher in parts; first the feet, and legs, then the head and torso. A travois can be made for moving an injured person if no other alternative exists. The victim is loaded onto the stretcher, tied down firmly at the feet, thighs, midsection, chest and head, and padding is placed around the head, neck and injured areas. The first-aider lifts one end of the stretcher and drags the victim along. WARNING: Such a setup is dangerous and should not be resorted to unless absolutely necessary.

In some cases, it may be necessary to leave an injured person as comfortable as possible and seek help. This is not a desirable situation, but if you are alone in the outback with a badly hurt person—one you can't safely transport—you have no alternative other than to do all you can for him, and then head for help. Leave him food, water, warm coverings, and if possible build him a shelter even if it's of the crudest kind. Mark the location of the victim copiously, and take the shortest route for help. In rural areas, head for the nearest house or farm. If a phone is available, dial zero and have the operator place an emergency call to the police.

20

Emergency First Aid for Your Dog

This brief look at emergency first aid is not intended to take the place of professional veterinary attention. It's meant to fill in the gap created between the time of an injury and the time it takes to bring the dog to a vet. After an injury, regardless of how well the dog looks, have it checked by a vet. There may be complicated internal damage, delayed reactions and a host of other physiological adversities that can't be spotted or treated without professional scrutiny.

The First Steps

The procedures for treating an injured dog vary considerably, but if a dog is hurt seriously, say it's hit by a car or for some reason collapses, proceed as follows:

Approach the dog from the rear. If possible, toss a coat or blanket over it to partially contain it and defend against shock by decreasing heat loss.

Next—and this is important—muzzle your dog with a piece of rubber tubing or a strip of cloth (such as a handkerchief or bandanna). Your dog may be the gentlest, most loving creature in the world, incapable of biting you ordinarily; but in the confusion of an emergency the same dog may bite you in a purely reflexive snap. Slip the cloth or tubing under the dog's muzzle, and tie a half hitch or simple overhand knot to firmly clamp shut the dog's mouth. (This won't interfere with breathing if the nasal passages are clear.)

If the dog is conscious and passive, talk to it reassuringly while mak-

An injured dog may reflexively bite you, hence it should be muzzled before first aid is attempted.

ing a quick examination. If the dog must be moved immediately, pick it up carefully, supporting it fully. Small dogs can be held to your chest, placing one arm under the belly and chest, and the other around its side to hold it firm. A large dog that is not acting aggressively or anxiously can be draped over your shoulders like a mink stole, only don't allow the head to loll, and clamp the hind feet together with one hand. If the animal is thrashing about or if it is aggressive (growling, etc.), lean over it and pin its buttocks to the ground with your shoulder. Extend your arm ahead, over and across the dog's chest, and grip the front legs. With your free hand, grab the loose skin at the dog's scruff (lower neck) and lift it up. Use the arm around the chest to do most of the lifting. This carry doesn't hurt the dog, nor does it allow it to hurt you. The main thing to remember is to always give the dog the impression that it is being held solidly. If the animal thinks it's going to fall, it will begin to struggle.

Just like human first aid, if you have a choice, treat the animal's injuries before attempting to move it. Stop all bleeding, check for stoppage of breath, treat for shock, splint leg fractures, etc.

Stopping Bleeding

Stop blood flow the same way you would for humans. Apply a sterile compress and press it on the wound, holding it there firmly until the bleeding stops. If the wound is severe, twist on a tourniquet; but do so only if a pressure bandage won't stop the bleeding.

Minor lacerations should be washed with water after the bleeding stops, and the wound dabbed with antiseptic. Cover the cut with a wrap of gauze or a pad of gauze bandage. Don't seal the gauze with tape; air circulation over the wound will help it heal.

A dog that resists carrying should be held as shown at top, one arm firmly around the chest, the other holding a handfull of scruff. A passive dog can be carried over your shoulders (bottom), but be sure to hold the legs and head firmly.

Stoppage of Breath

You can revive a dog by giving mouth-to-nose resuscitation. Open the dog's mouth, pull out its tongue and look into the throat for obstructions. Wipe away excessive mucous or blood with your fingers. Close the dog's mouth and hold it closed while exhaling into the dog's nose, then remove your mouth from the dog's nose to allow exhalation. Repeat the procedure.

Stoppage of the Heart

If the dog's heart stops beating (place your ear to its chest, or clamp your fingers around the dog's thigh for a pulse), you may be able to revive it with an external massage.

Lay the dog on its right side. Place your hands over its heart (on its left side, obviously) and press down firmly. Then release the pressure. Work fast, applying 60 or more push-release cycles per minute. Since the dog has already stopped breathing, alternate between heart massage and mouth-to-nose resuscitation. Don't give up easily; all of a sudden you may be rewarded with regular breathing and a strengthening heartbeat.

Poisoning

If you dog ingests a poison, induce vomiting unless the poison was a strong acid or alkali (kerosene, drain cleaner). To induce vomiting, give equal parts of hydrogen peroxide and water (two tablespoons for each ten pounds of body weight) or four to six teaspoons of salt mixed in a glass of warm water, or mustard mixed with water. After vomiting, or if the poison was an acid or alkali, give the dog milk mixed with a raw egg. (One-quarter cup per ten pounds body weight.)

If convulsions occur, restrain the dog to prevent injury. Bring a sample of the poison or vomitus to the vet for analysis.

Snakebite

If the bite is on a limb, apply a constricting band (not a tourniquet). If you have antivenin serum, inject it into a major artery; the easiest, perhaps, is the one on the inside of a leg or thigh. Using a sterile knife, open the skin above each fang puncture, but do not cut deep or make crosscuts. Use either your mouth or a suction cup to remove venom from the wound. The first quarter-hour is vital, and the bulk of venom can be sucked out if you act quickly.

Keep the dog immobile. Carry it rather than let it walk. Give no stimulants and get to a vet as soon as possible.

Shock

A dog in shock has a weak pulse, breathes in shallow gulps, has pale gums and glassy eyes.

Keep the animal quiet and warm. Cover it with a blanket or coat. Get to a vet.

Broken Bones

Do not try to set a broken bone. Don't even try to splint a fracture unless it occurs in a leg bone, and then support it with two sturdy objects as you would for a human fracture. Carry the dog carefully to a vet, using a rigid stretcher if possible.

Heat Stroke

The dog may suddenly collapse; it will have obvious difficulty breathing and it will be unable to move. Treat heatstroke immediately!

The best method is total immersion in water, holding the muzzle above the surface to allow breathing. The next best procedure is to douse the dog with all the water you have. The body temperature must be lowered quickly or the animal will die.

NOTE: Many dog owners don't realize how susceptible a dog is to heat dangers. A particularly common fault is to lock a dog in a car on a hot day. Even with the windows opened slightly, the car becomes an oven in a matter of minutes. In fact, in ten minutes the interior can reach 120 degrees—a literal oven. Also, on hot days afield, give your dog plenty of water and plenty of rest. A dog cannot cope with heat as well as a human.

Porcupine Quills

If you read dog articles in magazines and newspapers, you'll come across quite a few "simplified" methods of removing quills: soaking the quills in vinegar, cutting off the quill ends to release pressure, etc. However, most authorities say the best method is to muzzle the dog, hold it between your legs and, using pliers, twist out each quill. Start with the quill located in the chest area, and work toward the head. The important thing is to pull out the quills as soon as you discover them. The longer you wait, the deeper they penetrate.

Skunked!

No need to expound on the indelicate details. Wash the dog's eyes with a boric acid solution to relieve the burning. Scrub the animal down thoroughly with strong soap and water. If you'd like, rub with a concoction of canned tomatoes or diluted lemon juice to eliminate odor. (A messy job at best; some think too messy to bother with.) After the scrubbing, let the dog air out for as long as possible before bringing it indoors. A slight odor will linger, but most times it's tolerable.

Other Troubles

Other ailments such as burns, imbedded fishhooks, foreign matter in eyes, gunshot and frostbite are treated in the same manner described for humans in the previous chapter.

INDEX

Boldface numbers refer to illustrations.